ANTHONY DANIELS

Fool or Physician

THE MEMOIRS OF A SCEPTICAL DOCTOR

'Every man at thirty
is a fool or a physician.'
ENGLISH PROVERB

John Murray

First published 1987
by John Murray (Publishers) Ltd
50 Albemarle Street, London WIX 4BD

Typeset by Inforum Ltd, Portsmouth
Printed and bound in Great Britain
by The Bath Press, Avon

British Library CIP data
Daniels, Anthony
Fool or physician : the memoirs of a
sceptical doctor.
1. Medicine — History — 20th century
I. Title
610'.92'4   R149
ISBN 0–7195–4355–X

The extracts on pages 209, 210 and 212 from the story
'Rain' from *The Collected Stories of W Somerset Maugham* are
by permission of A. P. Watt Ltd on behalf of the executors
of the Estate of W Somerset Maugham and William Heine-
mann Ltd.

CONTENTS

PREFACE

Twenty years ago, while I was still at school, I went to Battersea Funfair. There was a small booth with the following notice attached:

MADAME GYPSY ROSE LEE
As Patronised by the Gentry and seen on TV

I entered. Across a small round table with a floral tablecloth and a water-filled glass that substituted for a crystal ball sat a somewhat bored-looking lady with large copper earrings and a scarf over her head to match the tablecloth.

'One 'and or two?' she said.

'What's the difference?' I asked.

'Five bob one 'and, ten bob two. Or a pound the tealeaves.'

I chose one hand.

She took it with a slight curl of her lip as if to say, I thought as much, and followed a few of my palmar creases with her long crimson nail.

'You'll be educated', she said. 'It'll take a long time.'

I did not demur.

'A lawyer . . . or a doctor perhaps. Yes, a doctor.'

I was taken aback.

'You'll travel a lot. And you'll live to be eighty-four.'

My five shillings' worth of prophecy was over. I *did* become a doctor and I *have* travelled a lot. Whether I live to be eighty-four remains to be seen.

ONE

England

'AND WHY do you want to be a doctor?'
I, a somewhat callow youth of seventeen, faced the men of the medical school interview board across the shining table.

It was not an unexpected or an unreasonable question to ask. Indeed, I had rehearsed my answer on the train. I had vowed against replying with any clichés about wishing to help humanity, relieve suffering, etc.

'I would like to help people,' I said.

'Have you ever helped people before?' asked a rather stern member of the board.

I did not know what to answer. I wondered whether relinquishing my seat on buses for old ladies counted.

'You say you want to help people. Have you joined the St John's Ambulance Brigade? Have you attended first aid courses?'

'No,' I said, shamefacedly.

'Why not?'

Having scored a small dialectical triumph, the member of the board wanted to pursue the point.

'I haven't had time.'

'Haven't had time to help people? You can't want to help them very much.'

He was right, of course. I didn't wish humanity any harm, but on the other hand I wasn't excessively anxious about its welfare either.

I had, in a manner of speaking, been found out. My looks of

dismay must have revealed more to the board than my answers, but not quite the depths of my discomfort. For the question 'Why do you want to be a doctor?' contained a premise that, in my case, was completely unjustified, namely that I *did* actually want to be a doctor. 'Why have you applied to medical school?' would have been a less tendentious question.

And the true answer would scarcely have secured me a place. I applied to medical school because I was middle class; because I had to do something; but more than anything else, because my father had pushed me into it. There had been a time, it is true, when I was ten or eleven, when I and a close friend of mine dreamed jointly of becoming doctors; of scientific fame and glory, of winning the Nobel Prize at the unprecedented age of fourteen by discovering the secret of cancer, which we felt must lie in the ugly, knobbly growths that affected all the apple trees in my garden. But those dreams had long since faded and my ambitions lay elsewhere. I wanted to be an historian or a philosopher rather than a doctor, but my father insisted – not unreasonably, perhaps – that it was unlikely I should ever be able to earn a decent living that way. Science, he said, and science alone, was the passport now to worldly success. He was not the kind of man lightly to be contradicted, and since biology was to me the most congenial of the sciences I chose medicine as a career, though I knew even then that I should never be wholeheartedly devoted to it.

Thus I entered medical school somewhat reluctantly, with reservations from the first. My career as a student was undistinguished, quite unlike those of doctors who achieve an obituary in *The Lancet*. I specialised in doing and knowing the least necessary to pass the examinations. Only occasionally did I exert myself beyond the minimum, to assure myself that I could, if I so desired, achieve excellent marks. I found that I could get by (or 'satisfy the examiners', as they put it) with very little effort, leaving myself free to study matters that then, but not now, seemed to me more important.

The course of study I prescribed for myself consisted largely of philosophy, with the result that while I can discourse with fluency on the ontological argument of St Anselm, my knowledge of the anatomy of the inner ear is a little hazy (not that it matters greatly: most doctors, other than specialists, treat ears with antibiotics and then, if they fail to improve, with referrals to specialists). I can also provide my patients with a satisfactory refutation of Marxian epistemology, but not, alas, a convincing explanation of how some of the drugs I prescribe achieve their effects. I now bitterly regret my inattention to my medical studies, for the fundamentals of a subject are never satisfactorily acquired later; but I was young and chose not to believe that anything I did then, or failed to do, would affect me for the rest of my life. I imagined that by taxing my brain with Descartes and Hume I was treating of questions larger and more important than why Mrs Smith's leg had swelled up. Now I should reverse my priorities; for, as Hume would have been the first to admit, toothache is quite sufficient to destroy any philosophy.

No-one was more surprised than I when it was announced I had 'satisfied the examiners' in obstetrics, a subject which I held (and hold) in total abhorrence. It will forever be associated in my mind with unearthly hours in the morning, flickering strip lighting, women in pain, blood and officious midwives screaming 'Push down harder! You're not trying! Push down harder!' at exhausted girls of sixteen, soon to give birth to illegitimate children destined for life in the slums. When a consultant obstetrician asked me what I had felt after witnessing my first birth, I said that I thought it a poor experience. Whatever the moral complexities of gestation outside the human body, aesthetically it must be an improvement. An evangelical Christian in my group, when asked the same question, said he thought it was 'a little miracle'. However, he was in the habit of seeing miracles everywhere.

Once qualified, I remembered the advice proffered by a senior consultant to a group of us at the outset of our clinical studies. He was teaching us how to examine patients; he had just discovered that he had cancer of the bowel, which he took to be a sentence of death. His life was at an end, he said, and now he realised that he had devoted it to a worthless ambition, namely to become a consultant in a teaching hospital. To achieve this he had led a deformed life for many years: he had been endlessly on duty at night, ruining his family life; he had toadied for years to men whom he detested; he had failed to develop other interests; and he had played silly academic games by doing research which he knew from its inception to be futile, since it was undertaken from a desire for promotion rather than from love of knowledge. Worst of all, he had lived his entire adult life in a single institution, knowing nothing of the world beyond. And now it was too late, he was dying.

'I know you don't like me,' he said, which was no more than the truth, for he had been an irascible and intimidating teacher. 'But I want to give you a piece of advice. You won't take it, I know, but I'll give it you all the same. On no account pursue a career only for power or prestige. To live an interesting life, that is the main thing. You don't appreciate it yet, but this is the only life you have, so make the most of it. Don't do what I've done. The world is much bigger than any hospital.'

His words, I think, fell largely on deaf ears, because most medical students are dazzled by the amateur dramatics of the casualty department and operating theatre: which is, after all, why most have chosen to be medical students. I, on the other hand, was receptive to his embittered message, because it coincided so exactly with my own feelings. Whenever I had been on duty in the hospital over the weekend I felt a sense of physical release, as though from prison, when I left the building. I knew it was a poor omen for a conventional medical career.

My first paid employment was in a small hospital in a town in the Midlands, where at the time (1974) there were still many small forges, hardly changed since the Industrial Revolution, in operation. Men worked in them at extremely high temperatures, and were allowed to refresh themselves *ad libitum* with beer, fetched from the local pubs in buckets. I was assured that some of the men drank forty pints a day without ever becoming drunk or addicted.

I had a suspicion that one of the consultants for whom I worked who told me this drank at least as much.

The hospital was completely undistinguished, except for a kidney dialysis unit. I was on duty one night in two, and sat in my room waiting for my bleeper to call me into reluctant action. Sometimes the telephone would ring at three in the morning to warn me of the impending arrival of a patient being brought by ambulance. I prayed that he would be D.O.A., dead on arrival, so that all I should have to do before returning to my bed was to certify him. The case could then be dealt with in the morning by our pathologist and Fred, our distinguished-looking white-haired mortuary attendant, who actually performed the post mortems.

My room was immediately above that of the Matron, a spinster who complained that I was intolerably noisy. At first I met her complaints by trying to be quiet, by creeping round my own room like a thief in the night. But I never succeeded in being quiet enough to satisfy her, and her complaints continued, both in writing and by insistent bangs on the ceiling with a walking stick. I decided to go on to the offensive. Whenever I was called up at night I crashed around my room as loudly as I could, knocking furniture over and dropping things, even jumping up and down on the floor. Her complaints ceased forthwith.

The consultant with whom I spent most time was a woman in her mid-fifties, a spinster for whom her patients were her family, her recreation, her whole life. Her devotion to them was absolute. On her ward rounds she examined each with minute care, read their notes from start to finish, and ordered long batteries of tests in case she had missed something, even when the diagnosis had been made weeks before. Though she was clearly a woman of the greatest kindness, her ward rounds were a terrible ordeal for all concerned – patients, doctors, nurses – lasting eight or ten hours. By the end of them one wished to scream, to kick the walls, to smash plates. And the worst of these ordeals was that they benefited no-one. I do not recall a single patient whose life was saved, whose diagnosis was made, whose prognosis was improved, by this minute sifting of details.

Though she was a very clever woman who, had she been a man, would have achieved far greater distinction within the profession, she nevertheless displayed an ignorance of what went on in her own hospital which was at once naive and utterly invincible.

In one of the geriatric wards there were two old-time nurses, who had returned to nursing. They were splendid creatures, ample of girth, one of them in crisp green uniform, the other in fine blue and white stripes. Each vast bosom was kept in order by a stiffly-starched apron of dazzling whiteness: one would get snow-blindness looking at it for too long.

These two nurses had a no-nonsense attitude to their calling. They didn't hold with new-fangled ideas, like science. They believed that when a patient was destined to die no power on earth – certainly not hospitals, conceited doctors, or nurses – could intervene. The geriatric ward was their domain. Visited rarely by a doctor, and then only to withhold antibiotics from a stroke patient who had contracted pneumonia, these nurses had an elemental view of their calling: to keep the ward clean, the bowels moving, and to suppress by sedatives any human noise in competition with the television. In their ward, television was not an entertainment but an invariable accompaniment to every minute of the day. The only way for the patients to avoid the flickering screen was to close their eyes; but there was no escaping the stream of banal banter. (It is strange how many nurses think paralysed people are also deaf.) The ward often presented the visitor with a bizarre, not to say hideous, juxtaposition of impressions: the smell of urine, two rows of passive, incontinent old people lying motionless in cots, saliva dribbling from the corners of their mouths, and television pictures of young people gyrating to the latest hits in stroboscopic lighting, or a breathless young woman in a leotard demonstrating keep fit exercises to overweight housewives at home – AND one two three AND touch your toes AND one two three . . .

And if the two nurses, who meant no harm by it, considered that one of their patients was being deliberately difficult, he or she was given the bath treatment. Into the bath the aged delinquent would go, where he or she would stay for a couple of hours or so. (Sometimes, on the other hand, the patients were left in the bath not as a corrective measure but because it was simply forgotten – until medicine time – that they were there.) As a method of sedation it was, I think, moderately successful, though a trifle old-fashioned.

Occasionally, however, the two nurses were called upon to exercise less custodial and more therapeutic skills. When other wards in the hospital ran short of staff they were seconded to them. And it was here that the trouble began. One of their duties was to keep fluid balance charts – the quantity of fluid a patient took in each day compared with the quantity he lost by all routes in the same period. These charts were as tablets from Sinai to the meticulous woman consultant, whom the two nurses hated as only female nurses can hate female doctors.

A couple of hours before the consultant's ward round, the two nurses would sit down together to make up the charts which they had failed completely to keep since the last ward round. Knowing nothing of physiology, they put down on the charts the first figures that came into their heads, and then sailed majestically round the ward clipping a chart to the end of each bed.

During the interminable ward round that followed, the consultant would pore over the charts, trying to unravel their physiological mysteries. For example, a patient would be shown as having drunk twenty litres less over a week than he urinated, though he demonstrated as yet none of the signs of dehydration. Or he would be shown as having drunk twenty litres more than he urinated. She took the charts to the office, where we sat round a table trying – for hours at a time – to reconcile them with any known laws of physiology or pathology. It never once occurred to her that they were entirely bogus, works of cheap fiction. She was too devoted to her patients, too conscientious herself, to imagine such a thing of others. Everyone else in the room went mad alternately with boredom and suppressed laughter. Eventually she came up with a rare diagnosis, the nearest that she could somehow reconcile with the figures before her, and order a battery of expensive and time-consuming laboratory tests to confirm or refute it. No-one ever dared tell her about the two nurses, who laughed most of all; and thus a stream of patients was subjected to all kinds of unnecessary tests, and the resources of the health service frittered away, because of the child-like innocence of this clever woman.

She died not long afterwards, of secondaries from a primary cancer that had been removed some years before. Her aged mother, with whom she had lived all her life, survived her. When I learnt of her death I was seized by melancholy. A good and talented woman (she had studied under some of the most famous medical scientists of her day, and had had their good opinion), she had not, I suspected, known much personal happiness. At best she had made an accommodation with life. Her death would have been greeted with secret relief by all those who had still to endure her ward rounds; and a week later, it would have been entirely forgotten that she ever existed.

It was in the same hospital that I met one of the best men I ever knew. His name was Dr Mehta. Dr Mehta was short and rather fat; he had given up attempts to slim, he said, because his wife's cooking was too good. He chain-smoked when out of sight of the patients, and spoke English with a lilting Indian accent that I found enchanting.

It is always more difficult to convey the essence of a good man than of an evil one. Suffice it to say that Dr Mehta inspired immediate affection and even love in almost everyone who met him, including the hard-bitten racialists of the Midlands. Quite unconscious of his charm, he was incapable of thinking a mean thought, and if anyone behaved despicably he immediately sought to excuse them. He was always equable, even when called out of bed at three in the morning by a hypochondriac with a trivial complaint. If ever he heard a racist remark directed at himself, he always said that there was far worse prejudice in India, as between castes, classes, religions and regions. He said it was natural that people should feel antipathy to conspicuous outsiders, and he admired the British for their hypocrisy in trying to conceal it. It showed, he said, that they knew what was right, even if they could not feel it in their hearts. He was always, in my opinion, much too kind about the British, whom he regarded as having reached the pinnacle of civilisation.

Dr Mehta had come to England to take one of the postgraduate qualifications that are still so highly regarded in India that even failure is considered as some kind of qualification. He had so far failed several times, originally because of nervousness, but latterly as even he began to suspect – because of racial prejudice on the part of the examiners. (One notoriously prejudiced examiner in Scotland was dismissed when it was pointed out that, in his entire career, he had passed only one out of several thousand Indian candidates.) Dr Mehta's medical knowledge was more than sufficient, but each time he failed he was condemned to spend further dreary hours committing yet more facts to memory. His boss wept for him, and demanded of the examiners why 'my boy' had been thus unjustly served. But nothing destroyed Dr Mehta's serene good humour, or his faith in the underlying benevolence of the world and of men.

The goodness of his character was all the more surprising when one considers his upbringing. He was a spoilt member of the Indian upper classes who had never, until he arrived in England, so much as carried his own suitcase. As a child he had been given everything he wanted. A keen follower of cricket, though never a player, he had only to mention (at the age of ten) that he would quite like to watch a match being played a thousand miles away and he would be instantly despatched in a first class carriage reserved to him, with two or three servants to attend to his wants. But he had survived this upbringing to become the most unselfish of men.

Casual racism is endemic in doctors' common rooms through-out the country, and it appals me, though I have never risked opprobium or ridicule by speaking out loud against it. Junior doctors talk among themselves of 'the melanotic index', by which facetious expression they mean the proportion of Indian doctors working in the hospital. When I hear it, I think of Dr Mehta and his most charitable interpretations of the prejudice he sometimes encountered, in what he considered the most civilised country in the world.

Eventually Dr Mehta passed his examination, but alas did not live long to enjoy it. He died shortly afterwards of a heart attack at a very early age. As far as I know he left behind no scientific work as a memorial, but all who encountered him were the better for the experience. And if his constant striving for a goal that was for long denied him by petty prejudice hastened his end, as I think it may, I hope those responsible are proud of themselves.

My time in that hospital was neither happy nor productive. Doctors are often accused of treating their patients as physiological objects rather than as 'whole human beings,' but the reverse is just as true: patients often treat doctors as mere curative devices. Whenever I tried in the wards to talk to the patients about some aspect of their lives other than illness they always brought the subject back to their constipation, or this pain that shoots from my left knee, doctor, twists round my waist and up into my right eye. Prolonged contact with the patients usually provoked a string of new, unfathomable complaints and left me with a feeling of impotent rage. So when I had a moment to spare I spent it not with the patients, as I had once idealistically thought I should, but in a corner, reading Russian novels.

My greatest excitement came with the death of one of my patients. He was a rich old colonel, dying slowly of an insidious disease. He and I had got along famously: I listened with genuine fascination to his stories of service life, of war in the jungle, and so forth. I looked forward to his periodic admissions to hospital, for he was one of the few patients who preferred not to catalogue almost lovingly the minute fluctuations of every symptom. On one occasion he had a heart attack while I was in the room and his heart stopped beating. His case notes had yet to be marked N.T.B.R. – not to be resuscitated – and I managed to bring him back to life.

Some time later I heard from a nurse that he was so grateful to me for his temporary reprieve from oblivion that he had decided, having no close relations, to leave his money to me. I believed it, of course; and from that moment the worm of greed grawed at my heart. His illness required repeated blood transfusions; and where previously I had rejoiced at his renewed accession to vigour after each one, I now began to feel, however hard I tried to suppress it, a pang of irritation that he was so uselessly lingering. I attempted to hide it from him by becoming more than usually attentive. Whether he noticed a subtle change in my demeanour, or whether the nurse's story was fabricated, I cannot say. However, when the colonel died (shortly after my departure from the hospital, I hasten to add), I did not hear from his solicitors.

I decided that if the greatest excitement I could expect from working in a British hospital was the off-chance of a legacy, I had better seek employment elsewhere. I learnt that a hospital in Bulawayo, in what was still then Rhodesia, sought house officers. By a strange chance, the hospital was recognised by the General Medical Council for registration purposes. (Every doctor, after graduation, must work a year under supervision in an approved hospital.) I received an offer from Bulawayo, and all the people who thought they ought to advise me warned me that to accept it was the end of my career, if not worse. It was tantamount to professional suicide, they said; I should never get another job when I returned to Britain; the régime had a terrible reputation for brutality; besides which, it was illegal for a Briton to give aid and comfort to the white rebels of Africa.

I did not find these arguments compelling. I could not conceive that my presence would bring aid and comfort to anyone (not even patients, let alone whole régimes); and as for my career in Britain, supposing I had one, I gave it no further thought.

TWO

Rhodesia

IT USED TO TAKE, so they said, ten minutes for a man to become a Rhodesian after stepping off the aeroplane.

I had not come to Rhodesia out of any sympathy for the régime – on the contrary, my attitude to the problem of southern Africa was that of any right-thinking person – but there was no doubt that the pleasures of having effortlessly become one of an élite were seductive, even if it was only to call down anathema on it from a secure position within. White immigration to Africa had for long been an outlet for the disgruntled mediocre, a chance painlessly to achieve distinction and status, a high standard of living, and to avoid the mundane tasks of life by employing a staff of servants. The Kenyan settlers persuaded themselves that while Kenya was the colony of the officer class, Rhodesia was the colony of the non-commissioned officer class. They may have been correct about the social origins of the settlers in the two colonies, but at a deeper level they were identical: they had gone to Africa out of irritation with the modern world.

Never having any intention to settle, my motives were different but not, I think, more creditable. I wanted to avoid the tedium of working in a British hospital, but more than that I wanted to recapture old certainties. In my earlier youth I had held (strictly theoretical) radical views. I wanted to change the world because I saw it as a mirror image of Dr Pangloss' version of it: all was for the worst in this, the worst of all possible worlds. Everything, I thought, must be swept away in an orgy of destruction and built anew on foundations of universal love and cooperation. Anyone who disagreed with this simple formulation did so either out of ill-will or self-interest. As I later came to realise, my radicalism was to my mind what puberty had been to my body.

In any case, such an attitude could scarcely have survived even the most casual or restricted of brushes with the real world. The apparent difficulty – or impossibility – of improving the food in a British hospital gave one pause for the amelioration of the condition of the whole world. In Britain, a country in the inexorable process of decline, the good no longer seemed so easy to distinguish from the bad, and the psychological rewards for knowing not merely what was wrong with the world but what was necessary to put it right melted away like snows in spring.

Righteous indignation, however, is one of the most satisfying of emotions, cousin as it is to sheer hatred, and I was reluctant to abjure it altogether. My problem, therefore, was to discover where in the world pure evil still confronted pure good, where I could demonstrate that I was on the side of the angels, but at the same time live comfortably and register with the General Medical Council. Rhodesia was the perfect solution. It had the added attraction of being the last remnant of an empire self-evidently soon to disappear forever, and I wanted to see it before it died.

I arrived in Rhodesia after the briefest of stays in Gabon. There at night, the jungle seemed to encroach threateningly on to the very edge of the runway, a tenebrous mass dimly perceived in the dark air. The damp night heat throbbed with the insistence of a drum-beat, the very fulfilment of one's fantasies of Africa. But Rhodesia (as it still was then) is a land of bright savannah, not of steaming jungle, and the officialdom at Bulawayo Airport was of British inspiration. The shock of the familiar is sometimes as great as the shock of the new.

The hospital to which I was contracted to work, Mpilo (or Health in Ndebele) was in the black township of Mzilikazi, named after the warrior king of the Ndebele. I thought it odd that a government based on the premise of natural black incompetence to rule, should allow a fierce black ruler to be thus memorialised.

But perhaps it was being more subtle than I thought: Mzilikazi had led the Ndebele, a defeated branch of the Zulu tribe, into what was now Matabeleland only half a century before the whites arrived, pushing the more numerous but less warlike Shona into Mashonaland. As a result, there was no love lost between the Shona and the Ndebele. The name Mzilikazi helped to keep alive the memory of their imperial past among the Ndebele, when they lorded it over another tribe, and thus to prevent unity with the formerly subject people whom they regarded with contempt; it served also to remind them that they too were colonists, relative newcomers to the land they had taken by right of conquest.

Mzilikazi was a vast area covered with symmetrical rows of identical one-storey houses, rectangular and with tin roofs. I at once made it my duty to find out what percentage were without running water, what without power, and what without sanitation, so that I could see the township in the worst possible light. I came to the conclusion that it had been built by callous men who considered the Africans not as human beings, with all their idiosyncracies and need for self-expression, but as robotic units of labour (though robots with an irritating tendency to break down – hence Mpilo). I contrasted the grey and dusty township of breezeblock and tin with my first glimpses of the white suburbs, which I had caught from the air: large residences in spacious gardens of manicured lawns and carefully tended flowerbeds, with large lush trees to give shade, most with turquoise swimming pools glittering in the sun (the white Rhodesians had more swimming pools per head than any other group of people on earth), and not a few with tennis courts. It was small wonder, I thought, that the Africans wanted to turn everything upside down.

The hospital itself was a large building of red brick in the parsimonious British municipal style of the fifties, with metal-framed windows and no embellishments. It was one of two large referral hospitals for the whole African population of Rhodesia, then about six million. Though only three storeys, it seemed to tower over the squat houses of the township, an architectural symbol, I thought smugly, of the literal and metaphorical ill-health of this society.

At first I lived in the doctors' residence in the hospital grounds. Every evening, after work, I walked across the small patch of untended wilderness separating the hospital from the residence, which the savannah had reclaimed for its own. I lay on my bed and tried to read, but the rhythmic chanting in mysterious union of the night insects made me restless, as though I were being called to the unknown. From time to time, the unreliable telephone next to my bed would give a croup-like ring, and I would curse the day I became a doctor.

'Doctor, the patient is gasping!'

I was expected to know, by some abstruse process of telepathy, to whom the nurse was referring. Usually, she had a surprisingly deep bass voice, for a woman. I was lucky if I managed to ask the location of the gasping patient before the receiver at the other end was replaced with a crash.

The first time I received such a message – at two in the morning – I jumped off my bed and ran through the sultry heat round all the wards of the hospital until I found the one in which the patient was gasping: except he was not gasping, he was dead. Not only was he dead, but he had been dead for some considerable time, in spite of the nurses' attempts to make his demise appear more recent by immersing him in a warm bath before laying him back in bed, ready for certification. It took only a few such fool's errands for me to realise that 'gasping' was a euphemism for dead. In future, when a patient was gasping I finished my chapter, I sauntered, I went back to sleep.

Nurses on night duty can see no reason why doctors, who are more highly paid, should be allowed to sleep soundly the whole night through. It was a viewpoint with which, as I was called up more often in the night, I came increasingly to sympathise. In any case, certification does not take long, though it is not entirely without its problems. While a recently dead person undoubtedly looks dead – there is a *je ne sais quoi* about death – when a stethoscope is clapped on his clammy chest all sorts of noises can be heard, which call into question the diagnosis of finality. A gurgling, a sound of pattering feet: can it be that the patient harboured in his chest during life a family of parasitic mice, who are now trying to get out? The throbbing of the arteries in one's ears can seem like a heartbeat, and the horror of certifying as dead a still-living man rises like a spectre to haunt the imagination of the young doctor. It is not the burial alive that draws beads of sweat from his brow, but the ridicule of his colleagues.

I soon moved with three other doctors, somewhat my senior, into a house in a suburb with the utilitarian name of Suburbs. The road was named after one of the great heroes of colonial society, Pauling, a railway engineer and big game hunter. The house was, by Rhodesian standards, ancient, dating back perhaps to before 1920. It was large and echoing, single storey, surrounded by a red-tiled verandah. The garden was exquisitely beautiful, with jacarandas spreading a perfumed shade and a dusting of purple flowers on the sun-dappled lawn beneath. Poinsettias grew to the size of trees, their leaves a flaming crimson. There was a swimming pool and a small orchard of fragrant citrus fruit and avocado trees. Every morning a go-away bird would settle in the trees and issue its plaintive instruction. To arise early and see the cool garden in the crystal translucence of the morning light was a positive pleasure. A table was set on the verandah for breakfast with a clean white cloth, the *Bulawayo Chronicle*, neatly folded beside one's plate (it invariably related with glee the misfortunes and disasters that had befallen the black-ruled states of Africa), and a cup of strong coffee. It was not difficult to see how one could be seduced by the colonial life, nor how one would tolerate almost any political system that enabled one to enjoy such a garden and such mornings.

The three doctors with whom I lived were unlike in their characters. The first was an Ulsterman, Conor McBride, a very competent physician (he is a consultant now in the province), of cautious frame of mind, who had so thoroughly assimilated his scientific training into his personality that he never said anything without the firmest foundation in fact. He never allowed himself flights of fancy, and his extreme caution sometimes provoked me, when discussing something with him, into an unscrupulous manufacture of facts to clinch my point. Perhaps, coming as he did from a strife-torn province, he was all too aware of the dangers of the inflamed imagination.

The second of the doctors was a Rhodesian, John Williamson, proud of his long Rhodesian ancestry, going back at least a generation. He was very quiet, and towns made him uneasy. Though it was possible to escape Bulawayo into the complete emptiness of the bush within half an hour, the city suffocated him. The solitude of the wide open spaces, of the immeasurable blue skies, of limitless horizons, was for him an almost physical need. Next to nature, he communed best with his bull terrier, an ugly, pig-eyed brute, but fiercely loyal. His political views were highly conservative, his mind filled with the exploits of the white pioneers of central Africa. The mere mention of African nationalism was enough to make him angry. His mind and body clenched tightly like a fist; he used to say he would be happy to die fighting to preserve his way of life; but at heart he was a gentle man, undemonstrative and modest, who never in my knowledge did anyone any harm, and whom only circumstances could have turned even theoretically violent. His ambition was to be a medical officer in a rural district, leading a useful, self-reliant life. What became of him I do not know. In my mind's eye, I see him killed in the long guerilla war, or fleeing southwards before the onslaught of the twentieth century. But if he is still alive, I imagine him carrying a deep bitterness, an unhealing wound, an unburst abscess within him, a fierce but impotent desire for revenge on the destroyers of the beloved country of his youth. Harsh indeed are the penalties for being born in the wrong place at the wrong time.

The third of the doctors who lived at Pauling Road, Giles Legatt, was a handsome South African with an American mother. He was somewhat older than the others, and at twenty-nine I thought him almost an old man. He was gregarious and carefree, seemingly untouched by life's sorrows. Possessed of a harmless vanity, at which he was able to laugh himself, he was concerned only that everything he did should be done with a certain élan, a style, a dash, to maintain an image he had formed of himself. He has, I believe, become an anaesthetist in Cape Town, which demonstrates only how time and the world extinguish youth's dreams.

We were happy, despite our differences. We employed two servants, Justin and Moses, who smoothed our paths, relieving us of all domestic chores. Moses was the garden boy (boy in the mouth of a white southern African bears no connotation of youth); Justin the houseboy. Moses was little more to me than a shadowy figure who flashed a smile at me when I left for work in the mornings. But Justin was an ever-present factotum who cleaned my shoes, washed my clothes, made my bed and cooked my meals, the latter with indifferent success. He had a knack of turning any meat, even the best beef or the tenderest lamb, into hard little indigestible pellets. With vegetables, it was another matter. He could turn them into an indistinguishable, savourless mush *à l'anglaise*, merely by immersing them in water. In time I began to suspect that his cooking was an act of passive political resistance, or at least protest. But he was so ingratiatingly cheerful, so deferential, as he placed his barely edible efforts before us, that it was difficult somehow to tax him on the matter.

Occasionally we would return home from the hospital to find Justin, sitting on a stool in the kitchen, propped up against the wall for vital support, with a fixed grin on his face. We knew then that he had found his way into the cupboard in which we kept our drink. Justin was a fastidious drinker: he spurned Rhodesian products and drank only the imported wines and spirits which were then hard to come by, and which we saved for special occasions.

Justin was the incarnation of the one subject (other than Robert Mugabe) that united all Rhodesian white women into a unanimous bloc of avenging termagants: the Servant Problem. Somehow those who never lifted a finger for themselves for months or decades at a time managed to persuade themselves that they were the most ill-used of women, martyrs in fact to the impossibility these days of finding decent, reliable and honest servants. And the strange thing was that they had no fear of expressing this opinion in front of the very servants who were the subject of it, whom they knew perfectly well understood English. The reason for this was that they could never quite persuade themselves that their African servants were fully human. If they understood English, it was only in the same sense that a dog understood an instruction to sit.

It was all too easy to fall into the same trap oneself. In addition to their wages, our servants received an allowance of food. Whenever we went to the butcher we asked first for meat for ourselves; then bones and scraps for the dog; lastly, cheap and crudely-hacked chunks of miscellaneous flesh and gristle called 'ration meat'. This was for the servants; and it was the expression, rather than the meat itself, which shocked me, for it too implied something less than human. But just as one rapidly adjusts to injustice when it is not oneself that suffers from it, so I soon came to use the term unselfconsciously.

I had vowed as well that I should never just accept the daily presence of the servants as a fact of nature, like the weather, without enquiring after their welfare or taking a personal interest in them. But my good intentions – if they were good – soon lapsed under social and other pressures. Only one of our servants, Justin, lived on the premises, for the law did not allow more than one African at a time to reside in a white household, both for fear of falling property prices and of sudden rebellion, when the whites might otherwise find themselves outnumbered even in their own neat suburbs. Justin had his quarters in a corner of the garden not visible from the verandah, but like any Rhodesian who had employed the same servant for forty years without ever knowing how he lived, I never visited him there, excusing myself on the grounds that it would have been an intrusion on his privacy. Just before I left Bulawayo, though, I did look into his quarters while he was out: to my relief, for I had a bad conscience about it, they were clean and neat, if bare and spartan. On the wall was a reproduction of a triptych by Van Eyck.

Each day was brilliantly sunny and, as winter approached, the warmth of the day was pleasant rather than oppressive. In the evening an open fire became, if not a necessity, then a comfortable luxury. The climate, as Rhodesians never tired of telling me, was the finest in the world (except for a couple of very hot months), rejuvenating and invigorating in its effect. Once a week, many of the (white) junior staff of Mpilo gathered in the early evening on the beautifully tended, green playing fields of Milton High School, a short walk away from Pauling Road, to play touch rugby. The succulent grass – well, but not over, watered – was cool and grateful on the feet. They were fine games, played in the best of humours, after which we returned to the house for a few beers and what the South Africans called a graze (a meal). We gave no thought to the historical legacy of the Milton High School's most distinguished pupil: Dr Hendrik Verwoerd.

Thus I found myself sucked with ease into colonial society. My theoretical views remained theoretical, and were tolerated as the inevitable result of having read too much of the British press. Let me stay a year or two, and I should become indistinguishable from any other Rhodesian.

So I thought. But an African porter in Mpilo told me he knew at once, before I opened my mouth, that I had not been born in either Rhodesia or South Africa. I asked him how he knew.

'Because of the way you walk,' he said. 'We can always tell Rhodesian or South African whites by the way they walk.'

It appeared they had a certain swagger, a get-out-of-my-way, lord-of-the-earth gait, and usually, in middle age, a beer belly overhanging the waist of their shorts which they used like the blade of a bulldozer. Or so, at any rate, the porter claimed. I was so flattered that I at once went out and bought him a lengthy history of Southern Africa, written by a liberal historian, in which I wrote a priggish inscription about the need and hope of change.

Though social contact between black and white was not

actually outlawed, it was difficult to achieve. I once invited a few of the black junior doctors at Mpilo back to Pauling Road, but it was not a success. John and Giles, both raised in southern Africa, did not object, but neither did they approve. There was an awkward, strained atmosphere, and it was difficult to find things to say. The harder we scanned our minds for suitable subjects, the blanker they became. They were also a little anxious to demonstrate that they knew how to behave just as, when one lunches with one's superiors, one is excessively anxious not to slurp one's soup. It came as a relief to all concerned when, in unison, they said it was time to go. It was nearly impossible in the Rhodesia of that time to bridge the political and cultural abyss which separated the races, even for men of goodwill. The time for gestures was over: a life-and-death struggle had begun. John and Giles were not displeased by the outcome of my little multiracial soirée, for it proved – whatever my extravagant ideas – that *au fond* I was one of them.

Contact outside the relative sumptuousness of our home was a little easier, however. In the casualty department of the hospital I used to have friendly discussions with a black doctor who, unusually for Mpilo, was a Shona rather than an Ndebele. One of the questions we discussed was the division within the nationalist movement, at which all white Rhodesians rejoiced, to put it mildly. It was essentially a division along tribal lines, though the leaders of the factions also favoured different economic policies for the emergent black state. From time to time statements healing the wounds were issued, declaring undying solidarity in the common struggle for freedom and justice. But the unity soon fractured along the old tribal fault lines, and before long the factions were once again sending each other letter bombs and other tokens of high regard. We discussed the question just after yet another healing statement had been issued, replacing the era of internecine war with that of fraternal solidarity. I was sceptical, and said so. I said that disagreement, and worse, would soon enough break out again.

'What you are saying is impossible,' said the Shona doctor

hotly. 'Quite impossible. It's all propaganda. We are united as never before and can never be divided.'

Possibly he believed it, I don't know. But I saw in his excited countenance the gleam of lies to come. For the first time the gleefully bitter little aphorism of the white Rhodesians, which they flung in the faces of the well-meaning liberals like myself, one man one vote once, seemed to have some substance. It wasn't freedom the Shona doctor was after, but power. I learnt that good causes are not necessarily espoused by good men.

On a couple of occasions I ventured out at night into the black township with one of the Ndebele doctors. We went to shebeens, the illicit liquor shops that were necessary because there were only a handful of legal outlets for drink for a population of two hundred thousand amongst whom drinking was almost the only relaxation. The shebeens were run in the homes of women of strong character and strong arms, who were not themselves above ejecting by force troublesome male drunks. A lookout was always posted for the police (then still called the British South Africa Police) who ran an extortion racket. In the small, barely-furnished and tin-roofed rooms of the shebeen, lit by pressure lamps, everyone was friendly and dropped the insincerely deferential or cringing approach to whites that was habitual elsewhere. I learnt that the Africans had derogatory names for us too which, absurdly, came as a surprise. I found the home-brewed maize beer disgusting – gritty and sour – and thought it better to admit it than attempt to drink it with a face puckered with distaste while saying how nice it was (and being served with more). I drank warm beer instead. But as everyone grew drunker, I grew more anxious to leave. I had seen enough of drunks to fear their swift changes of mood, their recklessness, and their propensity suddenly to remember old grievances. I left before I could become the object of anyone's drunken resentment.

There were two black sisters on the surgical ward on which I worked. (The Matron was a stern white woman with blue-rinsed hair who inspected the hospital daily for cleanliness, and always found it filthy, almost on principle.) One of the sisters was a large, maternal woman, whose kindly laughter seemed to flow through her considerable body in waves, but who was nevertheless quite capable of exacting instant obedience from her staff. It was never difficult to make her laugh, and one day she invited me home to dinner.

She lived with her aged mother, alone in a standard township house. Her mother, who was also fat, had come to live in Bulawayo after seventy years in a distant village, which she had never previously left. The town astonished her and so, I think, did my presence. At any rate, she sat in the corner all the time I was there and never said a word. The house, both inside and out, had an incongruously but strangely moving chintzy atmosphere, as though the sister had got hold of a book by Beatrix Potter and used it as a manual of house decoration. Around the front door was a trellis, supporting a pink climbing rose. The garden, if you could call a patch of ground crossed in two steps a garden, was divided into neat flower beds and a pocket handkerchief lawn. Inside there was a clutter of ornaments and furniture covered in floral fabric. On the walls were group photographs of family occasions, the women in elaborate hats and spotless white gloves, the men in as close approximations to business suits as they could afford, often with black-covered Bibles under their arms. The children sat at the feet of the adults, the girls in ribbons and chiffon dresses, the boys in velveteen suits with matching bow ties. I had never been an enthusiast for the bourgeois virtue of respectability, but there was something heroic – or perhaps tragic – in the struggle of these people to keep themselves respectable according to the lights of another people for whom the African race was forever excluded from respectability.

As I left her house, I met her next-door neighbour, who was one of the few black members of parliament permitted by the constitution of that time. His English was as impeccable and even elegant as his suit. We stood and chatted for half an hour. He knew that many of his fellow Africans regarded him as a government stooge; still, he was able in parliament to say in public what no other African could say without being detained. And he acknowledged that many of the nationalists were not democrats in any conventional sense; and while, like all Africans, he resented deeply the privileges the whites had accorded themselves, it was nevertheless true, he said, that the whites were absolutely essential for the proper running of the country, at least for the foreseeable future. The division of the land between white and black, for example was grossly inequitable; but at least the country was more than self-sufficient in food. His was not a message, he said, calculated to bring widespread popularity among his fellow Africans (indeed, he had received death threats from them, while the whites simply ignored him). But it was the truth, at least how he saw it, and he was not afraid to expound it, even at the cost, if need be, of death. For too long, he said, African leaders had deluded their followers with lies and false promises of new dawns; but in the long run, only the truth served them. I wondered as he talked whether he was not, after all, in the pay of the government, employed to sow doubt and intellectual scruples in a situation which required incisive action rather than tortured reflection. But, other than that he was well-dressed, he appeared to live no differently from the other inhabitants of Mzilikazi. He was either a dissimulator of the first rank or a man of astonishing integrity. As I shook hands with him to part I thought of him as a dead man, if not literally then as a public figure.

The other sister on the surgical ward was altogether sterner. It was difficult to make her smile, let alone laugh, though I managed sometimes. One felt she harboured (nurtured perhaps would be a better word) an inextinguishable bitterness in her breast.

She was the sister-in-law of Joshua Nkomo, the father of southern Rhodesian nationalism, and I mentioned one day that I should be interested to meet him. (He was, by the way, a regular attender at Mpilo outpatients, under the care of one of the white physicians. Racial hatred had not so far eroded either medical ethics or trust in doctors.) Then, one day not long afterwards, Sister Nkomo invited me to tea with the great man. I had never before met anyone of truly international fame, and I was excited at the prospect. My white colleagues thought that by seeking what amounted to an audience with a black man I was rather letting the side down (white men should always grant audiences to black, for racial prestige is indivisible), but were nonetheless intrigued by the outcome, and awaited my report from the den of iniquity.

His house in Mzilikazi was identical to a thousand – ten thousand – others, except for a white Mercedes and a Peugeot parked outside. As I entered, two men from the BBC were leaving, one of them holding a camera.

'Thank you very much, Sir,' said the interviewer, whom I did not recognise. He bowed a little. 'See you again, Sir. And if it would not be impertinent, Sir, may I wish you luck with your struggle.'

We bumped into each other in the doorway and he gave me a sideways glance, as if to say, 'And who might you be?'

Joshua Nkomo sat on a chair in the middle of the main room in the house. He was enormously fat and held himself like a Zulu king. The room was barely furnished; I noticed a crucifix on the wall. There were children – his grandchildren – playing in the small, dusty yard outside.

'What can I do for you, doc?' he asked.

I felt slightly foolish. I explained, what he obviously knew already, that his sister-in-law worked with me at Mpilo, and I had told her I should like to meet him.

'What do you want me to talk about, doc?'

The way he called me doc made me feel, strangely enough, like a very small boy which I suppose I was, wandering into the great world of events.

'Politics,' I replied, and tea, stiff with sugar as the Africans like it, was served.

At that time Joshua Nkomo was engaged in 'secret' talks with Ian Smith, the settlers' Prime Minister. He was therefore regarded with some suspicion, to say the least, by other nationalists, who feared he might do a deal with Smith excluding them from power. And the whites now regarded him (however many times they had arrested him or exiled him in the past) as the most moderate and reasonable of the bad bunch of nationalists, whose underlying motive, so they said, was only to get their fingers in the economic pie.

I asked him whether he thought he could achieve anything without resort to violence.

'When I was a young man like you', he replied, 'I thought that violence was the only solution.' He glanced at the crucifix. 'But now – as I get older, I realise that violence solves nothing. It only breeds violence.'

It wasn't quite an answer to my question but I was too shy not to let it pass. I had the impression, as he took a grandchild on to his knee, that he was not the kind of man who exulted in the deaths of others. His aversion to violence was genuine enough. But later, when negotiation proved as futile as I had always suspected it was, he began to dress up in military uniforms (a more unmartial figure could scarcely be imagined), and when his men succeeded in shooting down a civilian airliner and in massacring the survivors on the ground, he regarded it as a great success. This earned him the undying hatred of the whites; but I nevertheless retained my impression of him that afternoon and felt that he had resorted to such methods not out of natural bloodthirstiness but out of fear of political irrelevance as the guerilla war grew more desperate. He had, after all, devoted thirty years to the cause, for which he had suffered not inconsiderably. It was therefore understandable, if not commendable, that he did not want the cup dashed from his lips just as success became certain. But tribal demography, about which he could do nothing, was to make him politically irrelevant.

The result of my meeting was eagerly awaited at Pauling Road. I was unable to shed much light, except to say he was an amiable man, apparently without racial animosity, and that if whites could not reach agreement with him they would never find a more reasonable man with whom to deal. But there was no seeming imperative at the time to do a deal with anyone, and the whites thought the Indian summer of their rule would last forever.

My medical work, I must admit, played a small part in my life. I was the lowliest member of the surgical team. The hospital provided the best possible opportunity to garner 'experience' (the term used for the process of learning by the inexpert treatment of a wide variety of complaints), but I was not at the time much interested in anything remotely connected with my profession. I had four bosses, including a future Zimbabwean Minister. He was a Fellow of the Royal College of Surgeons, and seemed to bear the grudge that men often bear who have risen in the world despite all the obstacles placed in their path. Some of the white housemen said that he was a poor surgeon but I saw nothing that led me to that conclusion and their opinion may have been mere vexation at having to take orders from a black man. As to his character, I thought that his ambiguous position as highly paid employee of the government but senior member of the nationalist opposition accounted for his less than forthcoming demeanour.

Another surgeon for whom I worked was Mr Greaves. He was the best surgeon I have ever known. There seemed no problem he could not tackle with consummate skill. He was as comfortable, surgically speaking, in the skull as he was in the abdomen or the chest. He could operate on a day-old babe or a decrepit old person with as much facility as on a young adult in the prime of life. Furthermore (and this is a different skill altogether) he was the most acute diagnostician I have known. His accuracy was legendary. Everyone would give his opinion of a doubtful case; then Mr Greaves would be called to give his, and the matter was regarded as settled. He was, withal, a model of courtesy to his staff and patients, not at all given to the erratic and egocentric tantrums that are commonly supposed, not always erroneously, to be the hallmark of the surgeon. His staff was never afraid to call for his help, no matter the time of night; and he had a way of pointing out error that did not destroy the self-respect of him who made it. He had come to Rhodesia from Zambia at about the time of the latter's independence. He had retreated southwards not out of addiction to the politics of racial domination (so, at any rate, I felt must be true of a man who gave so wholeheartedly of his time and talent to the service of black Africans), but because he felt it inevitable, alas, that with the transference of power came a lowering of standards, an inattention to essential detail, that

would nullify his skill. He wanted, I concluded, to practise his
craft properly or not at all, and his experience led him to suppose
this would not be possible in newly-independent African states.
When Mpilo was put under new management, as it were, and the
top jobs were redistributed according to new imperatives, Mr
Greaves retreated, not to South Africa as some might have
expected, but to England. Whatever else they may have gained by
the new order, the black Zimbabweans lost the services of an
excellent surgeon and a good man.

The third of my bosses, Mr Peeler, I considered rather less
worthy. He was a urologist given to outbursts of rages, when his
face drained of blood and went as white as an ingot in a furnace. I
had the impression he enjoyed his rages, like a connoisseur. He
was the kind of man who thought everyone a fool, with one or two
exceptions, notably himself. He never asked a question unless he
thought it would go unanswered, confirming his view that the
world was composed of fools. I did not enjoy working for him.

The last of the surgeons for whom I worked was a woman, Miss
Schroder. Orthopaedics as a discipline requires not merely
stamina, but strength; if there was one attribute Miss Schroder
possessed (other than high intelligence) it was strength. I thought
of her as a recently-retired East European olympic athlete of
shot-putting or discus-throwing variety; in fact, she was a former
nun. She was also reputed to be a pianist of professional standard,
but she was not the kind of woman one questioned, other than
about work. Her particular interest was the place of surgery in the
treatment of tuberculosis of the spine, until research (hers included) proved that it had very little place.

My duties, like Gaul, were divided in three, between the
operating theatre, the wards and the casualty department. Of the
three, I liked the operating theatre the least. It was ruled over by
two white Rhodesian sisters who both had sky-blue eyelids and
that perpetual air of exasperation which, as I came to learn, was
characteristic of the white women of Africa. It must have been
years coping with the servant problem that brought it about.
Nevertheless, the theatre ran smoothly, if not happily. Our

anaesthetists were another source of friction. One was a rather silent man, Dr Cash, who appeared very relaxed, though perhaps he was only skilful and efficient. Once he had put a patient to sleep he was thenceforth to be found in the coffee room reading a newspaper or a book about southern African history by Oliver Ransford, his fellow-anaesthetist at the all-white Bulawayo Central Hospital. Perhaps Dr Cash was so confident of his prowess that he felt no anxiety for his anaesthetised patient; at any rate, I never knew of any who suffered as a result of his inattention. Our other anaesthetist was a woman, Dr Langridge, of whose good qualities I learnt ten years later from a doctor who had known her in her student days; but at the time she appeared to me sour and uncouth. She had had a difficult life; and perhaps the cancer that was not many years later to kill her had started its insidious progress through her body. But youth does not make allowances: it deals in absolutes. And there was much in her behaviour to dislike. Of very swarthy complexion, it was said she had an Indian mother, and in a society where race was so very important perhaps she was trying to prove by her abusive and contemptuous treatment of the Africans with whom she came in contact, which would have made Verwoerd himself blush, that she was, in the words of Frank Richards about Billy Bunter's schoolmate Hurree Jamset Ram Singh, a white man deep inside. If so, she must have had a very poor opinion of the white man's temper. My only form of protest as she was being particularly unpleasant was to gaze silently at the floor.

I learnt little in the theatre because I wished to learn little. Assisting at operations was, for me, a kind of slow torture. It is one thing to take infinite pains yourself, quite another to watch someone else doing it. And it is an ineluctable law of surgery that the assistant can never satisfy the surgeon. He either pulls the retractor too hard or not hard enough, but never just right. There is an old joke about a medical student who asks the famous professor of surgery: 'And how would you like your stitches cut today, professor? Too long or too short?' The layman thinks of the operating theatre as a place of drama. It is true there are moments of drama, or rather of crisis, but for the most part there is only tedium, exacerbated by the desultory conversation between the anaesthetist (if he is not wholly absorbed in his crossword) and the surgeon, concerning their sailing dinghies, dogs or vegetable gardens. I admired the surgeon's capacity for prolonged concentration, up to ten hours at a time; the concern for the welfare of patients that such an effort implies; and the coolness with which crises, when they arise, are handled. I remember Mr Greaves accidentally cutting an artery, and the strong instantaneous jet of crimson blood spattering his face and soaking his mask. It was enough to make even a brave man flee, but in one swift and sure movement of his finger he staunched the jet, and the crisis was over before it had properly begun. But for all my admiration, it was not work I could enjoy, and I never left the theatre without feeling great relief.

Because it was expected that many of the young doctors who passed through Mpilo were destined for remote out-stations where there would be little help available to them, they were all taught to administer simple anaesthetics. It had to be admitted that Dr Cash's enthusiasm for passing on the sacred flame of anaesthetic knowledge was as etiolated as was mine for receiving it. The second anaesthetic I gave under his distant tuition nearly ended in disaster. Mr Peeler was operating (sober for once and in relatively good humour). He noticed as he cut the flesh that little blood oozed out, and what little there was had an ominously dark colour, more blackish purple than red.

'The colour of this blood is a little odd,' he said with sardonic understatement. 'Do you suppose the patient is still alive?'

I was far from certain. I felt for a pulse and eventually I located a very feeble throb. Dr Cash was recalled from the coffee room and in a short time he had restored the patient to a condition more closely resembling life. It appeared that I had somehow managed to deprive the patient of an oxygen supply. Dr Cash said nothing and returned to his crossword in the coffee room.

Had the patient died it would not, I think, have been the end of my career. There can hardly be a doctor in the world who has not been responsible for somebody's death. And to kill a patient, or nearly to kill him, is, as the Americans say, a valuable learning experience, for the doctor if not the patient. In the Rhodesia of that time, to kill an African in the hospital through negligence or incompetence would have caused me no direr consequences than personal embarrassment, for there was none of the fuss attendant on a hospital death in Europe or America. The doctors of Mpilo were, for all practical purposes, a self-regulatory body outside the law. Only the ethical standards of the doctors themselves stood between the patients and the most fearful negligence. Yet, taken all in all, I do not think the patients would have been better served by a system of rigid external control. And I am not optimistic that they will be better served under the new dispensation.

Autres temps, autres moeurs. At Mpilo I treated a young child with serious burns with intravenous fluids. (In the unlit houses of the township, burns from kerosene lamps and stoves were very frequent, especially in winter.) I overestimated grossly the quantity he required and he died, not from his burns, but from my misguided efforts. When I was called to certify him dead I experienced a small crisis of conscience over what to put on the death certificate. In the end, I decided on the truth and to face whatever consequences there might be. But there were none: no-one ever so much as remarked on the death of the baby I had so incompetently caused. The mother accepted the loss of her child with that impressive but maddening African fatalism that is both the enemy and friend of the doctor: the enemy because it allows people needlessly to die from entirely curable diseases, the friend because when a patient dies it is only what the relatives expected in the first place, and is accepted with dignity rather than recrimination. As to losing a baby or two in the course of her child-bearing career, it is only what an African mother expects; while it causes sorrow, the loss is made good the next year. Losing a child or two out of seven or ten is not the same as losing one out of one point nine, and I am not sure it is wise to teach African mothers otherwise, until the means to prevent such deaths are available.

The second of my duties was to attend the surgical wards, clerking the patients and attending to their postoperative needs. The wards were bare but clean and not dreadfully overcrowded: there was only one patient per bed (not to be taken for granted in Africa), and there was room between beds for doctors and nurses to move. The beds were simple iron bedsteads, the mattresses lumpy, but the linen clean. The Ndebele service of the government radio station was loudly relayed all day, except during ward rounds, but no-one ever complained. It was largely tribal music interspersed with 'the latest hit, straight from the U.K.'

Our day invariably started with taking blood samples from the patients for the laboratory. Because of sanctions, or lack of money, or both, there were no disposable needles and syringes such as I had been accustomed to using. Instead, we had old-fashioned glass syringes and re-usable stainless steel needles of various degrees of bluntness. The barrels of the syringes were often so worn that they exerted little if any suction, and thus the simple task of taking blood became a sore trial to our nerves. It was impractical to use the veins of the arms (the usual place) to draw blood, for the needles were too blunt to force through the skin except at high velocity: instead, we used a technique known as the femoral stab. A vein and an artery run close together through the groin, and it was the vein we aimed for. The stab was precisely that: with the patient lying in the bed, the syringe was brought down sharply from what must have seemed, lying in bed, a great height and buried in his groin. If by mistake we entered the artery rather than the vein the syringe needed no suction: rather the problem was to prevent the bright red blood from shooting the plunger out of the barrel altogether. The patients accepted this barbaric procedure with exemplary stoicism (I cannot think of someone doing it to me without wincing). Not one of the patients ever cried out or protested.

There was an annexe to the wards called the verandah, built almost like a conservatory. It was here that the most hopeless cases lay. For a reason not fully understood, but presumed to be something to do with diet and possibly the consumption of maize beer brewed in crude iron pots, cancer of the oesophagus was very common in this part of central Africa. Every week two or three patients would arrive at the hospital complaining of difficulty in swallowing, and we knew at once it was a sentence not only of death, but of a repulsive, tortured death. Being by nature active people, surgeons were reluctant to admit there was little they could do for these unfortunates, other than palliate. As if the disease were not bad enough, they subjected the patients to what is known as 'heroic surgery'. For this disease, heroic surgery consisted of removing as far as possible the diseased portion of the oesophagus and replacing it with a section of the patient's own large bowel. It was a technique pioneered in Hong Kong, another region of high prevalence of cancer of the oesophagus; but the mortality from the operation alone was appalling, and before long it was discovered that even when the patient failed to die from the operation, he also failed to live longer than he would have done without it. But that was not appreciated at the time, and so we spent countless and exhausting hours over the operating table, performing these hideous operations. So much time, so much skill, so much effort, so much devotion, and all to no purpose, except to prove it was all to no purpose! For the same money and effort, we could have immunised a thousand children – perhaps more – against measles.

Another disease that was common and also relegated to the verandah, but that I had never seen before, was Kaposi's sarcoma, a slow-growing cancer of connective tissue which eventually fungated, memorable to me principally for its offensive smell. At the time it seemed merely a medical curiosity that such an otherwise uncommon tumour should appear so frequently in this part of Africa, but within a few years the condition had captured the headlines of the world, not for its own sake or the sake of the Africans whom it distressed, but because it had started to appear across the Atlantic as part of the Acquired Immunodeficiency Syndrome (AIDS). It was even suggested that central Africa was the home of origin of the virus that caused the syndrome. All this was quite unsuspected by me then (as by everybody else), and I found it difficult enough to conceal my disgust at the odious and foul-smelling deformities the sarcoma produced. I had no scientific interest in it at all.

The last of my duties was to work in the casualty department. It was perpetual night there, and the fluorescent lighting gave no indication of the time of day. I had never seen a casualty department so busy: sometimes the floor of the corridor was slippery with blood (and blood has a distinctive and rather sickly smell, at least in large quantities). People lay groaning on the ground, their faces swollen up like blue-black balloons from the beatings they had received; or with the ragged remnants of an arm which had been bitten off by a crocodile as they tried to cross a stream near their village; or clutching their stomach in which they had been stabbed; or, very occasionally, sitting with their skin clawed to bloody tatters by the leopard that had dropped out of the tree in whose shade they were sitting; or, very commonly, lying unconscious as the last survivor of a road accident in which four others had been killed. We saw children immolated by fires because their homes had no light; we saw the victims of the puff adder, their legs tensely swollen and in great pain, having trodden on the sluggish, camouflaged serpent as they walked barefoot in the bush; we saw every kind of accident which man can contrive to suffer.

Mpilo acted as a kind of magnet for the sick of the entire region, an area half the size of Britain. From far and wide people dragged themselves to its portals. Whenever the local medicine man's treatment with the African panacea, scarification, had failed to work – that is to say, when the illness was not self-curing, or was merely psychological – the patient would take himself, or be taken, to Mpilo. I remember an old lady in gross heart failure, her legs and abdomen swollen by oedema, who seemed to be *in extremis*. It transpired she had walked all the way to hospital from her village a hundred miles away, to fetch a supply of the miraculous pills that rid her of her swelling. There were, of course, rural medical stations much nearer her home, but she had faith only in the pills of Mpilo. She did not wish to be admitted to the hospital even for a rest, but had come only for her prescription after which, once obtained, she walked the hundred miles back to her village.

From time to time one of the white farmers in the surrounding district would bring a worker who had been injured on his farm. The farmer would demand instant attention for his worker, even if his injuries were trivial by comparison with those of patients long before him in the queue (there was always a queue). This, as I soon discovered, was not solicitude for the welfare of the worker, but impatience. I recall one such farmer arriving with a farmhand who had somehow managed to catch his genitals in the moving parts of the tractor, denuding himself of skin. The patient writhed in pain on the wooden bench. The farmer, who had that kind of deeply-lined face, wrinkled like a dried apple, that spoke of a lifetime in the sun, wanted a chat.

'Where are you from?'

'England.'

'Stay here, man. It's God's own country.'

With the patient groaning softly, this did not seem to be the moment to discuss my future plans, if any. I drew attention to him.

'Ah, he's quite a good boy,' said the farmer. 'He's been with me twenty years. Only careless, like they all are.'

I asked his name. The farmer did not know it.

Once, a man walked into the hospital with a dagger firmly implanted into his skull, right up to the hilt. There was no blood to be seen: his assailant had done a very neat job. It was astonishing he was alive, let alone ambulant and talking. He was put to bed in the surgical ward, still with the dagger in his head, where everyone in the hospital went to stare at him. The handle of the dagger was so firmly stuck that it seemed like a strange biological appendage. His skull was x-rayed from every possible angle (there were no computerised scans then) to build up a three-dimensional picture of the blade's location. A discussion about what should be done ensued. It was clear the dagger could not be left where it was; but it was not clear how to remove it without killing the patient. In the end, it was just pulled out, like Excalibur. This was done in the operating theatre and afterwards the patient appeared to have suffered no ill-effects, either from the original injury or from the removal. This all went to prove, said one of the white doctors, that most of an African's brain was completely redundant, and the remaining portion seldom used.

Several of my young white colleagues were younger Mr Peelers. They had faces of amazing ruddiness in men so young, as though they had been born angry and had remained so ever since. It was as though the world never quite came up to their expectations. Having been born in Africa, they knew the African: he was *an Aff, a munt, a kaffir*, and he needed to be whipped (literally) to prevent him from raping white women. They thought in such clichés, so perhaps it was only justice that the world thought of them in clichés as well. But yet I do not suppose they were bad doctors, or failed to do their best for their patients.

I certainly failed to do my best on one occasion, and it resulted in the death of a young woman. I had been on duty over the weekend, and though such weekends fell to our lot only once every five weeks, they were exhausting beyond measure. Starting on Saturday morning, we worked until Monday evening; and, largely as a consequence of drunkenness, saw an endless procession of victims both of violence and accidents in the unlit townships, so that we were rarely able to sleep more than two or three hours in fifty-six. We were either in the operating theatre or the casualty department. It was all the worse for me because I was only perfunctorily interested in my work. By the end of the weekend I was leaden-headed with sleep, scarcely able to think, with constant apparitions of my bed and delicious slumber before me. Towards the end of one such stint of duty I was working in the casualty department when a pregnant woman complained of a slight loss of blood. I took little notice of her and told her to wait – until the next doctor came on duty. She offered no protest and sat quietly on a bench. I went home to what I thought was well-earned rest; but next day, the doctor who had followed me on duty informed me that in the hiatus the patient whom I told to wait had quietly and unprotestingly exsanguinated. I was shaken – my hands indeed shook – and when I had recovered slightly I rehearsed my excuses mentally before the tribunal which never came. But for a short time I was less self-assured, less confident that I knew the answers to large questions. However, self-regard is the quickest-healing tissue of the body and before long I had recovered it in full. I was able to face the death of my patients with equanimity, though I have to admit that never again, as far as I am aware, have I been so negligent or caused a death (I leave it to philosophers to argue over the fine distinction between the two).

At various times the hospital was put on special disaster alert, when an even heavier load of casualties was expected. Mostly it was only a football match in the nearby stadium that provoked the alert: it amazed me that in those revolutionary times, there was supposedly sufficient energy left over for football violence. In fact, I do not recall a single casualty reaching the hospital from the stadium. The four of us from Pauling Road once attended such a match, and apart from momentary awkwardness at being the only whites in a crowd of twenty or thirty thousand blacks, we did not feel at any time endangered. On the contrary, the crowd was far better behaved than its equivalent in England (not that it would be difficult). Once we were asked to stand by when the police had shot eleven demonstrators dead in Harare, the African quarter of Salisbury soon to give its name to the entire city. But once more nothing happened. Some said that the police in Salisbury could shoot as many Shona as they liked as far as the Ndebele of Bulawayo were concerned; others, that it demonstrated the forebearance of the Africans.

Although I worked at Mpilo only six months – it seemed an aeon then – I was able several times to leave the city and see the country beyond. For short excursions there were the Matopo Hills, less than an hour away; there, great boulders balanced delicately on the tops of weirdly-shaped eminences, and the acacia forest was said to have the biggest population of leopard in the world, though I never saw one – only the results of its maulings. Up on the highest hill in the Matopos, at a place called World's View, was

the tomb of Cecil Rhodes, a holy place for the settlers; a large slab
of metal was let into a massive flat boulder, with only three words
standing in high relief on the metal: CECIL JOHN RHODES. His
tomb was now a favourite place for the dazzling blue, green and
turquoise lizards to lie, for the sun warmed the metal; while in the
evening, when it grew chilly, the two African soldiers set to stand
guard over the remains of the man who had engineered their
people's downfall huddled round a small fire they had built for
themselves and waited for the leopard or the guerillas. World's
View was certainly a well-chosen site for the grave of a man with
an insatiable greed for land, minerals and domination: empty mile
on empty mile of acacia forest and eccentric kopjes stretched
green and then blue into the far distance. If the Matopos had
contained gold or diamonds, Rhodes would have sunk mines and
built cities. Only their mineral uselessness preserved them for the
leopard.

   We explored the ruins of Zimbabwe, for which the new black
state was to be named. At first I thought this rather odd, as though
a revolutionary government in Britain were to rename the country
Stonehenge. But ever since the whites first came to the country,
some among them had gone to considerable lengths to 'prove'
that the impressive walls and citadel of the ruins could not have
been built by Africans, but were instead the work of the ancient
Phoenicians, the Arabs or even the Portuguese. Books to this
effect still appear in South Africa. The argument went something
like this: the Africans are stupid, therefore they could not have
built Zimbabwe, therefore someone else must have built it,
therefore we, the whites, were justified in taking their land. Stung
to a reply, the nationalist argument was a mirror image: we
Africans are *not* stupid, therefore we could have built Zimbabwe,
therefore we did build Zimbabwe, therefore a government of
blacks must be better than a government of whites. I believe the
archaeological evidence points indubitably to an African origin of
the ruins, but evidence in such a situation is quite beside the
point: passion decides everything in advance. But if the ruins
were indeed African, it would solve the inferiority complex that

even the nationalists felt vis-à-vis the whites, for it proved that
Africans could, unaided, construct something more than mud
huts, and that the famous lines of Aimé Cesaire were no longer
necessary for self-respect (or true):

> Hurrah for those who never invented anything!
> Hurrah for those who never conquered anybody!

Zimbabwe, then, was not so extraordinary a name to have chosen
in the circumstances.

With my two friends Patrick and Claire O'Brien, whom I had
known slightly in England and who by coincidence were both
working in Bulawayo, Patrick at Mpilo and Claire at the all-white
Bulawayo Hospital (which had just received by helicopter its first
casualty of the guerilla war amongst scenes of almost festive
excitement in the normally tranquil grounds), I drove the two
hundred miles to Victoria Falls. At that time it was still possible to
drive around the country without fear of attack, except for the
north-east border, though only a year later it was necessary to go
in protected convoy, and two years later whites started to sleep
with guns by their beds, even in the suburbs. But coming as I did
from an overcrowded island where every hill concealed a housing
development of little red-brick houses, the sense of space and the
freedom it conferred were exhilarating. You could drive for
scores of miles through cattle ranches without seeing another
person. Then quite suddenly, the land changed from being green
with vegetation to being parched brown with dust, so that it was
possible (literally, though not legally) to have a foot in each. The
parched area was one of the Tribal Trust Lands, the half of
Rhodesia's land surface set aside for the rural Africans. These
lands – where it was not permitted for us to stop – were
overcrowded and, what was worse, overgrazed with that great
African store of wealth, herds of goats. The villagers lived in huts
as primitive and poor, I imagine, as any to be found in Africa.
This, if anywhere, was the dark underside of the régime: not a
land reserve only, but a vast labour reserve where poverty and
destitution forced men off the land to seek work at whatever

wages employers paid. The land looked as though it would soon become, if it had not already done so, complete desert. I then took pleasure in indignantly attributing this to the greed of the whites, who had alienated to themselves half of the land (and the better half at that) when they were less than 4 per cent of the population. 'When the whites came,' said the Africans, 'they had the bible and we had the land. Now they have the land and we have the bible.' But whatever the historical cause of the problem, the solution was not obvious (at least outside the imaginations of theorists, of whom I was then one): an equitable and general redistribution of the land, with the population increasing by four per cent a year, would soon enough lead to the desertification of the entire country instead of only half of it, and at the same time destroy the country's agricultural surplus.

We reached Victoria Falls, having stopped for lunch in a region famed for both its malaria and bubonic plague. We had hired a house with a garden going down to the bank of the Zambezi, a mile or two above the falls and on the borders of a game reserve which had recently been closed because of threatened guerilla activity. Between the crocodiles on the near bank and the bazookas allegedly on the far, we experienced a not unpleasant frisson of fear as we sat in the outwardly peaceful garden, the pleasant and reassuring clink of ice sounding in our glasses as the sun went down and the river glided silently by. Later in the evening, hippo emerged from the water and used our garden as a path to their grazing grounds beyond. These animals, which I had always regarded as slightly comic, are ill-tempered beasts and very nasty when anything comes between them and their destination. It was wise to keep out of their way. Once when we returned from the small town of Victoria Falls at night we nearly collided with a hippo in the road, a large, dimly perceived amorphous black shape, the reflective glint of whose small eyes saved us both from a fearful accident.

The Rhodesian government, short of foreign exchange, was then trying to draw tourists from South Africa, and one of the attractions of Victoria Falls, other than the natural one, was the casino. Built high above the river on a bluff, it was a vulgar, if luxurious, concrete palace known as Elephant Hills. It was not conspicuously successful in attracting tourists, to judge by its strangely empty gambling salons: a few feverishly pinched and anxious faces around the roulette tables, but otherwise echoing with space. We won a few dollars and returned to our house. Not very long afterwards, the casino was destroyed by guerilla rockets: the tourists' instinct to stay away had been right, for guerillas usually have a strongly puritanical streak, and Elephant Hills presented an easy target.

Across the gorge below the falls was the single iron span of the railway bridge connecting Rhodesia and Zambia. Every day, from the lawns of the Victoria Falls Hotel, it was possible to watch a small farce enacted. This was the time of high-minded sanctions and of long-winded speeches. A Rhodesian locomotive would shunt a train of goods wagons on to the bridge, uncouple and then retreat. Two or three hours of apparent inactivity would go by, and casual observers might wonder what the stranded train was doing upon the bridge. Then, when it was hoped everyone had lost interest in the drama, a Zambian locomotive would approach the train as though in a fit of absentmindedness and couple itself to it, before dragging it slowly into Zambia. The significance of this was not lost upon the white Rhodesians who saw it, and they crowed in triumph. It was not so much the economic success they applauded, rather the ideological humiliation visited upon their high-minded neighbours.

Another time I took a week off to go with friends to the Eastern Highlands on the border with the newly hostile Mozambique, recently independent under Frelimo control. This part of the country was not yet closed to casual traffic, as it was soon to be. We climbed the highest mountain in Rhodesia, Mount Inyangani, about 8,000 feet high, and looked out over what must have been Mozambique, then considered by white Rhodesians as the fount of all evil. Frelimo was regarded both with fear and contempt, but its victory (more by attrition and its effect on the metropolis than by outright military campaign) was not thought to augur ill for the white régime, because the Portuguese were only halfway between black and white on the evolutionary scale. The vast tracts of empty land around us looked peaceful enough, but the war had yet to erupt in earnest. That evening, after stumbling down the mountain, we stayed at a place called Troutbeck where, in the same hotel, the Prime Minister, Ian Smith, happened also to be staying. We met him in the bar, he conservatively dressed, we dishevelled and grimy after our climb. Meetings with the famous are apt to be disappointing, for one expects their every word somehow to display the natural talent by which they reached their positions of eminence. This ridiculous expectation is rarely, if ever, fulfilled: and Ian Smith gave the impression of being a shrewd but essentially ordinary man who had gone into politics only reluctantly – to fight for what he regarded as the rights of the community from which he sprang – and wanted only to return to his farm, once things had settled down a bit. We talked to him briefly after we had been surveyed by his bodyguard. He asked how long we intended to stay. Conor McBride, one of the party, said a year.

'Why stay a year, man?' he asked. 'Why not stay a hundred?'

Did he really think, even at that late stage, it would last a hundred years? I think he did. He was a consummate (if amateur) juggler, and hoped to keep the balls in the air for a long time yet. He certainly believed that if we stayed we should become his supporters. Perhaps he was right: tribal politics, after all, is not confined to blacks.

The last of my excursions before I left Rhodesia was with a party of doctors from Bulawayo to the northern game reserves of Botswana, in a Land Rover and a saloon car. The border was still open: Botswana could not afford to choose its trading partners. One of the ways Rhodesian farmers evaded sanctions was to mark their goods *Produce of Botswana* and ship them to the rest of the world via Gaberone.

The Chobe River Game Reserve – recently visited by Richard Burton and Elizabeth Taylor on the honeymoon of their second (or was it third?) marriage to each other – had one of the largest populations of elephant in the world, so large in fact that it had recently been thought necessary to cull it by ten thousand. We camped by the river, in open tents. A game warden had recently been trampled to death by an enraged pachyderm, and a camper eaten in his tent by hyenas. The first night we slept fitfully, awaiting the entry into our tents of animals that were outside, making the noises of a Tarzan soundtrack. In the twilight a large herd of elephant had lumbered in slow motion through our camp on the way to the river. I was terrified that on their way back they would stumble into our tents and crush us to dust. The screams, cackles, roars and trumpets made us feel we were besieged by Nature herself; but by the second night we had adapted well enough. For city dwellers it comes as a surprise how black is night.

Daylight dispelled our fears. We went in search of game: we saw hundred on hundred of elephant. They seemed to be destroying the area, denuding the ground of undergrowth, pulling down the trees and tearing off their leaves, more careless of their environment than industrial man. It seemed they had pushed other game from the area: we saw only the occasional giraffe and a moth-eaten lioness sleeping in the shade of a thornbush. We deliberately provoked a bull elephant into charging our Land Rover. The driver pretended to stall the engine and then stalled it in earnest, producing an uncomfortable moment or two before restarting it just in time. And when we returned to the camp, as often as not we found that monkeys had wrecked it – had sprinkled flour, sugar and powdered milk everywhere, apparently for the fun of it.

We fished by a bend in the river, where a sandbar sloped gently into the water. With neither skill nor difficulty, we pulled out delicious bream-like fish every five minutes or so. Sometimes we caught an ugly catfish, black, slimy and with repulsive whiskers. From time to time small spotter planes circled above us, presumably South Africans on the lookout for guerillas. We were on the edge of the long spur of South West African land called the Caprivi Strip, between Botswana and Angola, where the small war between the South Africans and the South West African People's Organisation was brewing. Having circled us inquisitively for several minutes, the aircraft flew off, apparently satisfied that we were holidaymakers and not guerrillas.

We started to fish early in the morning. The hours slipped by quickly and we gathered what we considered a fine catch. Towards midday, with the sun directly overhead, we heard and felt through the ground the deep pounding of a thousand hoofs behind us. We looked back. Galloping across the horizon on a low eminence in the landscape was a herd of sable antelope extended over hundreds of yards, as noble a sight as any I can remember. Their movements were as graceful as the curve of their horns, and the dust raised by their hoofs rendered pastel the harsh colours of the land. In a few moments they were gone, I knew not where, and we returned to our fishing; but they were moments imprinted on our memories.

We were oblivious to everything except our growing pile of fish and the prospect of an excellent lunch. Suddenly, we heard an angry trumpeting behind us. A herd of elephant was coming to the river for a midday drink, and was not pleased to find its habitual place usurped. We hastily gathered up our catch, our escape route almost cut off. There was always the river, of course, but there were the waiting jaws of crocodiles, almost certainly. We ran along the river edge until we reached a steep bank, the trumpetings growing angrier. Someone dropped her fishing rod and was sent to retrieve it in the face of the advancing, ear-flapping elephants by her husband. We clambered up the bank to relative safety, but next day when we fished we were careful to leave the elephant's watering hole before noon.

I had completed my six months' probation. Somewhat to my surprise, for I did not think I had covered myself in medical glory, Mr Greaves asked me to stay another six months. I gave it little thought: to me then six months was an eternity and he might as well have asked me to stay six decades. The idea that I should know what I was to be doing a whole six months in advance filled me with horror. I refused and decided instead to take the train to Mozambique. Everyone thought I was mad.

THREE

Mozambique and South Africa

THE TRAIN from Bulawayo to Lourenço Marques (not yet renamed Maputo) was empty, with the exception of an indigent Portuguese woman who preferred the rigours of post-revolutionary Mozambique to the slights of Anglo-Saxon Rhodesia, and the guard, an elderly northern Englishman. He had emigrated at the end of the war, and now found the world as he had known it collapsing round his ears. It was one of the last trains to run from Rhodesia to the newly liberated, or at any rate independent, Mozambique. I had not only a compartment, but a carriage, to myself.

The train sauntered through the endless unpeopled savannah. As dusk fell I had dinner in the restaurant car, the guard doubling up as waiter. He also sat opposite me and talked while I ate.

'Why are you going to Mozambique?' he asked. 'They might kill you.'

'Why should they want to kill me?' I replied.

'For food.'

I laughed.

'You can laugh', he said. 'But you mark my words. Before long they'll be so hungry they'll be eating one another.'

I was unsure whether he was possessed of special knowledge, or whether he spoke from the general principle that blacks were cannibals.

'I wouldn't go if I was you', he continued. 'This is the last trip I'll be making. I'll take my retirement if they want me to go again. But if I was you, I wouldn't go.'

The advice was somewhat belated. I could hardly jump out of the moving train and walk back along the tracks. I finished my meal and went to bed, leaving the guard-waiter shaking his head lugubriously.

At about midnight the train jerked to a standstill, waking me with a jolt. The darkness was impenetrable; there was silence, except for the rhythmic throb of the insects. I waited for something to happen: nothing did. Half an hour later the train juddered into motion and crept slowly forward a few hundred yards, then halted once more in the darkness. Excited voices filled the air. We had crossed the border into Mozambique, at a small place still called Malvérnia after Lord Malvern, a surgeon and reactionary prime minister of the ill-fated Central African Federation. The hubbub seemed to continue for a long time, without resolution. Suddenly the door of my compartment slid open and a dazzlingly bright light flashed inside, scanning each corner. As my squinting eyes grew accustomed to the flood of light I made out two black figures standing in the doorway, both in battle fatigues. One was customs, the other immigration. Customs had an automatic weapon slung around his neck. There were people behind them straining to see what would happen.

'*Boa tarde, camarada*', they said.

Good evening, comrade: it seemed an odd way to greet a white coming from Rhodesia.

'Good evening,' I replied, but I could not add 'comrade': my voice would have cracked with the insincerity of it. At that time, however, when revolutionary élan had not yet foundered on the hard rock of political economy, everyone appeared well-disposed towards everyone else, and the name of comrade was not mere cant.

The men advanced into the compartment and asked me to open my case, whose contents they sifted with the muzzle of the gun. I imagined myself then the subject of a brief report in one of the Sunday newspapers back home:

UNIMPORTANT YOUNG DOCTOR
SHOT ON MOZAMBIQUE BORDER

The men continued polite (as did I), and still called me comrade. My lack of a proper visa, however, caused some consternation, and they referred me to a superior official who worked in Malvérnia station some way down the track. It was from the rickety, cockroach-infested station that the hubbub had issued. Despite the lateness of the hour it seemed the whole town had turned out for the train. Amongst the ragged crowd mingled boys of not more than fifteen in battle dress, seasoned veterans of the war, who also carried automatic rifles. They were not threatening, only vigilant; it was simply that a whole generation of children had grown up to whom the gun was as familiar as the pen. By some revolution-fanciers in the suburbs of the west this kind of education would no doubt be deemed admirable; but on that remote frontier, in the dim light cast on the station platform by a couple of naked, flickering lightbulbs, the whiteness of their eager, counterrevolutionary-seeking eyes set in dark faces moistened by the damp heat stood out, and seemed to me alarming.

The official, a half-caste, took a relaxed view of my lack of visa, and said I could obtain one when I reached Lourenço Marques. Before long I was back on the train and fast asleep as it chugged slowly at an even pace towards the capital.

By morning, when I awoke, we had gained the outer fringes of the city, a wasteland of miserable shacks much worse than the mud hut villages from which these slum dwellers had recently emigrated. But the city centre was pleasant enough, though growing dingier by the hour. The plaster on the walls which not long before had been pastel, Lusitanian shades, was now flaking and fading into dun colours.

I found a small hotel still run by a Portuguese family, who looked enviously at my dollars. They lost no time in telling me they wished desperately to leave Mozambique now that the *monkeys* had taken over. So much, I thought, for the Portuguese claim to a higher, non-racially prejudiced form of colonialism. Unfortunately all their assets were in Mozambique, and Mozambican money was not accepted anywhere now, not even in Mozambique. They begged me to pay for everything in dollars: as soon as they had accumulated enough of them to purchase tickets back to Portugal they would go, leaving everything behind them. It would mean losing all they had built over the years, but they had no desire to participate in the return to the trees they were certain would happen once the guiding and civilising hand of Portugal was withdrawn. Their bitterness against the Africans was of a depth indescribable; likewise against the Salazar dictatorship that had lured them to Africa with promises of a stability it could not maintain. Their resentment, I thought, would remain with them all the days of their life, a destructive, dominating, sterile passion. I paid for everything in dollars.

Though independent for so short a time, Mozambique had already acquired that universal symbol of the struggle for equality and justice, the bread queue. Famine did not yet stalk the land, only shortage; but at all hours of the day long lines of people stood down streets in which there were bakeries, or had once been bakeries. But luxury had not yet entirely fled the city. Conspicuous as they rattled over the cobbled streets were the new yellow Volvos in which the triumphant upper echelons of Frelimo sat back, chauffeur-driven importantly round the city. And when I asked the hotel owner whether there was still a good restaurant in Lourenço Marques, he told me, after he had sworn me to secrecy, that there was. It was down a narrow street not far from the hotel, with an entrance difficult to distinguish from that of a private house. One knocked twice; someone came to the peephole; the door was slowly opened an inch or two; one insinuated oneself into the gap thus opened, to be faced by a heavy red curtain; an infinitely cautious hand drew it back and one entered – hey presto! – the familiar world of tablecloths and waiters and the clink of cutlery against porcelain. It was not especially luxurious, except by the increasingly empty-shelved standards of Mozambique, but it was reassuringly comfortable for a bourgeois like me. One could support revolution *and* still have a decent meal in the Lourenço Marques of those days.

The restaurant was patronised by such Portuguese business-men as had chosen or been forced by circumstances to remain.

The waiters, also Portuguese, treated us as confidential clients of a shady undertaking. They glanced repeatedly towards the entrance, as if half-expecting a posse of Frelimo men suddenly to burst in and express with machinegun fire their indignation that while outside there were proletarian bread queues, inside there were survivors of a putrefying colonialism gorging themselves on partridges and prawns. They never came, the Frelimo men, but vigilance was maintained at all times; and though it is not creditable to have to admit it, the bread queues outside gave an added, even incomparable, savour to the partridges and prawns. Thanks to my foreign currency I was able to eat lunch and dinner there, and the impression grew among the waiters that, my slightly shabby appearance notwithstanding, I was an immensely rich person with limitless funds (I had precisely $800). Whenever I appeared in the doorway, they ceased immediately to serve men whose suits alone were worth half my worldly wealth, and danced attendance on me in a hundred small ways, pulling the chair out from the table for me, shaking the napkin over my somewhat threadbare knees, offering me a cigar and so forth. The game necessitated large gratuities which I could ill afford, but I played it to the end.

Lourenço Marques had once been famed for its gaiety and Latin insouciance, at least among the white farmers of Rhodesia and the Orange Free State, who fled there from time to time to escape Anglo-Saxon primness and Boer godliness. (Gaiety in this context, of course, largely meant prostitutes.) But the revolution had changed all that, and no predikant of the Dutch Reformed Church could have found fault with the cheerlessness that had descended on the city in the name of revolutionary morality. The monotonous iconography of revolution was everywhere: there were power stations and steel mills to be built, bumper crops to be harvested, with square-jawed workers – black, white and mestiço – forever marching with banners headlong into the Future. Above the city hall in the main square was a vast portrait of Samora Machel, the first president of independent Mozambique, his broad, round, bearded face looking rather stupid and vacant,

recognisable from miles around. In the docks I watched im-
promptu revolutionary street meetings, in which knots of fishermen gathered to listen to speeches urging them on to greater
production, coupled with inflammatory denunciations of everything that had gone before the advent of Frelimo. The fishermen
showed every sign of enthusiasm and before long were punching
the air with the clenched fist salute, chanting Frelimo! Frelimo!
But the effort exhausted them, and when they dispersed back to
their boats I noticed that they went straight to sleep in the shade of
the bows.

I considered remaining in Mozambique to work for a time, and
so visited the main hospital of the city. There were only sixty
doctors left in the country, one for every hundred thousand
inhabitants; the rest had departed. I was therefore confident that
my invaluable services would be eagerly seized upon by the
authorities, but the hospital – which resembled a battleground –
proved completely indifferent to them. A Portuguese doctor, who
seemed very leisured considering the carnage around him, told
me that the present régime was extremely hostile to the medical
profession, officially on the grounds that doctors were by nature
élitists, concerned solely to entrench their power and status over
other workers, and opposed to plans to bring socialist health-care
to every village in the country. The régime had boasted that it
could well do without doctors; but my informant believed the *real*
reason for the government's hostility, which it dressed up with
ideological-sounding justifications, was that the President,
Samora Machel, had once been a medical orderly and had had his
ego bruised by having to take orders from men who were both
more intelligent and better educated than he. Hence his thirst for
revenge, his persecution of doctors and curtailment of their
privileges. There was therefore no official anxiety about the
shortage of doctors; quite the reverse, the fewer the better. So
there was no hope of work for me.

There seemed little point in remaining, and I decided to leave
Mozambique. The bookshops had suddenly filled with the works
of Zhdanov, which I thought augured no good. Besides, there

were no cheap psychological rewards any more – the awareness of one's own moral superiority over one's fellows – in behaving with ordinary politeness towards the Africans, since they were now top dogs in their own country and politeness was prudent as well as desirable on other grounds. I booked a place on the train to Johannesburg.

The journey was uneventful. I asked the guard on the South African Railways what time we should arrive at our destination, and he snapped back 'The right time!' It was only later that I learnt the S.A.R. were a kind of employment reserve for less intellectually gifted Afrikaners, who resented ever having to speak English, the language of the eternal enemy. At the border the South African customs man riffled through my case and alighted on a copy of Shakespeare. He flicked through the pages suspiciously and then asked, with the intonation of a secret policeman reaching the crux of a delicate investigation:

'Are these *all* the plays of Shakespeare?'

I replied that they were, so far as I knew, and he grunted, as if to signify that that Shakespeare must have been a lazy fellow, as well as a dangerous liberal and kaffir-lover (just think of Othello).

I arrived in Johannesburg – Goli, City of Gold – and felt immediately the electric thrill of being once more anonymous in a big city. (All the cities and towns of Rhodesia were small, and after a few days in any of them one began to recognise the faces on the street.) I walked down Commissioner Street, a kind of narrow canyon between skyscrapers, and heard talk only of money as I went. More than any other city in the world, Mammon made Johannesburg; Mammon is its only interest; Mammon is its highest good. There is something infectious about this worship of wealth, and I too began to dream of transforming my dwindling supply of money into an unfathomable fortune by a sudden coup on the Jo'burg Stock Exchange.

The outward manifestations of the notorious system of *apartheid* were curiously few in the centre of Johannesburg. There were no signs to say where blacks might or might not go. The crowds mingled as they do everywhere else, and I saw no whites angrily pushing blacks off the pavement into the gutter simply for being 'cheeky' and daring to look them in the eye. One might even have been forgiven for failing to realise that the majority of the city's population was black, for thinking rather it was a white city with a substantial minority of blacks to perform the menial tasks. It was only after working hours that the great separation happened, when the blacks returned to their townships on pullulating trains, the whites returned to their carefully-tended suburbs, and the centre of the city became an eerie, uninhabited wilderness of sickly light cast on concrete by street lamps, and of long, dark shadows. When I asked some whites the way to Soweto, they not only did not know where it was, they did not know *what* it was.

I made little human contact in Johannesburg. Over half the population was quite beyond it, for obvious political reasons; while the rest, with whom it was theoretically possible to meet, were too busy, too absorbed in their own affairs, to notice an insignificant stranger in their midst. I remember only an inebriated economist of the Johannesburg Chamber of Mines whom I met in a bar. I think he had run out of drinking companions on whom he could inflict his small fund of stories and was delighted to find a new and willing listener. He told me that the only foreign country to which he had travelled was the Soviet Union, where he had been accorded diplomatic status and sumptuous hospitality. I expressed surprise, for the two countries were mutually hostile. I was forgetting one thing, he said, one great factor that united the two of them: gold. They produced between them nearly all the world's gold; they were both largely dependent on gold for their ability to import vital goods from the western nations. It was in their mutual interest, therefore, to keep the price of gold high by not oversupplying the market; this was why, every six months or so, a delegation went from South Africa to the Soviet Union, or *vice versa*, to hammer out an agreement on production quotas. It all sounded reasonable, or at least plausible, but whether it was true I hadn't the faintest idea.

I left Johannesburg for Cape Town, which I hoped would not

ignore me in so callous a fashion. I arrived by air, for once having decided to leave Johannesburg it appeared to me urgent that I should arrive somewhere else. Cape Town can, without exaggeration, be said to possess one of the most beautiful settings of any city in the world; and whatever the moral qualities of the early Dutch settlers, their architecture was not without merit. The city had a much more leisured atmosphere than Johannesburg, and some pretensions to culture. Neither had it yet succumbed to the ubiquitous herald of rising property prices, the skyscraper. There were, however, several large buildings in the self-confident Victorian municipal mode. It had the best university in Africa; it had a theatre in which grand opera was performed, from which nothing but the high price of seats and lack of interest excluded the Africans; it even had a bohemian quarter inhabited by artists and would-be artists. And as in Johannesburg, one might have thought that South Africa was an overwhelmingly white country: there was nothing to suggest the contrary.

I booked into an hotel, not quite the best but still very comfortable. What my plans were, or even if I had any, I cannot now recall. I was seven thousand miles from home, with little money and no job, but I was Micawberishly unconcerned: something would turn up. I set about exploring the city, climbing Table Mountain and wandering the alleyways of the Cape Coloured districts. These lively, volatile, violent people were the product of a complete mixing of the races – hottentot, white, Malay, black, Indian – which began in the days before there were sufficient white women to satisfy the settlers. Liaisons between the races were now fraught with danger, but the Afrikaans that the coloureds spoke was a constant, if unwanted, reminder to the whites that the first consequence of their arrival was miscegenation.

The coloured districts were narrow streets of one-storey houses, rather crumbling, painted pink or yellow or blue. There were mosques for those who had remained predominantly Malay, and churches of varying degrees of religious enthusiasm for the rest. There was life on the streets, children playing, old men chatting. At night, of course, they were dangerous, for knives were sharp and tempers short. The authorities were trying to destroy these districts, for they were impossible to police and control; they were dangerously independent. Furthermore, they were insanitary. The commonest cause of intestinal obstruction among children there was an impacted mass of the large parasitic worm, *Ascaris lumbricoides*; these repulsive worms are found only where hygiene is poor. The authorities, therefore, had some good ostensible reasons for trying to move the people elsewhere, to soulless estates or worse; but the people themselves were putting up surprisingly stubborn resistance, for they were attached to their homes, however humble.

I settled down to a quiet life of two large meals a day in the best restaurants I could find (with a bottle of Paarl wine at dinner), the mornings and afternoons spent in the South African Library studying the country's history and economics. The Library was nearby the neo-Palladian Parliament building, surrounded by beautifully tended gardens in whose midst was the well-known statue of Cecil Rhodes, pointing inland with his outstretched finger, his famous advice to colonial pioneers inscribed on the plinth:

YOUR HINTERLAND IS THERE

On Sundays the Library was closed – indeed, the whole city was closed, in the best British tradition – and I amused myself by attending services in the Groote Kerk, the large eighteenth-century Dutch Reformed Church at the top of Adderley Street. They were in Afrikaans, of course, and the congregation was coloured. It was the sermons I enjoyed. I didn't understand Afrikaans, a language, it is said, richer in terms of abuse than any other, but that did not impede my understanding of the sermons. They were about Hell.

What a wonderfully interesting place it sounded, and how easy to get there! Cinemas, books, sex, football and brandy all led directly to Hell, where the sulphur-breathing demons were even at that very moment stoking the eternal fires. The predikant, in black robes and a white lace collar, gesticulated and fulminated in the pulpit (even 'I love you' sounds like fulmination in Afrikaans), a fine aerosol of spittle bathing the front row of the congregation. But apart from the sermon, the service was dingy and whining, as only protestant services can be. It was Hell rather than God that inspired everyone. For some extraordinary reason of moral masochism, the congregation was profoundly consoled to learn that it was more sodomistic than any generation. Perhaps the fact that their present travails were considered the just deserts of wickedness rather than the blind workings of an indifferent fate lent their lives a significance they would otherwise have lacked. At any rate, they went away happy in the knowledge that the Judgment Day was approaching and the severest penalties would be meted out unto them.

In other idle moments, particularly on Sundays, I encountered the Devil on the streets of Cape Town in his new guise of the television. For many years the godfearing Republic had held out against the satanic contraption, only to succumb after a long rearguard action by ministers and other righteous folk. The shops selling television sets attracted large crowds of idlers – like myself – who marvelled at the novelty of the flickering pictures. There was correspondence in the newspapers about the inevitable overthrow of the established order now that God's will had been so openly flouted, and one angry reader who had been so misguided as actually to purchase a set advised readers – of the *Cape Argus*, I think it was – against doing likewise because televisions showed only paintings and music and boring lecturers (the South African Broadcasting Corporation was screening Lord Clark's *Civilisation* as a trial run) and not rugby.

In the South African Library I read as widely as I could into the history of the country, and it soon enough became evident that its problems had such deep historical roots, and were now so complex, that any conceivable outcome was tragic. Those who touted a sovereign remedy – like all purveyors of panaceas everywhere – were either ignorant or charlatans. But the psychology of the Afrikaners in particular fascinated me. Here was a people who throughout its history had always acted in the most blatant self-interest, without any regard for the rights or interests of others, and yet continued to think of itself in metaphors taken from the Old Testament, as Israel in the bondage of Egypt. There was something in its rejection of the rest of the world's morality that would have been magnificent, had it been in a better cause. Neither was it hypocrisy, for hypocrisy requires sufficient self-knowledge for at least half-conscious dissimulation. (It was the British in South Africa who were the hypocrites *par excellence*.) Nothing illustrated this peculiar state of mind better than a slim volume of memoirs by Hendrik Verwoerd's private secretary which I happened across in a bookshop. A man universally execrated elsewhere, he was there held up hagiographically as one of the world's greatest thinkers, a benefactor of mankind, whose herculean labours would one day be recognised at their true worth. The memoirs described Verwoerd's election as Prime Minister by the Nationalist Party's parliamentary caucus after Strydom's death in 1956. When the result was announced the caucus spontaneously broke out into a full-throated hymn of praise to the Lord for having thus guided them to so wise a choice. The Lord is to the Nationalist Party what History is to the Communist Party.

I managed to lather myself up into a not unpleasant state of frenzied anger against Afrikanerdom, which I palliated by writing long and vehement letters of denunciation home to my friends. Day after day I sat in the South African Library along with the other autodidacts (of all races, be it said) who had come to pursue projects of their own or merely to escape the Cape Doctor, a cold Antarctic wind that blew up Adderley Street. *I* had come to arm myself with facts and figures – so many blacks arrested under the pass laws each year, so many executed for high treason against a state to which according to the state's own theories they did not belong – with which to batter apologists of the South African régime, if I ever met any. I cannot now remember why this should have seemed to me so urgently important, but I do recall opening each new work of history or economic analysis with something approaching the excitement of a drug addict taking his fix after a period of enforced abstinence.

Whatever the purpose of my labours, they were soon enough interrupted by that pervasive wrecker of amateur scholarship, impoverishment. I had already moved from my hotel to the comparative discomfort of the YMCA (about my meals, however, I would not compromise). But even so, my funds continued to dwindle at an alarming rate, though I tried hard not to be alarmed. I still dreamt of coups on the stock exchange (requiring no capital whatever), or of stumbling into one of the members of the opulent Cape Town Club – where a portrait of the Queen rather than the State President still hung – who would instantly recognise my worth and offer me a job at an immense salary. But just in case neither materialised, I registered with the South African Medical Association to make myself available for any locum work that became vacant.

One morning, as I prepared to go to the Library, I received a call on the public telephone in the entrance hall of the YMCA. It was not an address to inspire confidence, but by then I had precisely fifty-two rand left.

The caller was a woman with a strong Afrikaner accent who sounded desperate. Her husband was a doctor in a small town in Natal who had suddenly fallen ill. Please, please could I come today to stand in for him? I was her last hope.

I had known all along that Mr Micawber was right, something would turn up. I pretended to prevaricate, to let the caller know that I was doing her a terrific favour; but not for too long, in case she withdrew her offer.

There was one further problem, however. How was I to get there?

No problem, she said. There was a flight to Durban from Cape Town in about two hours, and she would meet me off the plane. No problem at all.

Not for her perhaps, but a decided problem for me. The fare to Durban was thirty rand more than I possessed. I couldn't tell her, of course, otherwise she might begin to wonder what kind of down-and-out she had contracted to her husband's practice. I merely said that I should be there.

Having replaced the receiver I tried to think what to do. I had no-one to whom I could turn for a short-term loan. The only expedient I was able to think of was to sell my now considerable collection of books about South Africa back to the secondhand book dealer from whom I had bought them, including a precious copy of the memoirs of Verwoerd's secretary, which I was convinced would one day become a collector's item. The dealer no doubt found my manner of proceding distinctly odd, since I had made my last purchase from him only the day before; but since it enabled him to realise a profit of at least two hundred per cent he did not complain. And afterwards I had enough money to get me to the airport and buy a ticket to Durban. I arrived with exactly seven rand in my pocket.

FOUR

Natal

THE DOCTOR'S WIFE was waiting for me. We recognised each other when everybody else had drifted away and we were left standing there. She was as relieved to see me as I was to see her.

'Thank goodness you've come,' she said. 'I thought you might not.'

We walked to where her car was parked. She asked me where I came from and told me about the town where she lived. Coming from London, she said, I would like it, because I was used to towns. It had everything: shops, a tennis club, a bioscope (the South African word for cinema), Greek shops (cafés), a hotel, a swimming pool, and even a place where you drove your car and watched a movie through the windows. Yes, if I liked a busy life, it was the place for me; though personally, coming as she did from the Platteland, she preferred something a bit quieter and less hectic.

The car was a bright red Lancia of a sporting kind. In the back there were two children, a boy and a girl, separated by a plump African nanny. I was introduced to the children but not the nanny. The children were anaemic and querulous, wanting things the very moment it became impossible to provide them. They squabbled continually and tried to hit one another across the comfortable expanse of the nanny.

Mrs Van der Merwe – the doctor's wife – drove as fast as she could, which was very fast indeed. She was a thin woman of darting movements, who looked as though she had been suffering from anorexia or a deep-seated fever. She chattered compulsively from fear, I think, of silence.

The road followed the coast at first, and we passed through the various fashionable resorts in which the whites of the Republic took their holidays, served drinks on the beaches by waiters in starched white tunics and maroon fezzes. As I later discovered, Natal is the Land of the Maroon Fez: the whites of the province seem to have an extraordinary predilection for dressing up their servants in this headgear, and even distinctly squalid establishments provide fezzes for their waiters, soup- and egg-stained though they might be. The fact is, it is not possible to take a man seriously whose face is festooned with a fez, especially when his waist is simultaneously squeezed by a cummerbund.

As we drove past Umhlanga Rocks, where a famous modern pyramidal hotel overlooks the rolling breakers of the Indian Ocean, I enquired after Dr Van der Merwe's illness. It was not too serious, I hoped? (But on the other hand serious enough for him to require the services of a locum until I had saved some money).

There was a silence heavy with emotion.

'My husband's not ill,' Mrs Van der Merwe said at last. 'He's drunk.'

I inferred that his drunkenness was not of an impulsive or short-lived nature, otherwise he would scarcely have needed me.

'He's an alcoholic. He can go months without a drink, then he suddenly starts again, I don't know why. A week ago he was drinking two bottles of Scotch a day.'

Tears swelled up in Mrs Van der Merwe's eyes. She was still young and retained a certain rural artlessness. Just then, a squabble broke out between the children over possession of a small toy racing car. Without looking back or reducing speed Mrs Van der Merwe swung her hand round to strike the children. She missed, but accidentally struck the nanny full in the face. The children ceased squabbling, but the new-found silence was punctuated by the half-stifled sobs of the nanny.

'What are you snivelling for?' asked Mrs Van der Merwe.

'The Madam hit me.'

These were the first words I had heard the nanny speak.

'Well you should have kept them kids quiet, then, shouldn't you, eh?'

A few minutes later Mrs Van der Merwe returned to the subject of her husband. He was taking a cure at a private clinic, she said, where he had been several times before. The 'cure' usually lasted a year or less: I was not the first locum Dr Van der Merwe had needed.

We reached the town in the most English of South Africa's four provinces, Natal. Of course, there are more Indians than English in Natal, let alone blacks, but that does not prevent the province from being considered English. Surrounding the town were large, undulating fields of sugar cane, just then a dark rich green. There was a main shopping street, and one did not have to stray far from it to reach roads that were only dirt tracks in the rust-red earth. The Van der Merwes lived in a new housing development where, as Mrs Van der Merwe pointed out proudly, 'every house was individual'. In the sense that they were not identical, this was true; but despite the multiplicity of adornments, the wrought-iron grilles, the coaching lamps and so forth, the overall impression was one of uniformity. The Van der Merwes' house had a small garden which was almost entirely occupied by the swimming pool and surrounding patio; the house itself seemed to have been designed by an architect who could not decide between Frank Lloyd Wright and the Alhambra. But it was very comfortable, in a suburban kind of way, with baths sunk into the floors, deep pile carpets, and velvet-covered sofas that enveloped one as one sat down, and made if difficult to rise again. Mrs Van der Merwe showed me round all this luxury with naive Platteland pride. She even showed me the heart-shaped bed with satin sheets in her and her husband's bedroom, apparently unaware of any construction that might be put upon it.

'It's just like Hollywood, eh?' she said.

'Yes,' I said. 'It is.'

'It was all my idea.'

She had designed it while her marriage had still seemed a romantic idyll. She introduced me to a woman whom she called simply *the Servant*, whose name I was never subsequently to discover, if indeed she had one. She was short and very dumpy, and had the broad, splayed feet of one who had never worn shoes. According to Mrs Van der Merwe she had never been into a house other than a mud hut until she came to work for her. She never spoke and moved as though through treacle, carrying out orders with glacial inexorability. Facial expression, at least within the confines of the Van der Merwe household, had she none, and it was all too easy to assume she was an automaton. Apart from the fact that when one ordered a beer, a beer eventually arrived, there was nothing to suggest she understood any human language, living or dead. I found the sound of her bare feet slipslapping on the tiles of the kitchen floor, and her otherwise silent presence, slightly unnerving.

Mrs Van der Merwe then left me, to stay overnight with her mother who had moved from the Platteland to the town to be nearer her troubled daughter and her grandchildren. Mrs Van der Merwe said she would return in the morning to show me round the practice; and once the Servant had finished in the kitchen I was left alone in that house of plush and satin. It was strange and rather eerie, like being on a film set after all the actors have gone. Television had not yet reached that remote outpost, with all its music and paintings and boring lecturers (and no rugby), and feeling suddenly tired I went to a bed that was disappointingly rectangular.

The next morning Mrs Van der Merwe returned, and after a breakfast of *boerwurst* and eggs cooked by the Servant, who had reappeared at an astonishingly early hour, Mrs Van der Merwe and I drove in the doctor's green Jaguar first to the town's hospital for whites, where there was a single patient with a broken leg to be looked after, and then to the surgery to meet Mrs Botha, the receptionist.

Mrs Botha was a friendly, middle-aged woman with a careful,

blue-tinted coiffure who spoke English with some hesitation and a strong Afrikaner accent. She welcomed me to the town and hoped I would be happy there. She told me once that I should not believe everything I read about South Africa: most of it was propaganda and the world was full of communists. Mrs Van der Merwe said that Mrs Botha would enlighten me as to my duties and then departed the surgery by taxi, leaving the Jaguar to me.

'She's gone to see her husband,' whispered Mrs Botha conspiratorially once Mrs Van der Merwe was out of earshot. 'In the clinic.'

Mrs Botha turned out to be a valuable source of information about everyone in town, which she communicated with the air of one performing a painful but binding duty.

'You know about Dr Van der Merwe of course,' she said.

'I know he drinks . . . er . . . rather a lot,' I said. And I added, 'Sometimes.'

'They say when Dr Van der Merwe starts drinking there's dancing in the Highlands of Scotland.'

Mrs Botha shuffled some patients' records on her desk to make me think she was working, and only incidentally gossiping about her employer.

'I don't know why he wants to drink like that,' she continued, sadly puzzled. 'He has everything he wants: a beautiful house, a pretty wife, nice children. And . . .' She hesitated, as though unsure whether she should impart this. '. . . Dr Van der Merwe is very rich.'

'He has a Jaguar,' I said, for lack of anything else to say.

'He makes a lot of money in this practice – about two hundred thousand rand a year, mostly in cash.'

In the light of that sum, my wages – which had seemed to me quite good – of three hundred and fifty rand a week were not excessive.

'Of course' she continued, her facial muscles flickering, 'Dr Van der Merwe doesn't *have* to work, like the rest of us. He's a millionaire – a multimillionaire. So sometimes I wonder why he goes on working.'

'Perhaps he likes it,' I said.

I did not have to wait long before I discovered how Dr Van der Merwe made his fortune. He had bought deserted tracts of land some distance away, whereupon everyone thought he had gone mad. Shortly after, however, it was announced that a vast industrial complex was to be built there, and suddenly those tracts of worthless scrub, which Dr Van der Merwe had bought for practically nothing, were worth several millions. From this story I deduced – though I never found out whether my deduction was correct – that Dr Van der Merwe had powerful connections in the ruling Nationalist Party, and was perhaps even a member of the *Broederbond*, the secret society of Afrikaners to which all the most powerful people in the country belonged.

'So I don't know why he needs to drink like that,' concluded Mrs Botha. 'But of course, there has been a tragedy in the family recently.'

One of La Rochefoucauld's Maxims ran through my head: we are all strong enough to bear the misfortunes of others. And as I watched Mrs Botha's jaws working to tell me the story of Dr Van der Merwe's family tragedy, I thought of another: there is in the misfortune of our friends something not entirely unpleasing.

The family tragedy was as follows. Dr Van der Merwe's aged father had recently been hacked to death in his bedroom with a panga wielded by a garden boy, whom he had not long before fired for stealing. Dr Van der Merwe's mother managed to shoot the garden boy several times with the family revolver before he crawled away, trying to make his escape. He was captured, of course, and taken to the African hospital to render him fit for execution. While he was there Dr Van der Merwe went to the hospital to shoot him, but was restrained at the bedside. Now the erstwhile garden boy was in Pretoria, awaiting execution.

Mrs Botha was highly satisfied with the effect her story produced on me. I must have looked astonished, and could only mutter something about such a situation being 'not very nice'.

'We have to live with it all the time, doctor,' she said with the triumph of one who had known adversity and overcome it. 'We have to be prepared for everything. That's what the rest of the world doesn't understand.'

And every Wednesday afternoon Mrs Botha went off, with perfect coiffure and gritted dentures, to the local police station to learn to shoot, along with the other ladies of the town. She fully expected at some time to have to use her skill thus acquired.

Within five or ten minutes of meeting Mrs Botha I knew quite a lot about Dr Van der Merwe. Her attitude toward her employer seemed to be compounded of contempt for his weakness and envy of his wealth. She spoke of him with a bitterness she reserved usually for the blacks. She expressed surprise (and disapproval) many times in the succeeding weeks that Mrs Van der Merwe had not yet left him, for he would never change now, and if Mrs Van der Merwe divorced him she would certainly receive a generous financial settlement and was by no means too old to remarry. Her behaviour was therefore inexplicable.

On that first morning, after she had said all she wanted to about Dr Van der Merwe, she showed me my consulting room – the one for white patients only. It was no different from such rooms in England. I sat in a swivel chair and waited for the patients to arrive. The first part of every morning was devoted to white patients who – as Mrs Botha told me, not without a hint of distaste – were disliked by Dr Van der Merwe because they were less lucrative than black patients. They were more demanding of time, less accepting of treatment (though no less ignorant of medical matters), and frequently failed to pay their bills until pressed or threatened. Moreover, when they *did* pay their bills it was with cheques or other traceable means, and therefore taxable, whereas the blacks paid cash. But it would have been socially unacceptable in the town for a white doctor to devote all his time and skill to the care of blacks. Thus Dr Van der Merwe had a white practice out of social obligation and to avoid a reputation as a *kaffirboetie*, literally a kaffir's little brother, or lover of blacks.

My first and only white patient of the day was introduced to me by Mrs Botha. She bustled into the consulting room in advance of the patient and spoke in a low whisper, telling me all she knew

about her, and lingering on those details of her life that were likely
to be especially sensitive. About her private life she was astonishingly well-informed, if what she said was true. She also gave
her medical opinion of the case, a spinsterish English-speaking
nursing sister with backache that had prevented her from working
for several months. Mrs Botha spoke venomously of her alleged
symptoms, in whose genuineness she clearly did not believe; it
was her opinion that the woman was a malingerer who did not
wish to work, who would only be cured by a husband who gave her
plenty of sex.

The unlikelihood of this prescription ever being filled was
immediately apparent when the patient entered. She had the face
of a mouse and the character of a wasp. Small and insignificant,
with sharp, unattractive features, she was made for resentment as
a bird for flight. She launched at once into a tirade against
doctors. It was they, she said, whose tyrannical orders – make the
bed, lift the patient – had given her backache in the first place.
And having given her this priceless gift they were quite unable,
through stupidity or ignorance, to take it back again, though she
had consulted the most eminent specialists in Johannesburg and
Pretoria, and even Bloemfontein. None of them had been able to
help, and some had added insult to injury (literally) by suggesting
she was faking. What did doctors know or understand? They
couldn't even cure a simple thing like backache.

'Then why consult me?' I asked mildly.

'Insurance purposes,' she said, and produced a form for me to
sign. It was to certify she was unfit for work.

'Are you quite sure you can't work?' I asked.

The very suggestion was enough to transport her with rage.
Never had she been so insulted. Thenceforth she would cease
altogether to have anything to do with Dr Van der Merwe's
so-called medical practice. There were plenty of other doctors in
town (there were three). She would let everyone know that Dr
Van der Merwe had employed an exceptionally rude young man:
his practice would be entirely ruined.

It was not an auspicious beginning, and I hastily signed the piece of paper that allowed her to collect some kind of payment. I ushered her out of the room as quickly as I could, Mrs Botha rushing into the vacuum to find out what I thought of her.

'Well . . .' I said, anxious to reveal nothing that could be bruited round the town. But I agreed with Mrs Botha both as to diagnosis and treatment, and she knew it. That I had said nothing was of no account: by nightfall the whole of the town would be apprised of my thoughts.

When it was clear there were to be no more white patients that morning, it was time to attend the black patients. They had their own premises, adjoining but quite separate. Mrs Botha took me as far as the dividing line but no further. *Apartheid* – apartness – was for her a living reality, and I think it would have shocked her deeply to have stepped beyond that line, except in case of direst emergency. She hung back in the safety of the white premises as she introduced me to Aurora, the black nurse who assisted Dr Van der Merwe with the black patients. It was as though closer contact would have defiled her; as though blackness were a highly contagious disease.

Aurora was a large Zulu woman in her thirties who wore a white uniform with a couple of prominent stains. She greeted me with a broad smile, revealing a piano keyboard of teeth. She called Mrs Botha 'sister', though as far as I was aware she had no nursing qualification, unlike Aurora; it was just that, regardless of paper qualifications, in this town any white was *ipso facto* more highly qualified than any black. If Aurora was a nurse, Mrs Botha had to be a sister; anything else would have been *lèse majesté*.

Aurora showed me round. There were five cubicles in a row, enabling the doctor to conduct a succession of consultations without having to stop for a moment, a production line of patients, as it were. Time was money. As one patient left, another entered. Consultations were on a strictly cash before delivery basis: five rand for a man, three for a woman, one for a child. It was one of Aurora's duties to collect the cash, and she was unswerving in the performance of her duty. Often while I was listening to a patient's heartbeat I heard Aurora outside the cubicle arguing with a

prospective patient. Her implacable rule was: no fee, no consultation. Sometimes, in response to the patient's insistent and plaintive pleas for mercy, I would ask Aurora whether in this one case,
perhaps, she could relent, but she said no, rules were rules; the
patient was faking poverty and could pay if he or she really
wanted, besides which it would be all round the African township
by tomorrow morning that the new doctor saw patients for
nothing, and then there would be huge crowds clamouring for
free treatment. In every case she was right: after a prolonged
verbal struggle the patient always managed to produce the required banknote.

The time devoted to each patient was not long, not more than a
minute on average, though even this was insufficiently swift to
satisfy Aurora, who used to hurry me along. She invoked the big
crowds of patients waiting on the open benches outside which,
she said, I should never clear at my present rate of working;
though it seemed to me that after such a long wait they were
entitled to more than a minute of my time. She told me I was
mistaken on two counts: first, the patients did not want prolonged
conversations or consultations, they wanted injections; second,
the Africans were well used to waiting, all day if necessary, and
turned waiting into a social if not a festive occasion. She had told
me to hurry only because otherwise I should get no lunch, not
from concern over the patients. And as if to prove her right the
patients rejoined the crowd from which they had come after I had
finished with them instead of going home. Aurora later joined
them too, over kerosene stoves cooking maize porridge. Though
she had taken their money there seemed to be no hard feeling,
and raucous laughter echoed through the building from outside,
once Mrs Botha had departed for her lunch.

She was quite right about the injections too. Patients did not
consider they had been given the best or most powerful treatment
unless they had had an injection: pills were a very poor substitute.
They went away disgruntled, and Aurora took me aside.

'Doctor is not giving enough injections,' she said (she always
addressed me in the third person).

'I give them when they're needed,' I replied.

'That is not enough. Doctor must give more.'

She explained that so insistent were the patients in this matter that unless I gave them injections they would forsake Dr Van der Merwe and turn to his rivals, though Dr Van der Merwe's surgery was nearest to where they lived and hence the most convenient. The other doctors would welcome the opportunity to steal his patients, for he was far the wealthiest of the doctors, the one most trusted hitherto by the Africans and, until my arrival, had been completely impregnable. I decided, with less than a clear conscience (for then I still had some scientific scruple), to give more injections.

Often when I entered a cubicle I was confronted by a pair of bared, smooth brown buttocks pointing upwards, waiting to receive the needle. At first I was puzzled by this behaviour. The patients wished for no discussion of their illness, for the simple reason that they were not ill; they wanted only to be stuck with a needle. But I soon discovered what the injections they so badly wanted were for: in the case of men they were to make them *strong*, by which I presumed they meant sexually potent; while in the case of women they were to make them fat, which was how their Zulu husbands liked them.

'Dr Van der Merwe always gives them Vitamin B,' said Aurora, and I later learnt that he prided himself when giving unnecessary injections that at least he gave the patient a nutrient in which he might be lacking, rather than the sterile water to which the other practitioners in the town resorted in the same situation.

Aurora pleaded with me for a potion to increase her appetite, which was inadequate to maintain her weight at more than fourteen stones. The Zulu ideal of feminine beauty, it seemed, was that of the queen termite: to be so fat as to be utterly immobile. And it is true that when they reached this exalted state there was something magnificent about them. They were not disgusting, as white women would have been; their black skin shone with a healthy sheen and they looked serene as gentle waves rippled through their semi-liquid forms, aware that their husbands now could wish for nothing more.

But Zulu girls who were at university had a different request. They wanted something to make them slim, though most of them were slim already. The ideal of beauty had changed with education, to something more approximating the European ideal. These were the people, presumably, who used skin-lightening creams that were everywhere advertised. Deeply, passionately resentful of the whites, they had nevertheless absorbed many of their standards, and lost their own. I felt pity for them.

In the black surgery I used a different stethoscope from that in the white. There was apartheid in equipment too. The black stethoscope had a longer tube by far than the white. As Dr Van der Merwe later explained to me, this was so that the doctor did not have to approach so near to the patients when examining them. A colleague of his in the anatomy department of Pretoria University had recently discovered a special gland in the armpits of Africans which accounted for their smell. I tried to look serious, and said nothing; and it would be dishonest to deny that many of the patients did have what, to my taste, was an unpleasant odour. This I attributed more to the lack of running water in the townships where they lived than to any secretions of a unique gland. Later, with some indignation I learnt that Africans considered we Europeans smelled like something dead, a plucked chicken, perhaps. I also discovered (and it reveals something of my unconscious sense of superiority that I should have had to *discover* it) that it was not only we Europeans who had a richly derogatory vocabulary to describe Africans: they too had such a vocabulary for us.

Other pieces of equipment were the same in design for the blacks as for the whites (though always duplicated). It would have been very difficult, for example, to have produced an ophthalmoscope on the same principle as the black stethoscope; but I once scandalised Mrs Botha by using the white ophthalmoscope on a black patient after I had temporarily mislaid the instrument intended for black use. Though the ophthalmoscope did not actually touch black skin, it was forever contaminated.

During my first days in the town I was obsessively worried that the patients would not like me and therefore the income of the practice would fall catastrophically. At the end of every surgery I would take the bundle of cash – usually quite thick – to Mrs Botha, who counted it and entered it in a book. Cash, strangely enough, was able to resist the contaminating influence of black hands. I asked anxiously whether the total was similar to that earned by Dr Van der Merwe in one morning, and when the sum fell conspicuously lower I wondered whether I was not ruining my shadowy employer. But Mrs Botha assured me there was always a decline in the income of the practice when a new locum arrived. It was only natural, she said, because even Africans preferred the doctor they knew to a complete stranger. And in truth, I was not sufficiently experienced at the time to cope with such a practice, for some of the patients were seriously ill with diseases I had never seen before and about which I had scarcely even read. Venereal diseases of many kinds were especially common; even now I wonder whether there might not be people in Natal suffering the late consequences of syphilis because I failed to treat them properly.

In spare moments Aurora would talk to me of her children (all of them illegitimate) and of her truly noble struggle to keep them at school. One could not but admire the ardour with which education was pursued by many blacks in South Africa, despite the limited occupational advancement to which they could realistically look forward under prevailing conditions. (Educate a kaffir, I heard it said, and you spoil him for life.) Their thirst for knowledge was insatiable, and education valued for its own sake, unlike in the rest of Africa where it has become a scramble for a government billet from which to exact tribute from a subject population.

Aurora said she was a member of the Zulu Royal Family, though her exact relationship to the king was of such complexity that it escaped my comprehension altogether. But being of royal blood, she said she could detect it in others, and strangely enough she detected it in me. She was utterly convinced I was a member

of the British Royal Family, closely related in fact to Prince
Charles, and nothing I said was able to disabuse her of this bizarre
conviction. I tried to explain that the two families had, in all
probability, quite different customs. At no time in modern history, for example, had British kings ventured beyond the occasional mistress, let alone kept hundreds of concubines for their
exclusive use. But I did not fool Aurora. My manner was regal,
my blood royal, and that was that. She even began to bow to me,
and the thought crossed my mind that it was all an elaborate
satire.

But it wasn't. When one day I offered to take her home to the
black township in the doctor's Jaguar she was overcome with
gratitude. Her life was a hard, neverending round of toil. She
showed me her passbook, a maze of documents and stamps so
complex that it could never fully satisfy the requirements of the
law, and therefore would always afford a pretext to any policeman
who wanted to arrest her, turning every journey, and even every
hour spent at home, into a hazard. She had to be at work by
seven-thirty, it took an hour to get there by bus; before she left
home she had to prepare breakfast for the children. On arriving
home at six in the evening she had once more to prepare their
food, do their washing and mending, and clean the house. A lift,
therefore, was something precious to her: it gave her almost an
hour of unaccustomed time to herself. But when I asked her to sit
in the front of the car next to me, rather than in the back to which
she had instinctively gone to create some distance between us, she
started to sob. Only a man of truly royal blood, she said, could
have made such a request.

I was not quite sure what she meant by this: whether, being
royal myself, I respected royalty in others, or whether, being
certain of my own social standing, I was able to stoop unselfconsciously to gestures of equality. At any rate, she thought it of the
utmost importance, and sat in the front with great ceremony.

As we approached the township, however, her delight began to
give way to another emotion: apprehension. She had warned me
that it was illegal for us to travel thus closely associated, but I had

dismissed the law – if it *was* the law – with a wave of contempt, and in the first flush of revolutionary enthusiasm she had discounted it too. But later, sounder instincts prevailed. The township, she said, was full of spies who for small sums of money provided the police with any tit-bits of information they might find useful. Everybody had enemies among his or her neighbours, and it would be better if I let her out at some distance from her home where no-one would see us. I was disappointed, for I had hoped to be invited to see her children; but she admitted she was ashamed of her house (it was no place for a member of the British Royal Family), besides which such a visit would be highly danger- ous for both of us.

The days passed quickly. I was out of the house before seven in the morning and rarely home before the same time at night. The mornings were best: a roseate light spread through the rolling fields of cane and made them glow. At that time the black cane workers were trudging along the dirt roads to their fields, and the clouds of dust my passage in the Jaguar threw up must have added to their discomfort. But their wretchedness, with which I sym- pathised in the official part of my mind, as it were, only increased my satisfaction at riding in so luxuriously engineered a vehicle. I glowed like the fields.

The white patients began to attend in greater numbers, not because of illness or my medical prowess, but out of curiosity about a stranger in their midst. Some 'patients' even admitted they had nothing wrong with them; they had come only to look at *die Engelsman*, the Englishman. I think they found my appearance disappointingly ordinary, though I am not sure what they ex- pected. But all of them, without exception, were fiercely anxious to discover my opinion of South Africa: not of its landscape or climate, of course, but of its political arrangements. I was trans- formed into a figure of great authority, being a foreigner, whose approval of apartheid would vindicate the whole system once and for all. My disapproval, on the other hand, would only confirm what South Africans already knew: that the minds of foreigners had been completely tainted by the cryptocommunist liberal press, and that it was up to South Africa alone to fight on behalf of the besieged Western Christian Civilisation.

In general, I steered a middle course between condemnation and outright approbation. I said the problem was complex; there was no easy solution; the future was uncertain. This was invariably taken as an endorsement of apartheid as the sole solution, for they were by now so used to strident denunciations of their country and its policies that anything else sounded like high praise. Once assured that I was on their side, they confided to me their innermost political thoughts, thoughts that were in every case identical.

'The rest of the world doesn't understand,' they said. 'It doesn't know the African.'

I never found out what it was the rest of the world did not know about *the African*, except that it reflected no credit on him. Only once was I drawn to make a remark critical of apartheid. An elderly man came ostensibly to have his blood pressure checked, but before long he was trying to explain the underlying principle of apartheid.

'The blackbird and the sparrow,' he said. 'They don't mate.'

'Well, there's no need to make laws about it then, is there?' I said.

This did his blood pressure no good at all and he never came back.

Most of my time, however, was spent with the black patients. To my surprise, even though they had to part with precious cash to see me, many of them were not ill at all, or had illnesses so trivial that they would have righted themselves in a few days. I had assumed, wrongly, that only whites allowed themselves the luxury of futile consultations or suffered the curse of hypochondriasis. One man even came to me asking for time off from work to watch an afternoon football match, and offered me what for him must have been a considerable payment if I would sign a sick certificate.

'It's a very important match,' he said urgently. 'Please sign, please doctor.'

Again it seemed to me remarkable that in these historic times anyone, let alone members of the downtrodden races and classes, should concern themselves so intently with matters as inconsiderable as football matches or their figures. When the history of these days comes to be written no-one will record these things. But I had little doubt, on general grounds, that the man requesting sick leave to watch a football match was mercilessly exploited at work, and I signed the certificate, refusing all payment. He was extravagantly thankful, offering to kiss my feet; but this offer, too, I declined.

The evenings were long and rather lonely. But after a week or so Mrs Van der Merwe suddenly reappeared. She was agitated and her eyes were red-rimmed from crying. I poured her a drink, which she seemed to need, and tried to calm her. She had no-one else to turn to, she said, and wondered if I minded giving her some advice. I said I should do my best, but secretly doubted my capacity.

Dr Van der Merwe, it seemed, had 'escaped' from the clinic for alcoholics. They had telephoned to tell her so. He was sure to head back to the town, in fact he might already be there. He would certainly start drinking again. What should she do? She had made it a condition of their remaining together that he complete the course of treatment at the clinic.

Suddenly I felt myself a very young man, completely unequipped to deal with such a problem. What could I say? I could talk a little – but only a little – of the prognosis of alcoholism. She, however, wanted a line of action to follow, not statistics. If it were firm advice she needed, she had much better have gone to Mrs Botha.

As a precautionary measure she decided to search for alcoholic drinks in the house and to destroy them by pouring them down the sink. The search involved not only the expected places, but also the garage, the toolshed, and the bushes in the garden. To Mrs Van der Merwe's dismay we found not only a cache of empty bottles in the garage but several full ones as well. Dr Van der Merwe had planned his relapse in advance. It was not the moment to tell Mrs Van der Merwe of the futility of her precautions, pouring it away as though it were the last whisky in the world. Activity in such a situation had a calming effect of its own.

She departed soon afterwards, but returned at ten o'clock. She was more agitated than ever. She was sure she had heard her husband creeping about in the garden outside her mother's house. It was either he or burglars. In either case, would I mind coming to search there?

We drove through the already sleeping town to her mother's house. It was an old colonial farmstead with a stoep, that not long before had been deep in countryside. There were still fields behind it and there was no street lighting. It was a moonless night, and the southern stars studded the jet-black sky. I thought, as we stumbled through the bushes scratching our shins, armed only with a single torch, that if it was bandits she had heard, we should make easy targets. But we found no-one, and Mrs Van der Merwe decided that by now her husband, if it had been he, would have decamped to the other house; so we drove back again.

Her first thought when we arrived back – a thought expressed not without an element of hope – was that her husband had fallen drunkenly into the swimming pool and drowned there. She asked me to look. I scanned the pool with the torch – she did not want to turn on the floodlights lest the neighbours saw. But Dr Van der Merwe was not in the pool, either dead or alive.

'Are you sure?' asked his wife.

I said I was sure I should have noticed a body in the pool had there been one but she asked me to look again. Out of deference to her distress I did as I was requested, but in the meantime she found her husband and shouted for me to come quickly to the garage.

Dr Van der Merwe was lying across the back seat of the Jaguar, snoring stertorously and with his feet out of the window. It was my first glimpse of my employer. He was dead drunk. Mrs Van der Merwe and I carried him, grunting and snorting, into the house and up the stairs, depositing him like a sack of potatoes on the heart-shaped bed, where he started to snore again. I retreated to my own room, leaving Mrs Van der Merwe sobbing over her husband.

Next morning, as I was having breakfast, Dr Van der Merwe appeared freshly washed and shaved, with only bloodshot eyes to remind one of his previous condition. He was a slim man in his forties. Like his wife, he spoke English with a strong Afrikaner accent, though with greater facility. He said nothing of his unusual return to his house – perhaps he did not remember it – but talked unselfconsciously about the practice. His manner was pleasant and unassuming; there was nothing in it to suggest a deep or consuming psychological conflict that needed drowning in whisky. I was rather disappointed. He said he would come with me that morning to the surgery.

He stayed only a short time, in the course of which I discovered that he spoke fluent Zulu. To my surprise, Mrs Botha greeted his unexpected return warmly, and showed him great respect. But as soon as he had gone she started to disparage him again, saying that she didn't know how or why a woman like Mrs Van der Merwe tolerated such a drunken lout, and contorting the muscles of her face into an ugly spasm of hate.

'It's the money, I suppose,' she said.

From then on Dr Van der Merwe became a figure hovering in the background, suddenly appearing in the morning or afternoon, and disappearing again with equal irregularity. I presumed his appearances and disappearances had some connection with fluctuations in his consumption of whisky, but never settled the point. Sometimes he would come to work on two successive days, remaining the whole day, and I would think he had recovered his sobriety; but then he would go missing for several days, and no-one knew his whereabouts. When he was sober we would go together to the town's African Hospital where we had a few patients. The wards were large halls whose floor space was almost entirely occupied by iron bedsteads, making passage between them difficult and hazardous. In the children's ward there were not enough cots to go round: a baby was put in each of the four corners, with results not difficult to imagine. But most of Dr Van

der Merwe's patients were men who had been injured at work.
According to Mrs Botha, whose information on the subject may
have been distorted by her dislike of Dr Van der Merwe, it was
very lucrative surgery, for the medical fees were deducted from
the compensation to which the victim was legally entitled, frequently leaving him with very little as a result. An appropriate
name for the act under which injured workers received compensation, in Mrs Botha's opinion (which she held from no love of
injured Africans), would have been the Surgeon's Compensation
Board.

Dr Van der Merwe and I had once to amputate two fingers
from a man with a badly mangled hand. I was the anaesthetist, and
was not brave enough to mention my less than distinguished
previous career in this branch of medicine. All went well on this
occasion; but later, when I went on my own to the African
hospital, one of the sisters told me of the time when Dr Van der
Merwe, very drunk, had performed a similar operation but
amputated the wrong fingers by mistake. The whites of the town
had thought this very funny, she said. I was uncertain how much
of this story to discount as exaggeration: an atmosphere of racial
hatred is not conducive to the propagation of the truth, un-
varnished.

It was not only Dr Van der Merwe whose appearances and
disappearances mystified me, but his wife's and his mother-in-
law's too. They flitted in and out of the house for no reason that I
could discern. Mrs Van der Merwe's mother was a plump woman
with peasant features, etched by a life on the veldt, in striking
contrast to her daughter. She had not long left her farm, where
everything had seemed as straightforward as the seasons of the
year. Though she took a guileless pride in the rich furnishings of
her daughter's home, she found the ferment of the modern,
urban world baffling.

'South Africa isn't like it used to be,' she lamented. 'Nowadays
you have to call an African a Bantu. But if you can't call a Kaffir a
Kaffir, who *can* you call a Kaffir?'

On one of the evenings when Mrs Van der Merwe and her

mother came to the house, we discussed a far-off land called
Overseas. They were neither of them very clear as to where it was
(it was something like Terra Australis on an old map), or what was
to be found there, but they had a subliminal intuition that it was
different from South Africa.

'Tell me,' asked Mrs Van der Merwe, 'what are the natives like
in England?'

'Friendly,' I replied. 'But getting cheeky.'

They tutted: things were the same everywhere, then.

The irregular visits of parts of the family, followed by their
departures, gave my life an almost dreamlike quality. This feeling
of unreality was strengthened one morning when I arrived at the
surgery to find a police *bakkie* (pickup truck) parked on the ramp
outside. The back of the truck was open, except for a wire cage;
inside was a white woman with wildly straggling hair, stark naked
apart from a coarse grey blanket wrapped around her. She
cowered like a wild animal in a corner of the cage. The white
policemen stood by the truck discussing something.

I approached them. They explained that the woman had been
found earlier in the day wandering the streets of the town, talking
to herself, singing and laughing.

I asked whether she had been naked then.

'No,' replied the policemen.

It was the police, therefore, who for reasons of their own had
stripped her naked and wrapped her in the blanket, but I did not
pursue the point.

The two policemen had been discussing what to do with the
woman when I arrived: whether to take her in the white entrance
because she was white, or in the black entrance because she was
mad. The objection to the white entrance was that she might
frighten the white patients; to the black entrance that it was
undesirable for blacks to see mad whites, let alone naked mad
whites (it is forbidden in South Africa for a black doctor even to
attend the post mortem of a white). The two policemen could not
agree, and I was as a Daniel come to judgment.

I announced my decision: she should go in the white entrance.

It is true that her appearance caused some alarm to the only waiting patient, a woman well-advanced in pregnancy, who might have gone into labour, and to Mrs Botha who clearly regarded madness as catching and backed away accordingly; but the policemen told me later that I had made the right decision as to entrances, and they supported me.

I was asked to sign a piece of paper committing the woman to mental hospital. It strikes me now as having been a remarkably casual way to deprive someone of her liberty; but at the time I had few doubts she was quite mad. Her answers to my questions, even allowing that she was simultaneously wrestling with the blanket so as not to expose herself, were bizarre and nonsensical. Whether this was sufficient reason to lock her away is another matter; but at least my conscience is clear that her madness did not take the form of protest against the régime.

Shortly after this episode, Dr Van der Merwe appeared at the surgery and announced that he had made a complete recovery and was now quite ready to take over control of his practice once again. Mrs Botha had her doubts, which she lost no time in revealing to me; while I confessed that I was less than pleased at being thus unceremoniously turfed out of a job. But Dr Van der Merwe did not leave me entirely in the lurch: he arranged a job for me at Edendale Hospital in the black township of Pietermaritzburg, the capital, though not the largest city, of the province of Natal. Two days later I left the town for its small airfield, and flew in an eight-seater to Pietermaritzburg. I carried with me a large, but not yet large enough, bundle of green ten-rand notes.

Pietermaritzburg was, despite its name, the archetypal British colonial city. It was named for two heroes of Afrikaner history, Piet Retief and Gerhardus Maritz. Retief met his death at Dingaan's Farm when the Zulu impis attacked his laager. The Afrikaners, led by Pretorius (for whom Pretoria is named), had their revenge, of course, at the battle of Blood River, so called because the river ran red with the blood of three thousand Zulu warriors; and the Day of the Covenant is observed as a holiday

still, because before the battle the Afrikaners promised God that
if he vouchsafed them victory they and their descendants would
keep the day as sacred for ever. Even names of cities and holidays
fuel hostility within the Republic, reminding some of their glory,
others of their humiliation, but all of their enmity.

But Maritzburg, as it is usually known, was as peaceful as could
be when I arrived: the well-ordered streets exuded an almost
British smugness. The public gardens were manicured by a
hundred gardeners, mostly on their knees; the jacaranda trees
that lined the streets were in flower; and a pigeon was firmly
planted atop the head of Sir Theophilus Shepstone, worthy
Victorian administrator, streaking his broad and generous brow
with white as he stood before the magniloquent town hall. But I
was not to stay for long in this genteel world of neat herbaceous
borders, bowling greens as smooth as felt, and afternoon tea; I
was headed (in a taxi) for the unlovely underworld of the black
township.

Edendale was nine miles from the centre of the city, reached by
a single road. It was no accident there was only a single route
connecting the township with its metropolis: if the Africans chose
to riot the road, and hence the township, could be sealed off with
armoured cars and the rioters would, in the words of the police,
foul their own nest.

Their nest was, despite the Elysian connotations of its name,
foul enough already. The statistics showed that Edendale was by
no means the worst of the black townships in South Africa, with a
higher than average percentage of electrification and a lower
murder rate. But it was still an utterly cheerless place where no
effort had been spared to eliminate all trace, all possibility, of
individuality so as to forestall the development of a sense of
attachment. There was no street lighting off the main arteries,
giving the *tsotsis* their chance to use their deadly skill: the insertion
of a sharpened bicycle spoke with surgical precision into the
spinal cord of a victim to paralyse him and rob him of whatever
was worth taking, from money to passbook. And as in Mzilikaze,
only the hospital towered above it all, to patch up the inhabitants.

The hospital was of a dull red brick, a forbidding edifice. It was less clean than Mpilo, more crowded. Perhaps its workload was greater, perhaps it was less efficiently administered; at any rate, there was not enough ward space and the corridors were littered with beds in which lay patients in all stages of recovery and deterioration. I was seconded to the busiest department of all, that of surgery, as a very junior member of the team of Mr Malan, a dynamic young Afrikaner surgeon (he had taken his Fellowship of the Royal College of Surgeons). He was a true enthusiast, with an insatiable appetite for cutting open people's insides. He did it with determination and skill, and often they survived. I marvelled at his unflagging zeal, his boundless energy, his total absorption in his work, and envied him not a little. He had an even younger assistant called Hills, with brilliant flaxen hair and piercing blue eyes, who wanted to be a surgeon and was avid for 'cutting experience'. It was he who told me that Mr Malan's surgical enthusiasm was not purely disinterested. Mr Malan did not intend to spend the rest of his life as humble surgeon to Edendale Hospital: he hoped one day to go into lucrative private practice among the whites and was using Edendale to gain the widest possible experience. Such was the wealth of *clinical material* – as patients are known – in Edendale, so widespread was pathology, that he could there perfect the techniques he would one day use on the whites. For him, keeping a black patient alive was not a moral imperative but a technical exercise on a physiological preparation. But Mr Malan's ambitions did not end with private practice. Having made a fortune and invested it wisely, he would return to less well-paid academic life and seek the title of professor, to be called 'Professor' being the greatest balm to his soul he could conceive. According to Hills, Mr Malan had had a deprived upbringing and had risen in the world solely by his own efforts and determination.

The young would-be surgeon recounted Mr Malan's motives for so enthusiastically operating on Africans without irony or even an awareness that they might strike a stranger as unusual and not particularly laudable. After all, *his* ambitions were identical to Mr

Malan's, except that, not having had a deprived childhood, he had no desire to be a professor, only to have a large income.

More than once I discussed with him the futility – as I saw it – of providing elaborate surgical care for a population whose very conditions of life were a guarantee of ill-health. In the intensive-care unit of Edendale Hospital it was always possible to see men kept alive at great expense by elaborate machinery and the continual use of drugs who, if they ever survived beyond the hospital, would lead lives of terrible restriction; while all around the hospital (I presumed) children died for lack of simple and effective preventive measures. But it was precisely in the intensive care patients that the two surgeons took most interest, for they were 'the intriguing problems' – renal failure, intractable pain, septicaemia. They looked on the hospital as a laboratory in which to improve their skill; and, powerless to change the world, they might yet save a life or two. The young assistant told me he enjoyed what he called 'the fight against pathology', even if the success were not proportional to the effort. I had to admit (if only to myself) that his outlook, however mixed his motives, helped more people than my lofty generalisations; for if the truth were told, my disdain of surgery originated not so much from theor-etical considerations, as from a disinclination to exert myself long and tediously on behalf of others. And I am glad now that there are such people, whatever their reasons, for one day I may need their services myself. But I know I shall never be one of their number.

Although Mr Malan soon realised that I did not share his enthusiasm for surgery (and thereby I earned his scorn), he was as anxious as anybody I met in South Africa that I should express my approval of the political situation there. As we looked out over the township one day from the window of a corridor high up in the hospital, he asked me what I thought of apartheid. The township below was eloquent testimony to a certain malaise, to say the least; but as his question had not been asked for the sake of information, but rather to receive an *imprimatur*, I was non-committal (more – or less – I could not be). Mr Malan, being a highly intelligent man, then regaled me with the most sophisticated apologia for the régime that I heard in all my time in South Africa. It was difficult, he said, for people of widely different cultures to live together, as the whole history of the world went to demonstrate. Why not, therefore, give each culture – he avoided the word *race* – a chance to develop along its own lines, in its own time and on its own territory? It was *separate development* now, not apartheid. Any other policy would lead to irreconcilable conflict.

I pointed out, very mildly, that the European culture in South Africa seemed to need an inordinate amount of black labour to sustain it, but Mr Malan replied that the eventual aim of Separate Development was to dispense with this necessity. I did not counter with all the statistics I had taught myself in the South African Library, or mention the 87 per cent of the land surface the Europeans deemed necessary for their separate development. To have won the argument would not have changed Mr Malan's mind; but it would have earned his enduring hostility.

Much of my time, as at Mpilo, was spent in the casualty department. But Mpilo had been to Edendale what a fête champêtre is to a bear garden. Every day, but especially at weekends, there was an unending trail of death and destruction leading to the hospital. Never a car crashed but it had been packed with people like a tin of anchovies, inflicting the maximum of injury on the maximum number, with a fair proportion of death thrown in. Worse still were the results of violence in the township. A visitor to the department might have supposed he had stumbled on the victims of a ferocious civil war. Groaning on the blood-caked floor were men and women whose faces had been beaten out of all recognition by knob-kerries, wielded by insensate drunk husbands, jealous wives, avaricious thieves and highwaymen. Not being seriously injured in the medical sense – that is to say, they were unlikely to die – they were suffered to lie unattended for hours on end while attention was given to more serious cases, of which there were always many. At first I found the groans, half of pain, half of indignity, as nervewracking as the cry of a baby, and wanted to give the patients large doses of sedatives not for their relief, but for my own; but before long I was able to pick my way through the prostrate, whimpering mass of battered humanity with a heart as hard as Pharaoh's, selecting those in greatest need – not usually the loudest – for immediate succour. It was the people with stab-wounds who needed the closest attention, for long narrow blades can inflict deadly injury with deceptively few outward signs. The toll of knife attacks was terrible. The victims were more often than not drunks who were utterly incapable of any coordinated movement, let alone self-defence against the gangs of youthful robbers who lurked at night in unlit streets. At the weekends, when men were out with their week's wages in their pockets to have a good time, by which was meant drinking to the extinction of consciousness, the thieves operated almost without opposition. Over one weekend I counted forty victims of stabbing attacks (one man was brought in dead, who had been killed for the sake of two rand). Many had stabwounds of the chest, a kind of injury I had been taught must always be taken seriously, requiring a period of observation in hospital to wait for the development of complications. This I had learnt in a country where such injuries were rare, causing some excitement in the hospital; but in Edendale there were not sufficient beds to admit them all, so they were told to go home and return later if they found it difficult to breathe. Very few ever returned, and I concluded that either stabwounds of the chest were very much less dangerous than I had been taught, or our patients were dying quietly at home. At any rate, the police regarded it as no part of their duty to reduce the level of violence in the township at the weekends: they merely waited for Monday morning to collect the bodies from the streets, the ditches and the hospital, and take them to the police morgue.

All this violence raised several questions in my mind. If I were willing to excuse the perpetrators of these terrible crimes because the condition of their lives had made them criminals; if, in other words, *comprendre tout c'est tout pardonner*; then, to be consistent, I must similarly excuse the whites for their cruelties which, being a stern moralist at the time, I was very reluctant to do. If, on the other hand, men were more than just the playthings of their circumstances, and at some time were masters of their fate, then the trail of human devastation did not speak well of the Africans. My old philosophical temperament reasserted itself as I sought a fully consistent solution to this dilemma. Either all men were responsible for their actions, or none was. It little occurred to me that the world would scarcely fit my scheme of either-or; in other words, that there was an infinite shading of degrees of culpability, and I should be more blameworthy if *I* behaved like a *tsotsi* than if an orphaned slum youth did so.

My companions in the casualty department were two young South African doctors who, having received their training in such an environment, were vastly more competent than I; and a young Portuguese doctor who had left Mozambique shortly after its independence. He and I had frequent lengthy conversations on political subjects, though we took the precaution of holding them outside in the car park where we could not be overheard. Rather naively, as I now think, I took him at face value. He claimed to be disaffected with South African reality, his presence in the country dictated only by the excellence of the surgical training there and the experience he would gain, after which he intended to return to Mozambique and place himself at the disposal of the Revolution. Far more likely, he was an embittered young colonist who, anxious that there should be no such *dénouement* in South Africa as had occurred in Mozambique, had agreed to act as an *agent provocateur*. The country, as I had been warned, was full of spies and paid informers; but I nevertheless confided to him my unguarded thoughts, even while the question 'Is this wise?' ran through my head.

Unlike the other doctors, who had flats or houses in town to return to after the day's work was over, I lived on the premises, over the shop as it were. I was therefore isolated and lonely, enclosed in the dismal embrace of an institution, unable to leave it at night for fear of the violence in the unlit township. I had no means of my own to travel the nine miles to the city centre, and had therefore either to walk in the hope that someone would stop to give me a lift, or to travel on a black bus – that is, a bus reserved for blacks – where my presence was nothing if not conspicuous. Indeed, it created a sensation among the other passengers, and caused not a few drivers' heads to turn dangerously as they drove past. No doubt my presence on the bus was construed in some quarters as a political gesture, subversive or brave according to taste; in fact, I was only trying to get to the best restaurant in town.

At the weekend, and during daylight hours, I ventured out into the township. It was then perfectly safe. At first I was apprehensive, fearing I might be met with hostility, for whites were uncommon visitors (it was illegal for them to go without a permit), and usually they went only on some mission of oppression. But I was either ignored or welcomed with smiles, my demeanour not being that of a policeman, secret or otherwise. One Sunday morning I was walking along a dirt road, finding even the bleak landscape of the township under the open sky a refreshment after a week in the entrails of the hospital, when I was attracted to some choral singing in Zulu coming from a Methodist church, a simple construction of brick and tin. I entered quietly from the back, hoping not to be noticed. The altar at the far end of the church was a simple table, covered with a snowy white cloth lovingly embroidered with a floral border. On the altar were two jamjars filled with flowers, a tribute to the beauty of God's creation not easily come by in Edendale.

As though somehow sensing my arrival through the backs of their heads, the entire congregation stopped singing and turned to stare at me. Their astonishment was plainly written on their faces. Blushing, I sat on the rear pew. With the habit inculcated by a lifetime in the townships, and necessary for their survival, they sized me up and, deciding I was harmless, resumed their hymn, if anything with greater gusto. They were dressed in the chiffon finery of two decades before, when no woman went shopping without her white gloves. It was here once again that the bourgeois virtue of good orderliness seemed not ridiculous, which as a member of the intelligentsia I had always considered it, but heroic. Were these the same people that I saw daily in the casualty department?

The hymn, as it happened, was the last of the service. I had thought to slip out unnoticed after the service was over, already feeling awkward at having interrupted it; but the preacher, the moment the last strain died away, rushed forward to welcome me. It was a great moment, he said; and he wondered whether I should do them all the honour of attending a little feast and ceremony they were about to hold in the adjacent hall. His manner was ingratiating, obsequious almost, but it was clear that my acceptance gave him genuine pleasure.

I was ushered into the hall with great ceremony, and immediately sat at the head table as guest of honour. I was dressed casually while they were all in their finest; I had come idly, drawn by their singing, while for them it was an important day; and yet, purely by virtue of my race, I was the guest of honour. Such were the rewards and pleasures of being a white liberal (this was a year before the great Soweto riots). It spoke eloquently, I thought, of the deep longing of the blacks to be recognised and treated as fully human by the whites for whom, despite themselves, they had a kind of abject respect. Things, I believe, are different now.

The ceremony and feast were to celebrate the graduation of a batch of black nurses from Edendale Hospital. The official presentation of diplomas had already taken place within the hospital: this was the proud tribute of the township to its new nurses.

Food was continually pushed towards me during the ceremony, the choicest morsels available. I was the only one eating during the speeches, but I consoled myself with the thought that it was evidently expected of me as the guest of honour. No sooner had I finished one chicken leg than another was pressed into my hand. I even listened to the hymns sung by the nurses' choir with a drumstick suspended halfway between the table and my mouth. Then came an address to the audience by the man who would have been guest of honour had I not arrived.

He was dressed in a dark business suit with the exaggeratedly wide lapels that were the fashion of the time. A man at my side translated from his Zulu. First he extended a welcome to me, and said how honoured he was – they all were – that I should attend. But it was obvious to all, he continued, that I had neither been born in South Africa nor lived there long, or else I should not be sitting where I was now. Just let me stay a few years, however, and I should be indistinguishable from all the others. Turning to me, he appealed to me in Zulu to go home, if I wished to remain a decent man.

He went on to tell the nurses that qualifying was a great personal achievement, but they should use their education to serve the people from whom they sprang. It was strange to hear nurses spoken of as highly educated, but in Edendale they had joined an élite. He said they must never forget their diplomas were not the result of their unaided efforts, but of those of their parents and the whole of their community as well, who had all made sacrifices that they might learn.

He spoke of a future that was coming, one in which the lion would, as it were, lie down with the lamb. He had just returned from a trip to West Germany where all men were equal, he said, and there was no apartheid. At this point an elderly man in a battered and grease-stained brown homburg hat jumped up and asked whether this meant that in Germany black and white sat next to one another in the cinema. This, for him, was the *ne plus ultra* of liberation. Certainly, replied the speaker. And had he been in such a cinema, asked the old man. Yes he had, only last week in fact. The man, half-incredulous, half-bewildered, removed his hat from his head the better to scratch it, and sat down.

The speaker finished what he had to say and the feast began. I was expected once more to eat as though I had gone hungry for days. I managed before long to make my excuses and slip quietly away: the other guests at the head table were constrained by the need, out of politeness, to speak English and to attend to my wants before their own. I left having exchanged assurances of high regard and in the afterglow, as I walked back to the hospital, I wondered why such meetings could not be expanded into political arrangements. It was naive even to wonder, of course: the township had as many *tsotsis*, as many nationalists of contending factions, as many police informers, as respectable Methodists; and as for the whites, there were probably only a handful who could even contemplate the prospect of sitting at the same table as a black without being overcome by nausea. Not everything can be solved by gestures of goodwill.

Feeling ever more isolated and dejected in the hospital I decided to leave. I manufactured a pretext – the illness of a close relative at home in England – and, to my shame, Mr Malan could not have been kinder or more considerate. As luck would have it, a friend of mine was visiting South Africa. His brother was a doctor in Zululand, with a practice in the lush green rolling hills that shaded blue into the distance. He lent us his pickup truck to travel the country, so that while I should have been going home to comfort my dangerously ill relative I was sojourning in the Drakensberg, the long mountain chain with saw-tooth peaks like a dragon's crest.

I was indeed fortunate, as I later discovered, to have left Edendale when I did. The day following my departure the Special Branch of the police called for me. I had offended in some way. Perhaps they had heard about my bus rides into Pietermaritzburg; or there had been an informer in the midst of the Methodists; or they had read my letters home; or the Portuguese doctor *was* a police spy. To everyone in the hospital my fortuitous departure must have looked as though I had some knowledge of the Special Branch's movements and was therefore engaged in some secret political activity. In fact, it was only the luckiest of coincidences. Several doctors were arrested that day, blacks amongst them. (So effective had been the segregation of doctors within the hospital that I was unaware till then that there *were* any black doctors working there.) So while I was enjoying the beauties of the Drakensberg, several of my erstwhile colleagues were enjoying the amenities of the prison service.

My friend and I drove through the Orange Free State, staying in small towns which, though far from ancient, seemed timeless, like flies in amber. We stayed in the hotel of one small *dorp* and asked for dinner. We were served a steak of remarkable toughness, which our knives were not merely unable to cut, but upon which they made no mark. We complained, but the proprietress, aware of her monopoly position, said we could take it or leave it. We said we should leave it, but certainly not pay for it. At this point she began to defend her steaks which – she said – were famous throughout the Orange Free State. We weren't surprised, we replied, and told her that if she considered the meat edible we should like to see her eat it. She hit upon another solution: we should take the steaks to the local policeman and let him decide whether or not they were edible. This would have given rise, no doubt, to a scene of great local interest and colour; but we had no confidence in the independence of the local policeman's gastronomic judgment, and we merely drove on to the next *dorp* – without paying.

We went through the Transkei, one of the allegedly independent Bantustans, where the land had been overgrazed and overcropped to dust, and into Swaziland where the sparrows of the Transvaal sought temporary congress with the blackbirds of the Mbabane brothels. We gambled in the casino there and lost. We drove to the impoverished mountain kingdom of Lesotho, half of whose men were away working in the mines of the Witwatersrand while the half that remained were drunk. The roads in Lesotho were scarcely distinguishable from the land they traversed, and we pursued an eccentric course over kopjes and mountains, thoroughly lost. We attained the small capital at last, and went to the central police station for directions. All the policemen were barefoot and drunk; when the chief of police entered – he had shoes – they struggled to rise and salute, but fell back in their chairs. So we had our directions from the chief of police, who was relatively sober. Meanwhile the Prime Minister, Chief Jonathan, was riding up and down the main street in his Mercedes, outriders in white helmets flashing their lights and wailing their sirens, to impress the population with his importance.

I departed South Africa for Malawi. I hired a car to go to Zomba, and in addition to the usual clauses in a hire contract I signed a promise to pull my car off the road, get out and stand to attention, should the President or any of his ministers go by. At my hotel I was given an information sheet for tourists. The people of Malawi, it said, so loved His Excellency the Life President Ngwazi Dr H. Kamuzu Banda, that if any of his opponents dared enter the country, they would chop them up and throw them to the crocodiles.

I thought it time to go home.

FIVE

London

I RETURNED to England hoping I should be able to see in it the vividness of a foreign country, but a year away had not been nearly long enough to undo the familiarity of a lifetime. True, after the open spaces and the brilliant southern skies everything looked a little greyer, darker, smaller, more overcrowded; but these were impressions heightened rather than newly formed. All the same, England was never again to be the obvious centre of my universe. I knew that I could – and would – uproot myself in search of a warmer, more colourful life. And strangely enough, while South Africa was accounted 'provincial', I had felt far closer to events of world significance there than I ever had in England, whose historical destiny was now irrevocably played out.

I had no immediate urge to bring medical succour to my fellow citizens, believing I had a more vital task to perform in telling of my experiences in Southern Africa. This was a belief which, as we shall see, was not in any way reciprocated; but in order to accomplish my self-appointed task, I accepted an offer of open-ended hospitality from my old friend Dr Richard Francis, and went to stay in his garret flat in a vast Edwardian house in Edgbaston, Birmingham, where he was then living. Every morning, after he and his girlfriend (now his wife, also a doctor) had gone to work I would sit down at a desk and write what was to be a devastating and definitive exposé of South African society, in novel form. It was not, of course, concerned *only* with South Africa; my ambitions were more universal. I wished to lay bare the evil that lurks in all men's hearts. I did not find it quite so easy as I had at first supposed.

The house in which I lived was once the family home of a prosperous merchant or manufacturer, built on a generous scale, with a conservatory and several ornamental turrets, large gardens and a laurel-lined drive. But the proper upkeep of such a house was now beyond the means of anyone in the city (there being no manufacturers left) and it had fallen almost into ruins. The laurels were overgrown, the panes of the conservatory broken, the tiled and wood-panelled entrance hall was gloomy by day and by night pitch black. The stairs, also unlit, creaked more theatrically than in any horror film; and in winter the whole house was irradiated with a terrible Siberian cold, so that in the mornings one had to open the windows to let it out. The house had been divided into three flats, with large numbers of rooms left unoccupied, except for pieces of broken plumbing, chairs with three legs, and ancient undisturbed cobwebs.

On the ground floor lived the lessee, Richard's landlord Dieter, and his wife Julia, both of whom subsequently became close friends of ours. Dieter was from East Germany, a refugee from communism in the early fifties who had come to an England whose prospects, then, had seemed brighter than any country's in Europe. A graduate in physics and mathematics, he spoke English with an accent, but with a command superior to ninety-nine out of a hundred native speakers. He had shrewdly bought property while it was still cheap and was now able to live off the rents, which allowed him to pursue his interest in philosophy. (He is presently writing a doctoral thesis at the London School of Economics on the philosophical foundations of Elizabethan science.) Julia was a woman of inexhaustible energy and good humour, who was able simultaneously to bring up a small child, keep the flat, conduct research into the health care of the old (she has her Ph.D), edit books on the subject, prepare lectures and cook delicious meals for any guests who turned up, all without fuss. The rooms of their flat had been restored to their former glory, their warm oak-panelled walls hung with Victorian seascapes, Persian and Turkish carpets strewn carelessly on the floors. When the weather was fine we took Sunday lunch with them on the garden lawn, surrounded completely by old oaks and elms so that the noise of the city was excluded completely and it was possible to imagine oneself in a country house. Dieter had just discovered some fifty-year-old wines in the cellar and we tried to drink them, but they had turned to vinegar and were auctioned off at great profit. As to rent, Dieter was embarrassed by the whole subject, and never brought it up, even when arrears were owing.

Sandwiched between his flat and Richard's garret lived an ill-assorted couple: a Bangladeshi factory worker known as Leonard and a large, slatternly woman into whose business it would not have done to enquire too closely. I never saw her except in her nightclothes, which were crumpled and soiled as though by weeks of continual wear. I think she spent most of her life in bed, and the rest of it flitting to and from the bathroom down the corridor, like an apparition. Leonard was morbidly sensitive to noise, providing it was somebody else who was making it. He would bang on the ceiling at the faintest sound from above, shout angrily and complain to the landlord; but when he played his own dance music, of a bygone era, the whole house vibrated. His partner attributed his detestation of noise to a sensitive, artistic nature blighted by the daily grind of factory routine; but we thought he was mad. One evening he appeared at our door brandishing a knife, foaming at the mouth and eyes wildly staring. He would kill us, he said, if he heard any more noise. We laughed, but not entirely convincingly. He was a nice, kind, gentle man, his partner said, but capable of anything once something she called 'his goat' was up. We believed it. Leonard made returning to the garret at night an exciting experience. It was quite impossible to avoid the creaking stairs – they all creaked – and in the utter darkness of the narrow corridor Leonard might have done us grievous harm had he sallied forth with his knife again.

The only time I have seen a ghost, in whose existence I naturally do not believe, was in that house. There had been a dinner party in the garret – Richard was a superb cook, always on a lavish scale – and, slightly tipsy, he and I decided to freshen up by taking a walk on Edgbaston golf course, which adjoined our garden. The clubhouse, by the way, was once the home of William Withering, the discoverer of the antidropsical properties of the foxglove, one of the greatest discoveries in the history of pharmacology. A low mist clung melodramatically to the ground, eerily dispersing the moonbeams. When we returned to the house a slight breeze rustled through the leaves of the laurels, and we felt a chill. When we were within a few yards of the stone entrance, I saw a vague triangular shape of diaphanous white glide noiselessly by into the house, where it swiftly disappeared. I turned to Richard.

'Did you see anything then?' I asked.

He described exactly what I had seen. It was later (at least, I *think* it was later, though I cannot swear to this) we learnt that early in this century a Dominican monk had been murdered in the entrance of the house. The Dominicans, of course, wear white habits.

At first my writing seemed to go well. But it soon became clear that raw experience was not sufficient to fashion a novel. I needed some organisational principle; above all I needed imagination, since unhappily life does not fall of itself into well-constructed plots for novels. To aid me I drew on two books I had read, one by Father Cosmas Desmond which described the destruction of black shanty towns by the white authorities, relocating them to far-off sites quite unfit or unprepared for human habitation; the other by the Swedish anthropologist Bengt Sundkler, about the many messianic Zulu churches, each with its own ritual, that flourished in the fertile soul of oppressed Zulu communities. All that was left for my imagination was, rather artificially, to draw the threads together.

The plot, so far as I remember it, concerned a young doctor who arrived in a small South African town to stand in as locum for, not surprisingly, a drunken general practitioner. At the time of his arrival the white townspeople were agitating for the removal of the black township to a remote site, both for aesthetic reasons and because they wanted to lay out a golf course in its place. One morning, practically without warning, bulldozers appeared at the township and, after the inhabitants were ejected from their shacks with such of their moveables as they could carry, the township was unceremoniously flattened and swept away. The people were taken in trucks to open wasteland at a considerable distance, given a few materials (but only a few), and told to build anew. While the whites congratulated themselves on the smoothness of the operation, into the town, unnoticed by them, moved an old Zulu who claimed to be a prophet. He carried with him an archbishop's robes which he had bought (or stolen) from a theatrical costumier's in Johannesburg. Dressing up in his robes he soon had a following among the dispossessed and managed to inflame them with millennarian visions, organising the black nannies of the town into what he called 'The Tenth Plague of Egypt'. On a single night, at a prearranged signal from him, they were to smother the white firstborn in their charge; whereafter Israel would be free from the bondage of Pharaoh. The night came and the firstborn were duly smothered, but only executions followed, not liberty. As for the whites, having lost their firstborn, they were more than ever determined to build their golf course.

The purpose of the story was to act as an antidote to the facile optimism about the wisdom and goodness of the oppressed which was then current amongst the intelligentsia, without siding with the oppressors. I sent the manuscript, which seems to me now to have been impossibly melodramatic as well as dated even then, to several publishers, some of whom – so they said – came close to publishing it; it was only financial considerations that gave them pause, and saved me from the embarrassment of attaching my name for ever to so immature a piece of work.

My literary activities were twice interrupted by the need to earn money. I looked on this necessity with the amused contempt of an artist for philistines. On the first occasion I took over the practice of an Irish doctor who suddenly felt the urge to go fishing. When I arrived at his surgery I could at once see why. It was in one of the worst slums in Birmingham, in an ugly two-storey building in the middle of a large tract of land from which all the other buildings had been erased. It reminded me of pictures I had seen of Hiroshima after the bomb, an isolated building surviving in a field of rubble. Surrounding this devastation were row on row of red brick houses, back to back for miles without end, only ancient and obsolete factories and the new grey tower apartment blocks providing variation for the eye. Along the gloomy streets shuffled bowed, defeated people in jumble-sale clothes, their complexions sallow, their teeth rotten, their minds and powers of expression stunted since birth. They were my patients.

The land around the surgery had been cleared to make way for more of the tower blocks. It was still the dream of town planners to move people from horizontal to vertical slums, and no evidence that it might not be wholly desirable was going to stand in their way. The entrance of every such tower block I entered in the course of my duties smelled powerfully of urine, as did the lifts; all the windows in public places were smashed, letting in freezing draughts; the spaces between the tower blocks acted as wind tunnels, setting up violent gusts of wind strong enough to blow down old ladies on their weekly shopping expeditions from their lonely flats high above. There were small patches of grass around the bases of the towers, on which the Housing Department, out of solicitude, had planted the following notice:

PLEASE DO NOT WALK ON THE GRASS
It Is An Amenity To Be Enjoyed By All

Those who lived on the ground floor of these towers suffered the attentions of the drunks and vandals who threw stones at their windows and banged on their doors in the early hours of every morning. With a fine sense of irony the council named these prefabricated concrete slums after the heroes of British socialism: Beatrice and Sidney Webb Towers, R.H. Tawney and William Morris House, G.D.H. Cole and William Cobbett Place.

The doctor's surgery was directly above the offices of the local schools medical service, a department concerned – insofar as it was concerned with anything at all – with keeping scandals from the pages of the local newspapers. The visitor realized at once that the principal aim of the staff, modest but achievable, was to reach five o'clock. Long-term objectives centred round Friday afternoons. As for my doctor, he had long since given up practising an art or science even remotely connected with what he had learnt at medical school. A quarter of a century or more of service in the slums had knocked any nonsense about coming to a diagnosis before treatment out of him. His surgery lacked even the elementary instruments of diagnosis: there was no ophthalmoscope, no thermometer, not even a sphygmomanometer (for measuring blood pressure). It was evident from his perfunctory notes on each patient that his whole rule of medicine was, give the patient what he wants, even if what he wants is not good for him. It was the doctor's quickest way on to the golf course, putting the slum and its hopelessness behind him.

Giving patients what they wanted often led to ludicrous results. They requested repeat prescriptions from the receptionist, who wrote them out and presented them to the doctor for his signature. Being young and relatively enthusiastic, this was a practice of which I could not approve, and I resolved personally to see all patients seeking a renewal of their prescription.

A blowsy woman with the kind of sallow flesh one gets from eating a diet mainly of fried carbohydrates appeared in my consulting room one morning. She was put out at having to see me. It appeared from her records that she had been taking ampicillin, an antibiotic, continuously for seven years. She had come to obtain more, which by now she regarded as a right.

'I see from your records', I said, 'that you've been taking ampicillin for seven years.'

'That's right,' she said, a little belligerently.

'Have they worked?' I asked. It was impossible now to tell from the notes for what condition they had first been prescribed.

'No.'

'Well,' I said, as pleasantly as I was able, 'I usually find that if they haven't worked after the first seven years, they're not going to. I think we've given them a fair trial, so I'll stop them.'

The patient looked aghast, then indignant.

'What about my 'eads?' she said.

'What heads?'

'These dizzy 'eads and 'eadaches what I get?'

'But ampicillin is not an analgesic. It's for infections.'

'I'll be terrible without them.'

'But you said they hadn't worked.'

'They 'aven't, but I'll be useless without them. I can't do without my antibionics. I mean my 'eads, doctor, what about my 'eads?'

I nevertheless refused to renew the prescription, reiterating what I fondly imagined were my cogent reasons.

The patient stalked out angrily and I heard an altercation outside my door. The receptionist flew into my room and said she would resign immediately unless I gave the woman her prescription. She had threatened to beat up the receptionist if she did not get what she wanted.

I could, of course, have gone to the police, but at the mention of that idea the receptionist repeated her threat. I gave in and wrote the prescription. It was, I decided, the responsibility of my employer to do something if he so wished, and I did not want him to return to discover that during my tenancy all his staff had resigned. But I doubted whether this little scene was quite what Aneurin Bevan had had in mind when he called the National Health Service into being.

I was requested often to make house calls. Mostly the reasons were trivial, and the receptionist who answered the telephone and demanded to know all the details of the patient's illness before passing on his message to me (so much for medical confidentiality), somewhat inconsistently advised me against pandering to the whims of the patients by complying with their requests. I never refused to go, however. I was afraid that on the very occasion I refused to go, the seemingly trivial complaint would turn out to be fatal, with all the unpleasant legal consequences; and I was curious as to how people lived. This curiosity would not, I daresay, have lasted beyond a few weeks, had the job been a permanent one.

I discovered that the human race, at least in this Birmingham slum, was divided into two great classes: those who have only to feel the slightest twinge of discomfort before running to the doctor and those who will endure excruciating agonies, days and even months of torture, before resorting to him. 'I didn't like to bother you, doctor,' they say, as if doctors had better things to do than attend the seriously sick. (A variation on this theme is the patient who calls at four in the morning, saying 'I didn't like to call you while you were busy, doctor,' or, 'I hung on as long as I could for you, doctor'.) The slightest twingers seem to be by far the more numerous class, to judge from the patients one sees, but occasionally one comes across notable examples of the agony-endurers, and one is impressed by the nobility, if also the futility, of their suffering.

I was called out one day to a slum dwelling of particular squalor in the middle of a short terrace of houses that had been condemned as unfit for human habitation and scheduled for demolition. All the others had been abandoned. It was small and gloomy, a house that had never in its ninety years of existence been either warm or dry, even in summer. Only fungus flourished there, a slow stain that seeped through the walls and created a map of a fantastic archipelago on the peeling wallpaper. The furniture was mouldy and decrepit, with wobbly legs and filthy upholstery. On an old sofa lay a man in his sixties, covered by threadbare blankets. He was too weak even to lift his hand from the pillow. He had been lying there for three months, passing blood from his rectum. He now had so little blood left that his heart was failing: his legs were swollen, he was short of breath. Standing by him were his wife and daughter, both fat, the latter with dyed blond hair with jet black roots. I asked why I had not been called sooner.

'He said we wasn't to bother the doctor, he knew you must be busy. He didn't want us to call you today but he was too weak to stop us.'

There was no telephone in the house and I wanted to call for an ambulance. It was no easy matter to find a public phone still in working order in that blighted landscape. When I returned to the sick man's house I found his daughter feeding what she called 'me babby' with a dirty bottle containing a fizzy sweet drink, the malign chemical concoction of a giant food company. I was filled with despair, and understood more than ever the state to which my employer had been reduced.

The second interruption to my literary labours was more pleasant. I stood in for one of the doctors in a two-man practice in a small Shropshire town. The contrast with Birmingham could scarcely have been greater. The town itself was pleasant, much of it more than two hundred years old, and the surrounding countryside, in which half of the patients lived, was idyllically beautiful. The agricultural policies of the government had not yet destroyed the hedgerows and, while in Birmingham the sky was always overcast if it was not actually raining, in Shropshire the sun seemed always to shine. No doubt this is a trick of memory; but the joy of driving down the narrow, winding country lanes in the warm sunshine, crops ripening golden in the fields, mice and voles and weasels scurrying across the road in front of the car, on my way to visit old people who lived in rose-clad cottages, and who offered tea and buttered scones when I arrived, is with me still. It was a traditional world in which a triarchy of notables still ruled: the squire, the vicar and the doctor. I was accorded an extravagant degree of respect which, being a young man, I ascribed to my person rather than my station. If I went into a shop the other customers immediately stood aside – there was a hush too – on the assumption that whatever *I* had to do must be more important than what *they* had to do. It is of Shropshire that I think when I wish to recall the pleasant things I have left behind in England.

A doctor, however, deals largely with the darker, or at any rate the more sordid, side of life, which manifested itself even in this town. I soon realised that half the patients in any surgery came from a single road in the town, a small estate of council houses that were quite characterless, if decent and on a proper human scale. The council had gathered there all the misfits and awkward characters of the district: alcoholics, unmarried mothers, mental patients, psychopaths, ex-prisoners and uncontrolled epileptics, an agglomeration of all the people the rest of the town shunned or feared. These people absorbed attention as a sponge absorbs water, except that it made no perceptible difference. Their problems remained the same, no matter how many times they were visited by doctors, social workers, home helps, district nurses, child welfare officers and the like. These people looked on the welfare agencies as a kind of Prince Charming, whose function was to transform their lives with a kiss, into something more closely resembling life as seen in advertisements for Martini; and when Prince Charming failed, they were correspondingly resentful. Experience taught them nothing: their expectations never changed, nor did their embitterment at the failure to meet them.

There was poverty in the countryside, of course, but nothing as depressing as in the city slums. The cottages of the farm labourers, though far from commodious, at least overlooked the beauties of nature. Their problems, as intractable as those of the slum dwellers, seemed somehow less crushing, and sometimes even comic, or tragicomic. In a shingled cottage not far from the town lived a simple labourer and his wife, who had an enormously fat daughter of subnormal intelligence. The labourer and his wife were having supper one evening when they heard a thump on the kitchen ceiling: it was their first intimation that they were grandparents, the child to which their daughter had just given birth having fallen on to the bedroom floor upstairs. She was so fat that her pregnancy had gone unnoticed; indeed, one might have thought it biologically impossible to look at her. But she turned out to be exceptionally fertile, though the identity of the father of her children was never discovered. Some time after her first child had been put out to adoption, she appeared at the doctor's surgery complaining of severe abdominal pain. Appendicitis was suspected, but the operation that started out as an appendicectomy ended up a caesarean section. Her third child was delivered in the lavatory of the waiting room at the surgery, from which the doctor, as he passed heard issuing a peculiar stifled gurgling. Rushing in, he had to rescue the baby from the bowl of the lavatory.

Now she was pregnant once more, and the doctors were valiantly attempting to administer antenatal care to the uncomprehending woman, in the hope that she might at last give birth in more appropriate circumstances. The nettle of sterilisation had not been grasped, mainly for fear of the press, to whom the story would have been a godsend, if only for one edition. The strange thing was that the parents of the girl were quite unmoved by her problems, which exercised so strongly what are called 'the caring professions'. They had their cross and were content to bear it as best they could.

Much of my work was of not a strictly medical nature – something for which a tyro like myself was unprepared – but more like pastoral care. For example, there was a list of old people to visit each week, not because they were ill but to alleviate their loneliness. With great tact, the doctors pretended to have come to measure their blood pressure or some such thing, so they should not think they were the object of pity. There is no doubt they came to rely on the doctor's visit and went to considerable trouble to provide him with refreshment. I thought this a noble enterprise, a proper task for a doctor. The town's doctors visited alike the rich and poor, the clever and foolish, without distinction. It was an intimation of the best tradition of medicine, its highest ethical ideal: to bring comfort wherever comfort can be brought. But I rapidly came to the conclusion that if this ideal were to be upheld, the doctor must not waste his substance on those beyond help.

One such hopeless case presented itself shortly before I contracted the illness that brought my career in Shropshire to a premature close. I was on night duty, and about midnight I received a call from a woman so distressed that she was scarcely able to explain why she had called. Unusually for Shropshire – or for my recollection of it – the night was foul, raining like a monsoon and blowing cold gusts of wind.

'Come quickly, doctor. 'E's tried to kill isself.'

If I had not quickly asked who 'E was and where 'E lived, the woman would have rung off.

As I had suspected, 'E was a denizen of the infamous road of misfits. (Several years later, on the other side of the globe, I met a man who came from a village nearby, and when I described the road to him he was able to identify and name it at once.) My heart sank. I drove to the house where the woman was waiting for me. The brief walk through her small front garden, littered with garbage, soaked me through. Inside a scene of desolation greeted me. Strewn across the floor was the washing of a decade. I was shown to the front room where, before asking me to sit down in an armchair, she ran over it with a rag, itself none too clean.

'The dog's just 'ad pups,' she explained. 'But being a doctor, you won't mind.'

She said that her daughter was upstairs, also beginning her labour pains, but that was not why she had called. It was her husband she was worried about.

Her husband was a fat man with a grizzled, unkempt beard, lying like a beached whale on the sofa opposite. He was muttering something about a bitch, his wife I think he meant, rather than the newly delivered dog.

'Actually, 'e's not really my 'usband, doctor,' she said. 'Not yet. We just live together. We're planning to get married next week.'

'Fuck,' interposed the groom-to-be.

'Are you quite sure it's wise?' I asked.

'We met in the mental hospital,' she said, ignoring the question. 'He's just come out of there.'

Too soon, it appeared from his present state. He was diabetic, epileptic and an alcoholic, recently discharged from a programme of rehabilitation.

'I want to die,' he muttered from the sofa, between fearful but incoherent imprecations.

To this end he had drunk ten pints of beer, swallowed anticonvulsants, sleeping pills, antidepressants and tablets for diabetes, with possibly some aspirin thrown in for good measure, though he refused to tell me whether he had or he hadn't. I was supposed to know, being a doctor.

'I want to die,' he reiterated. 'So you can fuck off out of it.'

'That's no way to talk to the doctor,' said the bride. ''E's 'ere to 'elp you.'

'No-one can help *me*,' he said, with something akin to pride. 'Tell 'im to bugger off and leave me alone.'

Had I been braver, that is precisely what I should have done. His judgement that no one could help him was almost certainly correct; and at gone midnight, soaked to the skin, I cared infinitely more for my bed than for the continuation of his poor life. Only a vivid mental picture of the judge at my trial leaning forward to ask me the precise scientific grounds on which I based my conclusion that the patient would be better off dead prevented me from abandoning him completely.

The first task, from the medical point of view, was to get him to vomit. I asked for a spoon and approached him with it. He swung his arm to hit me, but fortunately he was seeing at least two would-be medical attendants, and it was not difficult to evade his blows.

'Please open your mouth,' I said, and he clenched his jaws together as tightly as any child trying to infuriate its mother.

'Open your mouth,' I shouted. 'Come on, don't be stupid.'

I was losing my temper and the patient was less cooperative than ever. My rage amused him. I am not going, I thought, to be defeated by a drunken swine like him, so I grabbed him by the nose and firmly held his nostrils closed. His physiological hold on life being stronger than his emotional one, involuntarily he gasped for air with his mouth wide open. I wiggled the handle of the spoon down the back of his throat, certain then he would vomit.

He gagged, but by a supreme effort of will managed to keep himself from vomiting. He smiled at me in triumph and offered the back of his throat for me to try again. No matter which end of the spoon I used, I was unsuccessful. By now the patient was positively crowing.

'You see, I'm as good as dead already. No-one can save me now.'

'But we're getting wed in two weeks . . .' protested his bride, who was also watching me closely.

'Are we fuck!' he said. 'You know what you can do with your fucking wedding.'

I hit upon water as a method of making him regurgitate the pharmacopoeia he had swallowed. It was not perhaps the correct thing to do, medically speaking, but I was determined that one way or another I would empty his stomach. He was now overconfident, certain he could confound me whatever I suggested. He offered to drink as much water as I liked. He drank the first two pints with a flourish which astonished me, when I considered his previous intake. But by the fourth and fifth pints he was visibly discomfited, and all of a sudden his body was convulsed by a terrible peristaltic wave starting at his feet, and he let fly a lava of vomitus, so repulsive that I had to turn away. When it was over a bucket was full, and he was somewhat chastened though still defiant.

The next stage was to get him to hospital, but he said he refused to go. I invoked the Mental Health Act, which permitted a doctor to admit a patient against his will if he were a danger to himself or to others because of mental illness, providing either the nearest relative or a qualified social worker agreed to it. I doubted that the man's future wife counted as the nearest relative within the meaning of the act, so I had once more to brave the torrential rain to find a call box from which to summon a qualified social worker, who lived in Shrewsbury, sixteen miles away. It took him half an hour to arrive, and in the meantime I had to listen to the alternate anecdotes and abuse of the patient. There was little point in calling an ambulance until the papers were signed. Fortunately the social worker was not one of those to suffer a crisis of conscience about depriving a man of his liberty, least of all at two in the morning, and he signed without delay. It took another half hour for the ambulance to come from Oswestry, but when it arrived the patient declared flatly he would not get in it. The social worker had gone, the ambulance men refused to drag a man against his will into their vehicle ('Not our job,' they said), and I could not do it alone. There was nothing for it but to call the police. The town's only policeman, however, was fast asleep and not on call. It was the Wrexham police I needed, and they took another half hour to arrive. But when they came the patient behaved with sweet reasonableness, as though he had never done otherwise. Seething with anger and resentment, I returned to my bed at gone four, in the full knowledge that the next day would be ruined by tiredness, and all in a worthless cause. As I left the house I heard the woman say 'But I still want to marry 'im, doctor,' and I knew then that I should never understand the human heart.

Two days later I had a peculiar sensation to which I could not at first put a name. I found I was unable to breathe deeply, though there seemed nothing tangible like pain to stop me. Accustomed to searching for illness in others, it did not occur to me for some time that I might be ill myself, or that the peculiar sensation was breathlessness. Eventually I consulted my partner who diagnosed pneumonia, and I saw the shadow on my x-ray with a kind of detached surprise. I made a short-lived resolution to be more understanding of people unable to describe their symptoms. I was put to bed in the cottage hospital next door to the surgery, where I behaved less than well, making difficulties over the medicine prescribed for me, and reducing the kindest of nurses to tears. Several times each day I suffered sudden drenching sweating attacks, so that the bed had to be changed, and I was too weak even to walk to the door of my room. Ill for the first time in my adult life, I understood the power and wisdom with which the patient invests his doctor, well beyond anything he may deserve: it is the response of someone who needs to believe that help is at hand.

After two or three weeks, I was fully recovered and it was time to find more permanent employment. It gradually became clear to me that my novel would not win me immediate fame or fortune, and I needed to eat. I looked into the rear page of *The Lancet*, where advertisements appeared for medical posts. I had seen enough of the blood and thunder side of medicine in Southern Africa; now I wanted to plumb the depths of human folly. The bizarre had always interested me, and I applied for a junior post in psychiatry at a hospital in the East End of London.

The interview was held in another hospital in the slums, a converted workhouse which one of the consultants working there once had the temerity to describe in *The Times* as a rat hole, no more than the literal truth and therefore especially calculated to infuriate the Health Authority that employed him. By common consent it was (and is) in one of the worst three boroughs in the kingdom, a wasteland of slums, derelict and pestilential building sites, vandalised amenities; an area of the world where man has created such ugliness that it is possible to travel for miles without casting an eye on anything in the slightest degree pleasing, where the degradation of the surroundings is equalled only by the brutalised lives of their inhabitants. Or so it seems to outsiders, to whom the borough is a foreign land, though they may live only a few miles away.

The post was not in the hospital in which I was interviewed but at an affiliated institution, the —— Hospital, at the bottom of a short residential road. It had been founded in 1843 to serve the then considerable Central European community in London, and had moved into its present building in 1864. A watercolour of the time shows it to have been a rather splendid example of medium-scale Victorian architecture, with pleasant grounds; but subsequent ages, with an insensitivity often attributed to the Victorians, had contributed a hotch-potch of additions, obscuring completely the original design. Age too had played its part by dulling the crimson brick to a gloomy brown-black. The hospital had severed any special connection with the Central European community at the inception of the National Health Service, but some traces of that connection remained. There was a magnificent Blüthner grand piano in the doctor's residence; the library was filled with German medical journals from the heroic age of bacteriological discovery; the entrance hall was inscribed with the names of the hospital's patrons, an alliance of the crowned heads of northern Europe – the Kings of Prussia, Saxony and Denmark, and Tsar Nicholas I – and of bankers, the Barons Rothschild and Schröder among them. In the committee rooms hung portraits of the solemn aristocratic dignitaries who served on the board of governors in the hospital's distinguished past. Before departing for the Crimea Florence Nightingale had visited to learn the methods of the protestant deaconesses who served as nurses, and were accounted good by the standards of the day; some of London's most famous physicians, providing they spoke German, had consulted there, including Sir James Paget of Paget's disease, and Sir Herman Weber, at one time physician to Queen Victoria, of Weber's syndrome, and Frederick Parkes Weber, of the Surge-Weber syndrome.

But there was no disguising the decline into which the hospital had slipped. The only members of the staff remaining from the old days were a radiologist and a distinguished laboratory technician, an elderly lady with a pre-Anschluss doctorate in biochemistry from the University of Vienna, a woman of the widest culture in the Central European tradition, fluent in several languages, a first-rate pianist, a Goethe scholar, who was sadly isolated in the philistine environment of the British National Health Service, but who nevertheless needed her work there. She had retired from it but a few weeks when a cancer manifested itself and within a few weeks more had killed her. The hospital had now only two departments, psychiatry and medicine, the former expanding, the latter contracting.

The two junior doctors in the department of medicine were both from the Indian subcontinent and, by an unfortunate coincidence, well-placed to bring the civil discord of Bengal to the hospital. One was a Muslim from Bangladesh called Dr Iqbal, the other – now my firm friend, and a well-known research cardiologist – was an aristocratic Brahmin whose family had been driven from East Bengal during Partition, losing almost everything in the process. It would not be going too far to say that the relations existing between them were those of extreme distaste, historically conditioned. The only good my friend, Dr Khoka Chaudry, could find to say of Dr Iqbal was that his cooking was better than the hospital canteen's, though often somewhat lacking in salt. Dr Iqbal used to cook for himself in the doctor's residence, and Khoka and I would sneak spoonsful of his delicious Bengali curries. It was Khoka's revenge for the injustices of Partition.

Their boss was a locum who was, I think, the most peculiar consultant I had ever met. It cannot be often that a consultant physician's behaviour is so objectionable that he is banned from all the pubs within a mile radius of his hospital, least of all in the East End, but Dr Pascal had managed it. He was constitutionally hypomanic, that is to say, overactive, restless, jocular and without normal social inhibitions. Entering the hospital canteen, he would shout across it in a booming voice and with a salacious leer, 'How many times did you have sex last night? You look as though you need it more often.' He would clap people on the back – hard enough almost to propel them through the adjacent wall – and cross-question them on the details of their private lives. Once, before I knew his character, I referred a young female patient to him because she had an abnormality on her chest x-ray. When her notes returned with her from Dr Pascal, they bore a detailed account, scrawled across several pages in writing that clearly betrayed loss of control, of something more closely resembling a sexual assault than a medical examination. Fortunately for Dr Pascal, the patient was too deranged either to appreciate what had been done to her or to give sufficiently coherent evidence to be believed. Being a coward and reluctant to act as an informer of any kind, I kept silent; but like everyone else, I thenceforth refrained from referring patients to him, sending them instead to other hospitals in our group.

Not that Dr Pascal was altogether without his adherents. One could always tell the days on which he held his out-patient clinic by the trail of elderly ladies approaching the hospital with bagsful of groceries, cooked and uncooked, butter, eggs, chickens, fish, vegetables, cakes, which he received like an African potentate accepting tribute. Quite what he did with it all was a mystery, for it was far more than he and his wife could possibly eat: but he always gave more appointments to those who gave him much than to those who gave him little.

His ideas of medicine were frequently unorthodox, too; so unorthodox, in fact, that Khoka sometimes felt obliged secretly to tell the patient that unless he cleared off to some other hospital he would not survive much longer. On one occasion, there was a patient with a condition called pyloric stenosis, in which the outlet to the stomach is obstructed; the patient becomes dangerously dehydrated through loss of fluid. Against all sense, Dr Pascal instructed that the patient be given powerful diuretics, drugs to make him lose yet more fluid, on the grounds that the pylorus, the muscle obstructing the outlet to the stomach, was engorged with fluid, the true cause of the problem. It was one of Khoka's reasons for despising Iqbal, his immediate superior, that he adhered slavishly to the theories of Dr Pascal, outwardly at least, and followed his instructions unto death – the death, that is, of some-body else. But Khoka arranged while he was on night duty for the transfer of the patient to another hospital, thus saving his life.

The hospital was a safe haven of employment for other eccen-trics, like the switchboard operator, a man known only as Sylph, on account of his enormous girth. On the few occasions when I saw him other than seated at his antiquated switchboard, he appeared a lumbering giant, well over six feet tall, as out of place as a walrus on a lawn tennis court. The swivel chair was Sylph's natural habitat, and he left it only with the greatest reluctance. He wore spectacles with one lens blacked out, for he had lost an eye; his right hand had only the thumb and index finger remaining, the latter as powerful through overuse as an eagle's talon; his left hand had been replaced entirely by a metal hook which he used with great dexterity. There was a rumour he had been mutilated in the War, either trying to defuse an unexploded bomb, or having a hand grenade blow up in his face. It was also supposed he had been highly decorated, though I never heard him speak of this. He hinted darkly more than once that he was still engaged in top secret work, something for the police or MI5 in his spare time. Into details he could not go; but he had been responsible in his time for the capture of several notorious criminals and even some spies.

I do not know whether this was phantasy or fact; I suspect it was fact. But I do know that Sylph unashamedly listened to our calls, for everyone heard the clicks when he cut in or out. He was not in the slightest apologetic about this, and frequently offered his opinion on the matter discussed, after the caller had rung off. As a judge of human character Sylph was amongst the best I have known, with an unrivalled instinct for social distinctions and an uncanny ability to sniff out untruth. He had been telephonist at the —— Hospital since the end of the War and I suppose he must have heard everything in over thirty years of eavesdropping. One did not begrudge him his vicarious knowledge, and somehow I felt he had put it all to good use. He was a genuine student of human nature, and it was as well if you worked in the —— Hospital to keep on his right side, for otherwise your telephone calls would be strangely subject to sudden disconnections, crossed lines and other annoyances. If, on the other hand, he liked you, he would rescue you from awkward situations with a timely intervention. When a patient called to say that her pills were not helping, she was no better, in fact she was worse, she was now desperate and (rising to a crescendo) unless someone did something she would . . . In cut Sylph, gravely to inform the doctor that there was an urgent call on the other line, and the desperate patient, more often than not a regular, would find herself unceremoniously cut off. There would be a deep chuckle on the line, followed by, 'I thought you needed some assistance, doctor – goodbye.' At other times, if a lecture we were to attend promised to be particularly boring, we arranged with Sylph beforehand to call us away by our bleepers.

The switchboard was in the porter's lodge at the gates of the hospital, a small room fusty with smoke, not infrequently mixed with fumes of alcohol, in whose unhealthily overheated atmosphere our porters spent most of their day – at any rate, as much of it as they could, chain-smoking and drinking endless cups of tea, often with hip-flask chasers. They were as idle and slovenly a group of men as one could hope to find, and yet one could not be angry with them. Their uniforms were stained with the slurps of a thousand meals; the knots of their ties never reached their collars; their shoes were scuffed; their hair was as tousled as if they had spent the previous night riotously; they walked with an unwilling shuffle; and yet, with me at any rate, they were friendly and obliging. They carried on a ceaseless verbal war with Sylph who, several grades more intelligent, usually emerged victor from these skirmishes. Sylph called Thomas, our middle-aged Jamaican porter with a greying halo of frizzed hair, the Black Bastard; to which Thomas responded by doubting whether other parts of Sylph's anatomy had not been affected by the explosion; to which Sylph retorted with animadversions on the intellectual achievements of Thomas's race. It was possible, by the way, to joke with Sylph: when Richard called me at the hospital from far away, and Sylph failed to locate me quickly, Richard told him to pull his hook out. In general, only those porters deeply involved in their union were less than cooperative. They were dour, sullen men who seemed never to do a day's work, though they believed themselves the most ill-treated and exploited of men; their main goal in life seemed to me to find new interpretations of the union rules to make the smooth running of the hospital impossible, and to necessitate the employment of yet more staff, though there was already not enough for them to do. They were perfect functionaries of the Circumlocution Office, miserable and stupid, who bored the others into voting for them at union meetings. One suspected they were henpecked at home.

Immediately beyond the hospital gates was a Victorian gothic church which had once been closely associated with the hospital, serving the Central European community. In 1880 there had been a scandal when it was discovered the Protestant deaconesses had been forcibly dragging their Jewish and Catholic patients into the church to hear services, in contravention of the hospital's specifically nondenominational charter. The whirligig of time, however, had brought in its revenges: there were now so few Lutherans to form a congregation that every other week the church was given over to West Indian immigrant Pentecostals, so that funereal intimations of hell and bourgeois heaven gave way to joyful dithyrambics in tongues previously unheard on earth, splitting asunder the gloomy walls of the church. A few hundred yards away was a market, where the reggae music of the West Indians mingled with the Cockney shouts of the barrow boys, the smell of Greek and Turkish Cypriot bakeries competing with the sharp odour of dispirited English chips soaked in vinegar. And in the market I discovered real treasure: a small shop, hardly bigger than a kiosk, in a dilapidated wall, in which worked Morris, merchant of smoked salmon whose fish were the finest I had ever tasted. I took to eating four to eight ounces of the finest salmon at a sitting at least twice a week; and Morris took such pleasure in my pleasure that he invariably cut an extra ounce or two for which I did not pay, in addition to the slices he fed me while I was in the shop, just to see my face light up.

Morris was a Jew in his late fifties whose strength was phenomenal. Even now his muscles were of stony hardness. In his youth, in his native Poland, he had been a professional wrestler, among other things; but when the Germans and Russians invaded Poland in 1939 he found himself in the eastern zone, and for no reason in particular – none was needed – he was transported to a Siberian labour camp by the Russians. There he saw hundreds of thousands of men, all destined to die of a regime of hard labour and starvation rations. Several times he was made to walk the gauntlet between two lines of Russian guards, who beat him from side to side until he reached the end, where at a table sat a commissar determined to extract confessions from him, his crimes nameless, unspecified, but unforgivable. He decided to die escaping rather than live the chronic death of the camps and, speaking by now accentless Russian, he walked five thousand miles to Persia, where he reached the British zone and joined up with the British Army. The peasants he met helped him on his way, thinking he was a Russian.

His wife, who helped him in the shop, had been a young girl during the Nazi occupation. She was taken to Auschwitz, and Morris wanted her to show me the number tatooed on her arm. She broke down and wept. 'No, Morris, no. I can't.'

In the shop hung a photograph of the Queen. In their case it was not an empty gesture. Their patriotism for the country which had given them thirty years of peace and freedom was intense. Morris spoke with contempt of those intellectuals who derided democracy on theoretical grounds, never having lived under a real dictatorship. As for those who toyed with communism, the thought of them was enough to put him in a towering rage, and he clenched his powerful fists.

At the time of my arrival at the —— Hospital there were two psychiatric wards, one called Tuke and the other Conolly, after the two famous psychiatrists who liberated British lunatics from their chains early in the nineteenth century, bringing a régime of 'moral treatment'. Practically every institution for the care of the mentally disordered in the country has its Tuke and Conolly wards, psychiatry as a discipline having few such heroes to whom it can turn for names. The two wards were painted in colours which were, however, the spectrological contradiction of Tuke and Conolly's work. Tuke was a bilious yellow while Conolly was a deeply jaundiced orange. Both were floored with dark brown carpet tiles with the surface consistency of sandpaper, specially designed to absorb urine, and then to emit for ever, despite all counter-measures, its smell. This and the food trolleys which brought the patients' meals two hours before they were due to eat them gave rise to the characteristic odour of mental hospitals, described once as *piss and chips*. The wards were both in the 'new' wing of the hospital, built in the thirties, with metal-framed windows for maximum draughtiness, a clanging metal entrance door, conveniently noisy for notifying the staff when a patient was trying to effect an escape. The nursing office was near the entrance, in which the nurses spent an inordinate time drinking coffee, creating a pea-soup fug with their chain-smoking and, in some cases, picking certain winners at Kempton Park. Sometimes patients would obtrude and ask for a cigarette, a light (it was assumed that all patients were potential fire setters), or the key to the bathroom. The first rule of psychiatric nursing being never to accede to a request at once, this meant further intrusions by the patient, whose persistence in search of his trivial goal could be taken, if necessary, as a clear indication of his disturbance.

In charge of the nursing on my ward – Conolly – was Mustafa, a short and fat Levantine fluent in Turkish, Greek and English, who was always studying to improve himself. With few exceptions, Mustafa saw madness as moral failure, and believed the patients could do better if they tried harder. Somewhere inside him there was a psychiatric Ataturk trying to get out, but he was never able to impose discipline because the patients were irredeemably anarchic. It was a viewpoint to which I was cyclically sympathetic and antagonistic. At times I found it difficult to swallow the official psychiatric ideology that the patients were ill, that it was their illness causing them to behave in antisocial or self-destructive ways, and that they could not pull themselves together even if they wanted to. This ideology turned the patient into something less than fully human, depriving him of his free will; he became an object without being a subject. In such moods I found it difficult to credit that the patients actually believed their delusions, which were so obviously false that even a child would find them laughable. When, for example, a totally insignificant man who had never left the borough in his life insisted that the secret services of all the powers were after him, I felt like shaking him and asking what made him think anyone would waste time and money persecuting a little squirt like him? There is an extraordinary condition called Cotard's syndrome in which a patient becomes so deeply depressed that he believes, all evidence to the contrary notwithstanding, that his body is rotting away, and even that he is already dead. I remember a woman who believed that all that remained of her was the tip of her nose, the rest of her body having crumbled to dust. I never quite rid myself of the suspicion that the patients were pulling our legs, having a joke at our expense, until it occurred to me that my suspicions were themselves the beginning of paranoia. All the same, sometimes I felt like slapping the patients on the face, as they slap hysterics in the films, and shouting 'For God's sake, don't be stupid'. Failing which I should have liked to resort to the eighteenth-century remedies of iced water baths, or a prolonged session in the whirling chair, to set their thinking straight again.

At other times, however, I had no difficulty at all in thinking of the patients as ill. This depended not so much on the patients themselves as on my mood; and then Mustafa's characterisation of the patients as lazy, dissembling, malingering degenerates merely irritated me. A man does not jump from a sixth-floor window to escape from his pursuers unless he really believes in their existence; and if the only evidence that they exist is the man's hallucinatory voices, then he is ill without qualification.

There were yet other times when the question of the patient's illness was an equivocal one. I remembered as a student having seen a girl who claimed that her mother was poisoning her, a claim that was sufficient to mark her down as mad; but it turned out that her mother really *was* poisoning her, which taught me, or ought to have taught me, the lesson that one must at least listen to patients with an open mind. Once, not very long after a Bulgarian emigré who broadcast for the BBC had been killed on the streets of London by a stab with a poisoned tip of an umbrella wielded by an agent of the Bulgarian secret service, an emigré from another east European country appeared at my outpatient clinic, to tell me that the secret service of his former homeland were similarly intent on killing him. He too had worked for the BBC, though in a humbler capacity; and as proof of his claim he brought to hospital a suit which, he said, had been marinaded in a poison which would seep slowly into his body as he wore it. The suit smelt as if it had been recently dry cleaned, nothing more, but the man insisted that I smell it over and over again. Before the murder of the Bulgarian emigré I should have unhesitatingly accounted him mad; but before the murder, if anyone had told me he was about to be killed with a poisoned umbrella, I should have thought him mad too. Even if, as seemed likely, his suit had not been poisoned, one could understand in the circumstances him thinking it had. Only one thing about him worried me, and cast doubt on his sanity: in common with many paranoid people who claim to be the victims of far-reaching plots, he had sought help from doctors rather than the police, indicating perhaps a subliminal awareness that there was something wrong with him rather than with the world around him. But he had an explanation for his paradox, and not a bad one: had he gone to the police they would at once have concluded he was mad and sent him to see a doctor. So he decided not to waste time, but to consult a doctor straight away.

I decided on balance that he probably was mad, a conclusion strengthened by his willingness to be admitted to mental hospital. He thought it a good place to run to ground for a time. Unfortunately he did not live in the area from which our hospital drew its in-patients and he was transferred elsewhere. I never discovered his fate; but as he left our hospital in an ambulance a line ran through my head: 'There are more things in heaven and earth, Horatio, than are dreamed of in your philosophy.'

Mustafa abandoned his career in psychiatric nursing to take up more lucrative employment in fast food, and was replaced by Andrea, a large Barbadian with a ready smile and a loud laugh. She had once been a wardress in Holloway Gaol, and was not therefore easily intimidated by disruptive behaviour. There was also a Jamaican nurse on the ward who, in sharp contrast to the prevailing informality, was known always as Nurse White. She was tall and held herself intimidatingly erect at all times. She was often in charge when Mustafa or Andrea were off duty, and she carried out her alloted tasks with an efficiency as unyielding as her backbone. Her enemas, in which she rejoiced, always produced what was described in the nursing notes as 'a good result' and she allowed nothing to interrupt her routine.

One afternoon, at four o'clock, a patient attempted to strangle herself in the lavatory with a nylon stocking. She was a Chinese woman, no longer young but still unmarried, who had announced to the world that she would kill herself on such and such a date at such and such a time (unless, that is, a certain man with whom she was having an affair agreed to marry her.) Her threat was taken seriously, since she had made it in public, and face would require that she made at least an energetic attempt, even if she did not really wish to die. A guard was placed on her but as four o'clock approached she persuaded him – an inexperienced youth – to allow her to go unaccompanied to the lavatory. There she wrapped a stocking around her neck and pulled hard on each end. When found, her heart was still beating but she was unconscious and not breathing. I was called, and with the help of another nurse respired her artificially. This we had to do for about ten minutes, until the patient began to breathe for herself. Our labours, however, were interrupted by Nurse White, who flew into the room, and glared at the nurse who was helping me.

'Nurse!' she exclaimed. 'What are you doing? Don't you know it's medicine time?'

I explained that Nurse was helping me to save a life, but Nurse White looked at her watch and reiterated that it was now gone four o'clock, time to give out the pills. My shout of laughter made an enemy for ever of Nurse White.

The day began on the ward at nine o'clock with a ward meeting. All the patients were expected to attend, after their greasy breakfast. Most of them would far rather have gone back to bed, and sometimes they had to be dragged, protesting, to the meeting. They sat in chairs lined against the walls of the day room, the focus of which was the ward television whose screen was smashed regularly, not, as might have been justifiable, in response to the programmes, but out of pique or minor frustration. A smashed television was replaced at once, much sooner than a broken window or medical instrument; and in their priorities thus revealed, the authorities were probably not mistaken. There was also an old gramophone and some records, warped by time and misuse. On the walls were two pictures: a reproduction of *The Hay Wain*, and a photograph of the Matterhorn. In lulls in the meetings I wondered whether Swiss lunatics behaved with more decorum than ours, and supposed that they did.

The purpose of these meetings was never clear to me, but I had a vague sentiment that, as the only member of the medical profession present, I was expected to take the lead and to guide the proceedings in such a way that they would be *therapeutic*. This was a word bandied about by psychotherapists and whose true meaning I never discovered, except that it had nothing to do with pills or *cures* as generally conceived. According to the nurses the meetings were supposed to give the patients something called *insight*, another term of almost mystical application. The inchoate theory behind this search for insight seemed to be that once a patient knew where his symptoms came from, what traumas had provoked them, and what effect his behaviour had on others, he would regain his balance; which is rather like expecting a patient with tuberculosis to stop coughing once he knows the disease is caused by *Mycobacterium tuberculosis*, and that coughing spreads germs. In most cases, giving the patients insight consisted of telling them a few brutal home truths. If a patient complained that her husband was no longer interested in her, one of the nurses would have no hesitation in providing her with a long and comprehensive list of possible reasons. No unattractive trait, no habit or physical blemish, passed unremarked; and while what was said was usually true, I doubted it did much for the patient's or the Ward's morale. Well meaning, one had the impression of elephants treading on eggshells.

The meetings were dreary, with just occasional moments of superlative comedy, of a rather grotesque kind. Mostly the patients drowsed in their chairs and let their cigarettes burn yet more holes in the upholstery. Those with hearing aids had a perfect means of withdrawing into a world of their own; they switched off and went to sleep. I asked one old paranoid lady to turn hers back on but she refused, saying it only made her voices louder; and others when asked to do so adjusted them to emit a high-pitched whistle, just to annoy the staff. The patients were for the most part inarticulate, scarcely able to express everyday needs, much less describe emotional conflicts or frustrations. I recall a West Indian man, at best semi-literate, whose conversation consisted of verbal fragments, even after he had recovered from a period of profound depression. To express his gratitude he bought me a bottle of good champagne on the day following his discharge from the hospital, and a bottle on each of three subsequent days. The rest of the staff thought he had gone mad again, but it was a madness I was reluctant to treat. One day he went to the offices of the Department of Health and Social Security to collect a payment, but finding they were closed he expressed his displeasure by burning them down: the catharsis of the deed, as it were. He paid, however, for his ability to express himself only in flames, not words. He is detained at Her Majesty's pleasure in an institution for the criminally insane.

The only subjects on which the patients regularly became eloquent were constipation and weekend leave. Except for the rare occasions when they suffered from food poisoning, practically all our patients were constipated, their diet consisting entirely of eggs, reconstituted mashed potato, corned beef or sausages, and suet puddings with lumpy custard. The kitchen staff made off with the fresh vegetables, an old tradition of the —— Hospital, as I later discovered, and perhaps of all hospitals. Combined with a sedentary life, apart from occasional fights, this diet brought almost all bowel activity to a halt and provided the patients with a continuing pretext to avoid all psychologically distressing subjects, about which I too had qualms.

From time to time, however, such subjects could not be avoided. Mustafa noticed one morning that one of the patients, a woman of mousy appearance, was sobbing all the way through the meeting. In fact, she had been crying every since her admission to hospital three days earlier.

'Why are you crying, Mrs . . . ?' asked Mustafa.

'I don't know, doctor,' she said, addressing herself directly to me, in spite of Mustafa's insistence that she speak to the whole meeting.

I suggested she must have some idea.

'My husband says he don't want me no more. He says he won't have me in the house.'

She needed some prompting to disclose why this might be. Eventually she thought of a reason.

'Well I did try to poison him.'

'How?' I asked.

'I put my valium in his mashed potato.'

'Did you crush them up first?'

'No, I never.'

'Didn't he find them, then?'

'Yes, he did.'

'And what did he say?'

'He said: there's a lot of pills in this mashed potato.'

'And what did you say?'

'They must've fallen in while they was cooking.'

The next day she tried rat poison in the soup, but it altered the taste and he detected that too.

'You must admit, Mrs . . .' I said, purveying insight, 'there seems to be a certain element of danger attached to having you home.'

'I know, doctor. But I wouldn't do it again, doctor. I love him.'

In the same meeting, the subject of husbands having arisen (the great majority of our patients were women), a lugubrious lady with a *basso profundo* voice and a hirsute face of terrible ugliness said that hers had recently killed himself by jumping out of their nineteenth-floor window.

I had read that it was best for the bereaved to talk about their loss, so I asked how she felt about it, using my very best intonation of sympathy.

'I knew I shouldn't have married him. He always had funny ways.'

Her life with him had been unbearable from the start, forty years ago. Even on their honeymoon – in Clacton – he had been so ashamed of her ugliness that he refused to walk at her side, but made her walk a few yards behind him, to pretend that she was nothing to do with him. Every so often throughout their married life he had tried to kill himself, and she would find him with slashed wrists or an electric fire in the bath, or hanging in the cupboard by the cord of his pyjamas. He was a pig, a pig, she asserted, and life with him had been hell. The world was a better place without him. But strangely enough after his death she lost her appetite; she grew thin and could not sleep; and before long a blood disease manifested itself that proved rapidly fatal.

After the meetings were over the patients were herded off to occupational therapy until lunchtime. No schoolboy ever crept more snail-like to school, or thought of more excuses for not going, than our patients on their way to OT (as it was universally known). I was never sure whether OT was supposed positively to do them good or merely to keep them out of harm's way. At any rate, they looked on it as a conspiracy to keep them from their beds, where they would have spent every hour of every day, if given the opportunity. As it was, they shuffled in a slow-moving, sedated line up the stairs (they were not allowed to use the lift – it wasn't therapeutic), like the *zeks* out of some *gulag* of madness. When they reached the OT department they were divided into groups, each to pursue some 'constructive' activity, the theory being that one could divine the state of their mind from the pottery they made or the pictures they painted. The atmosphere in the OT department was strangely reminiscent of that in a primary school or kindergarten: the patients had to seek permission to leave for any reason, and there were examples of their artistic efforts pinned up on the walls. There were cookery classes too, but few takers for the small dry cakes that were generally produced, no-one vouching for the purity of their ingredients. *Le patron ne mange pas ici.*

On two mornings a week, however, some of the patients were diverted from the OT stream: they were the ones to receive electro-convulsive therapy (ECT), or, as one patient put it because patients are not allowed to eat or drink before it, the electric breakfast. Much has been written of this curious treatment: of its discovery in an Italian pig slaughterhouse (worse still, in the time of Mussolini); of its first application to schizophrenics on the erroneous assumption that epileptics rarely suffered from schizophrenia; and so forth. In the days when it was given without anaesthetic and without muscle relaxants to reduce the vigour of the epileptic convulsions induced by the electric current, it must indeed have been horrific; and not infrequently patients broke their legs or even their backs as they thrashed about. But these days it is a relatively sanitised procedure, feared though it still is by many patients. Others come to hospital demanding to have it; but it was easy to avoid by the simple expedient of drinking something before the anaesthetic, whereupon it would be cancelled for the day.

The treatment took place in a long room with five beds, with curtains between. There was no room, or set of rooms, in the hospital where the treatment could be given individually, so that patients waiting their turn could hear the strangled cries, gurglings, jerkings on the bed, and sometimes the sudden, eleventh hour revocation of consent to treatment (which was seldom heeded, however, because the patient's signature was on the form and that was that). Without at first a very clear idea of what I was doing – I might have been electrocuting the patients for all the technical knowledge I possessed – I placed the electrodes on their heads and pressed the button. Their fits disconcerted me, but I soon grew used to them. I was soon convinced, too, that the treatment worked in some patients, or at least exerted a profound effect. There was an old lady so depressed that she was virtually mute; her apathy was such that she urinated where she sat or stood. After the treatments she was dancing little jigs in the dayroom, and making broad jokes. She might not have been well, but she was certainly different.

During my first weeks in the hospital I was left astonishingly to my own devices, considering my total inexperience of psychiatric patients. I had to learn the scheme of the psychiatric interview, a peculiar kind of conversation which, especially when carried out by a tyro, must leave a sane man wondering whether the doctor is mad. One asks the patient whether he hears any voices, other than those of the patients who are invariably shouting outside the interview room just as one asks the question; one asks also whether he feels his thoughts and actions are controlled by outside forces – a special machine, for instance, that beams invisible rays to him; whether he considers life worth living and if not, whether he has ever seriously considered doing himself in; and whether he thinks there is anyone against him, trying to poison him, following him in the street, putting it in his mind that he should kill himself, etc. And finally, to give him a chance to express his *insight*, he is asked what, if anything, he thinks is wrong with him.

The other junior doctors in the hospital were extremely diverse in their characters and outlook. Dr Smith was a tall, lean man, precise but old-fashioned in his dress, who had been successively a dentist, a radiologist and a psychiatrist, but had yet to find work that suited him. The world did not quite come up to his expectations: it was messy and disordered, and Dr Smith's mind was neat and logical. His every word was a gentle sigh of protest. His wife had just left him, probably for a Spanish matador or Texan oil-driller; and when once a distinguished lecturer came to our hospital to give a talk about his research into the biochemistry of the rat's brain, and the chairman of the meeting said 'That's all very interesting, Dr C., but after all, Man is not a rat,' Dr Smith murmured, with deep conviction, 'Oh yes he is'.

Dr Delia Lefort-Corby was the daughter of a prominent New Zealander, who once ran a *cordon bleu* cookery school (she made an admirable version of the New Zealand national cake, the pavlova). She wanted to be a psychotherapist, to which end she was herself undergoing psychoanalysis by one of the most prominent analysts in the country. As the analysis deepened, so did her interest in the minor fluctuations of emotional tone to which we were all subject; particularly, of course, her own, which tended to a somewhat solipsistic attitude to the world. In the end, one could hardly say Good morning to her without her puzzling out what one *really* meant by it, so that lengthier conversations sometimes became a strain. I am told this is a stage through which all analysands pass. In her spare time she wrote romantic novels about doctors and nurses for a pulp fiction publisher, under an assumed name which she was too ashamed to reveal.

Dr Robert Lathering was an intellectual with curly hair and a goatee beard who always wore corduroys. He was a man of (theoretically, at least) radical convictions, a Marxist with not a single proletarian taste. He took a deep interest in anthropology and the culture of immigrant minorities, not – I felt, perhaps unfairly – for the latter's intrinsic worth, but to distance himself from the bourgeois culture which, as this very reaction demonstrated, was so much a part of him. His flat was a clutter of *ethnoiserie*, ju-ju figures from all over Africa, Hindu gods, and so forth. He had an immense number of books, and was much impressed by that class of French intellectuals whose style of thought and writing is oracularly obfuscating. (Personally, it came as no surprise when Louis Althusser murdered his wife: I always thought his books had shown unequivocal signs of madness.) After dinner, Robert would ask what music I should like to hear, bearing in mind that he had nothing later than twelfth-century Byzantine, unless it came from the other side of the world, and could therefore properly be classified as ethnic. Conservative in my musical tastes, I chose gamelan music from Bali. We discussed at length the philosophical foundations of psychiatry, which soon led to wider epistemological questions. His Marxism provoked me to adopt ultramontane arguments, which in turn provoked him to mild Stalinism. I enjoyed these discussions, for they were only a kind of mental gymnastics: Robert was as much a revolutionary as the writer of Jennifer's Diary in *Harpers and Queen*. He later wrote a book in which he castigated psychiatrists for failing to appreciate the cultural dimensions of mental illness, supporting his arguments with a wealth of empirical evidence. The book was written in prose of exemplary clarity which surprised me, since he had always expressed himself in words of marshmallow; I sometimes see his reviews in a literary journal.

Dr Felicity De'ath I knew only briefly, before she moved on to an institution of greater prestige, the Maudsley Hospital. She was a woman of the utmost conscientiousness, very competent, and infectiously nervous, so that in her company you wanted to smoke a cigarette and bite your nails, though normally you did neither of these things. Having worked for a time as a doctor in a Palestinian refugee camp, a tabloid ran a front page story about her, accusing her of helping Palestinian terrorists in Britain and elsewhere. This turned out to be completely untrue, and the newspaper had both to retract and pay a large sum in damages; but a retraction never having quite the same force as an accusation, no-one was quite sure, until she went to the Maudsley, that a bomb might not one day rip through our wards. (Quite often they looked as though this had already happened.)

Dr Bruce Fell was a research assistant who was a former heroin addict, taken on after rehabilitation. He had led a wild life, gambling, drinking, whoring, brawling; as a student he had wanted to be a pop star, and had managed once to record a song that was number one for several weeks in the Singapore charts. On reflection I do not think it entirely a coincidence that when I went with him on holiday to Scotland I should have crashed my car at fifty miles an hour into a stone wall. As we were crawling round the smoking wreckage, groaning and covered in blood, a severe Scots female who had witnessed the accident offered the no doubt correct observation, 'You were driving far too fast,' but no further assistance; had I not broken my hand, my foot and my nose I should have attacked her. Bruce was not an entirely reformed character when I knew him; but I saw in a medical publication the other day that he is now helping to rehabilitate heroin addicts in London: the poacher turned well and truly gamekeeper.

There were two consultant psychiatrists then at the hospital. Dr Gilchrist was interested primarily in the psychiatry of old age, and spent much of his energy trying to set up a department devoted to it, a thankless task (though he eventually succeeded), for the specialty, though socially important, was not glamorous or technologically advancing, and therefore not fund-attracting either. Dr Gilchrist had a genuine sense of mission towards the elderly, the most neglected of the neglected, and he treated them with a kindness free of the condescension that so often taints their treatment. The old people of the area, who were almost all poor, sometimes desperately so, were fortunate to have so committed an advocate. He was not without his quirks, however. While talking to him he would slither down the chair until he was almost perfectly horizontal, and seemingly certain to end up on the floor; and to lose weight he had put himself on a diet consisting entirely of apples, of which he had eaten so many that the corners of his mouth grew raw and inflamed.

Dr Halperin was a small man of volcanic energy, who gave you the impression that, wherever he was, he really ought to have been somewhere else. He repeatedly glanced at his watch; he looked at the clock; his feet seemed to itch. He was a very busy man. His main interest, however, amounting almost to a passion, was in research: he had published an immense number of scientific papers and always had several trials of new drugs in progress. Sometimes he would stand on his dignity, but for the most part he was approachable and even took his staff to dinner at his club from time to time (though the food, as he himself said, was superior boarding house). A fluent speaker, even without preparation, and an able summarizer of other men's work, there was, as he was all too aware and as he sometimes freely admitted in unbuttoned moments, after a few sherries, a certain deficiency in his scientific work, a lack of brilliant inventiveness, which confined it to the second rank even in its own limited field. It was not often quoted by others; it was to science what craft is to art. He once said that he was really a medical journalist, and a good one, rather than a medical scientist. Journalists are not without their value, of course, but Dr Halperin's ambitions had once soared much higher.

By chance or design and in their separate ways – Dr Gilchrist through the bureaucratic infighting necessary to set up his new department, Dr Halperin through his research – both consultants had to a considerable extent withdrawn from day-to-day contact with the patients. Even if it were by design one could scarcely blame them. The spectacle of humanity that passed through the two wards was hardly elevating; the patients were not only mad, but mostly unintelligent and uncouth as well; and the varieties of human misery being infinite, too prolonged a contact with that underworld would have warped one's whole vision of the human race and indeed the universe. It was the nurses who bore the brunt of the patient's behaviour; they who ignored the insults, cleared up the messes, put out the fires, doled out the fags, suffered the noise, blocked out the screams, prevented the escapes, heard the complaints, forced down the drugs, bore the ingratitude. It was this constant exposure to all that was vile and petty in life, as much as a certain lack of training and in some cases a natural insensitivity, that made the nurses crude and on occasion even cruel. They were not, after all, a body of angels, but of men and women, and they were not highly paid. Our expectation of social niceties are so deeply ingrained that when they are not observed few of us can cope; it is difficult to live with brutishness without becoming brutish oneself. Perhaps it is presumptuous of those who have never entered this realm of mayhem to criticise the guardians of the mad.

The variety of human misery is, as I said, truly infinite. The Russian writer Korolenko once wrote, 'Man is born for happiness as a bird for flight'. As Alexander Herzen remarked in another context, this is rather like saying, 'Fish are born to fly, but everywhere they swim'. Even where there were no external causes of misery (common enough as they were in the East End) it seemed that men and women so arranged their lives that they suffered and inflicted exquisite tortures, experiencing miseries of the utmost refinement. Simple, obvious solutions never occurred to them and when pointed out, were invariably rejected on spurious pretexts; for after many years of living in uttermost despondency they had actually grown attached to it, and were frightened to exchange it for the chance of happiness.

I was on duty one night in the hospital when a curious couple arrived. The woman was in her early sixties, with absurdly jet-black hair, heavily made up, especially round the eyes, and with little golden Maltese crosses dangling from her ear-lobes.

Her husband followed meekly behind her.

'Doctor,' she asked, 'can't you lock him up?'

Not wishing to appear disobliging, I asked for how long.

'The rest of his life, of course. He's dangerous.'

He didn't look dangerous. On the contrary, he looked decidedly inoffensive: but so, perhaps, did Dr. Crippen.

'He's just tried to kill me, doctor.'

'How?' I asked.

'He fetched a crowbar to me.'

However odd her appearance, it had not been affected with a crowbar.

'I hope you'll excuse my asking,' I said, 'but if your husband had just attacked you with a crowbar, how come you are not dead – or even marked?'

She evidently considered my question naive.

'I set the dog on him of course.'

It transpired she had for years kept a Dobermann which she had trained up to attack her husband at her word of command. Her husband, it seemed, tried to murder her once or twice a decade, ever since they married nearly forty years ago.

'Is this true?' I said, turning to her husband, who up till now had been silent.

'Yes, doctor. You see, it's like this . . .'

He explained that he was the caretaker of a large bank building in the City, above which he and his wife lived in a small flat. By day the building swarmed with life, everyone rushing hither and thither; by evening, when he returned to his flat, his head reeling, the whole of the City had emptied, leaving the vast ornate banking halls to ghostly echoes.

'And when I gets home of an evening, doctor,' he said, 'all I wants to do is sit and relax with the evening paper. But she', he said, pointing to his wife, who never saw a soul all day, perched all alone as she was on the top of that great building, 'only wants to talk. That's what she does: talk, talk, talk. And when she talks them earrings – they go jiggle, jiggle, jiggle. I just couldn't stand it no more, doctor, so I came home with this crowbar.'

I looked at her earrings, which were quivering with indignation, and saw what he meant. I thought of the lieutenant's explanation of why he pushed his wife off the pier into the sea in Strindberg's play *The Dance of Death*. 'She was standing there,' he said. 'And I thought she ought to go in.'

'Well, what are you going to do about him, doctor?'

'There's nothing *I can* do about him,' I said.

'There must be. I mean, he's just tried to kill me, and you're a doctor.'

'You can try the police,' I suggested.

'But I mean, if he tries to kill me, he must be sick in the head.'

I pointed out that it by no means followed.

'But he may try to kill me again,' she said.

'He might,' I agreed. 'In fact, judging from his past record, I think it highly likely.'

'Then can't you lock him up to prevent him?' she asked.

I quoted the eighteenth-century judge, Lord Mansfield.

'As long as an act remains in bare intention alone, it is not punishable by our law.'

'Cor, you're a funny doctor,' she said.

I said it would make as much sense to lock *her* away for life, since she was the only person with whom he ever became violent.

'I'm afraid you must make the decision for yourself: either you stay with your husband and risk being murdered, or you leave him and face the resulting difficulties. Doctors cannot help you.'

'Come on, Henry,' she said to her crowbar-toting husband. 'Let's go. He can't help us.'

She left, her husband trailing behind her, the two of them to resume their tortured lives, indissolubly linked by ties of mutual hatred.

The flood of wretchedness that lapped at the hospital doors induced in me, at any rate, a feeling that we were psychiatric King Canutes, vainly ordering back the tide. It was different, perhaps, for Robert Lathering with his Marxist faith in the Beautiful Future, when all human problems, all *contradictions*, would be resolved in the synthesis of the dialectic; different too for Dr

Halperin, juggling with his mathematical scales of human happiness and misery to prove that one drug was superior to another in the treatment of boredom, loss of faith, bad marriages, leaking roofs, battered babies, incoherence and unintelligence. I had no such hope or faith to sustain me, and I descended into a not unpleasant state of nihilism.

> Every night and every morn
> Some to misery are born.
> Every morn and every night
> Some are born to sweet delight.

The circumstances and characters of our patients seemed to weigh so heavily against the chance of improvement that fatalism (always so easy to adopt in respect of other people) was almost the only defence against despair.

For more than two years our ward was home to a woman of fifty who had spent much of the previous twenty years in and out of mental hospitals. She had contracted syphilis first at the age of seventeen, and had been subjected to a prefrontal leucotomy in the hope it would improve her morals, at a time when enthusiastic surgeons were performing the procedure on out-patients. (The first grateful patient ever to receive the operation later shot the surgeon, the only Portuguese ever to win the Nobel Prize for medicine, in the back.) Her husband infected her again when he returned from the army. He was a waster, seldom keeping a job for long, acting as pimp to his wife when he ran short of money for the betting shop. When the money was spent he would turn on his wife, accuse her of being a prostitute, and send her out again. Not surprisingly, his wife began to develop signs of the emotional instability which eventually confined her more or less permanently to mental hospital. When I knew her she was slightly shrivelled: her teeth were not her own, and without them her face was that of a wizened old lady. With them her skin was stretched unnaturally taut like parchment over her skull. She painted her lips (inaccurately) a vivid red, caked her cheeks with white and pink powder, and used heavy eye make-up – black, blue and sometimes green.

Her mood was so volatile that it would change from profound depression to hilarity and back again in the space of a single sentence, though her hilarity was never free of desperation. Her husband's visits grew less and less frequent, until he would just leave a packet of cigarettes at the porter's gate once a month and flee. When his wife was short of cigarettes – the currency, no, the lifeblood, of the mental hospital – she would evade the nurses' less than watchful eye and make her way to the rubbish tip behind the nearby market, where she offered herself to vagrants, by then the only takers, first for the price of a packet, but towards the end for a single cigarette and even a few drags. Her laugh was like that of a hyena, punctuated by sudden screams of Joe! (her husband's name). Shrieks of Joe! Joe! pierced the air, fracturing the silence of the night, so penetratingly that neighbours of the hospital complained. Then suddenly, when all seemed hopeless, there was a ray of hope. Joe had been injured at work and awarded several thousand pounds in compensation. It seemed briefly that the money might liberate her, at least for a time, from the utter sordidness of her life. She dreamed of a fur coat, or a holiday, as a token of Joe's love. Instead Joe, who had never had money before, bought a pair of vastly expensive lizardskin shoes; he went to a plastic surgeon in Harley Street to have the wrinkles in his forehead removed because he thought they made him look old; and he bought a fast car, painted lavender, with imitation leopardskin seats. For his wife he bought two hundred cigarettes, and the money was gone.

Her decline was swift. Her shrieks grew more insistent, more hopeless than ever, she lost weight, she aged, she became incontinent. Before long she was intolerable. No sedatives calmed her, no words soothed her. If ever a soul lived in torment it was she. Then, one morning, she was found dead in bed. An inquest was held and a verdict of misadventure returned: she had died of an overdose of sedatives. A rumour started to circulate the hospital that someone on the staff had poisoned her, for it was no easy matter to tolerate, night after night, her tormented screeching. And if she were murdered, which I do not believe, it was a crime of the smallest magnitude and perhaps not even a crime at all.

As alarming in some ways was the case of a fourteen year old girl referred to the hospital because she was 'depressed'. Normally our hospital did not deal with children, and yet this girl had already lived through so much (except, that is, a proper childhood) that it seemed absurd to consider her still a child. Her mother had died when she was nine, since when she had acted as mother-substitute to her younger sister and, on several occasions, or so she claimed, as wife-substitute to her father, an alcoholic of violent temper. Otherwise left much to her own devices (she had never attended school in any regular way) she escaped the home by joining a gang that roamed the blasted streets of the district. She soon came to lead the gang, though it contained male youths three years her senior. Now she wore the aggressively ugly clothes of modern fashion. She led her gang into battle against other gangs, but more than anything else she had led it into experimenting with drugs. They bought uppers and downers, amphetamines and barbiturates, indiscriminately outside the pubs of the very worst slums. Sometimes neither the purchaser nor the vendor knew exactly what was in the pills or capsules, in which case a sample was fed to the dog of one of the members of the gang. If it went to sleep, or barked and wagged its tail excessively, it was concluded the drugs might be worth taking. But one day the dog died of an overdose, and thenceforth the trials were conducted on the youngest member of the gang, aged ten. But though she led the gang and had tried every substance that could alter the mind of Man – fumes of glue and petrol, tranquillisers and sedatives, opiates and hallucinogens – she felt something was missing in her life, though she was unable to say what it might be. She had tried slashing her wrists and taking overdoses, but still things had not improved. I listened with foreboding, all too aware of my powerlessness to affect the course of her life.

Not long before, I had been walking through the small rear garden of the hospital in which, strangely enough, was the most prolific cherry tree I have ever seen, there being no birds in that part of London to destroy the fruit. It was evening and I was revolving an important question round in my mind – where to have dinner – when I noticed a young man on a garden bench, his hands running with blood. He was a well-known psychopath (a sufferer from what, in the eighteenth century, was called 'moral insanity', in other words, a complete lack of the normal moral and social restraints on behaviour) who had tried to kill himself, or at least made gestures in that direction, on innumerable occasions. This time he had drunk a whole bottle of vodka, then smashed the bottle and slashed his wrists with the jagged edges, sufficiently deeply to produce much blood and to require stitching, but not deeply enough to endanger life. I approached him and asked him to come into the hospital, where I would attend to his injuries; but he muttered some drunken, threatening curses and waved the broken bottle about in the direction of my face. I was reluctant to have it cut to shreds while trying to help a man for whose fate I cared nothing – less than nothing, for I had inscribed him in my mind as a permanent liability both to himself and to society – so I went to fetch help. I found a porter whose mind and actions were normally so slow that he was a living refutation of the law of the survival of the fittest. We returned together to the garden, by which time the psychopath had climbed the iron fire escape and was up on the roof, seventy feet above the ground. He swayed drunkenly on a nine-inch ledge, hanging on by one hand to the iron railing. We rushed up the fire escape after him, but when we reached the roof the psychopath warned us not to come any closer, or he would jump. I disbelieved him, and we ran forward to grab him. Whether by intention or accident I do not know, he slipped off the ledge. By luck each of us caught one of his wrists, gritty with dried blood, and we held him dangling from the roof, seventy feet above his death. We held him through the railings but we were not strong enough to haul him up.

'Let me go you bastards!' he shouted, and then, 'Help, I'm falling!'

A small crowd gathered in the garden to watch, but stunned by the drama, or so used to television that they expected a replay of the incident, they stood rooted to the spot. The dead weight of the psychopath was beginning to tell, and we felt that before long he would escape our grasp and fall. Fortunately, just then the police arrived, bringing with them a woman who had undressed in the streets – there being no quicker method of gaining admission to hospital – and they rushed up on to the roof. Without hesitation they climbed over the railing and on to the narrow ledge, and hauled up the psychopath. Had he struggled he might have pulled them over with him, but they displayed no fear at all. I was impressed by their unflinching courage.

Having repaired the psychopath's wrists, I went on my way. It occurred to me that I was so far inured that had the psychopath fallen and smashed himself on the ground I should not have lost a moment's sleep by it, nor even lost my appetite for dinner. He was little more to me than the subject of an anecdote. But his double exclamation seemed neatly to encapsulate not only his, but everyone's attitude to authority and the welfare state.

It was the bizarre, the gothic, the depths of human contradictoriness, that had interested me when I decided to pursue psychiatry, and secretly I hoped – though I told no-one, for it would have been a grave heresy – that the attempts of researchers to reduce everything to a surfeit or deficiency of a few chemicals in the brain would fail. It is not that I disbelieve that human behaviour has a neurochemical basis, only that, should discoveries be made as to what it is, they are certain to be abused. Although supposedly a psychiatrist, I side with Hamlet when he tells Rosenkrantz that the heart of his mystery is not for plucking.

But I am still hopeful that we shall never understand ourselves fully. There are cases every day that defeat the neurochemists and would have baffled Shakespeare himself. I recall a spinster in her fifties who lived in a council flat with her brother and aged mother, who appeared to be suffering from standard (if I may put it so) paranoid delusions. She believed that her neighbours, a simple and inoffensive West Indian couple, were pumping poison gas into the flat, and had moreover invented an electronic thought scanner that could, and did, read all her thoughts. She heard them talking about her, plotting to kill her, and referring to her in the most abusive terms. It seemed a straightforward case, until I interviewed her brother. He had a slightly odd appearance, with a scar on his forehead (a benign brain tumour had been removed the year before), and a pushed-in face, like a piece of pottery that had been squashed before it was fired. Though only an unskilled worker, presumably on a small wage, he insisted on travelling everywhere by taxi, and he smoked his cigarettes through a long ivory and silver cigarette holder, like a proletarian Noel Coward. He dressed in an anorak with a rabbit collar and always carried a blue duffel bag over his shoulder.

'How long has your sister been like this?' I asked.

'Like what, doctor?'

'Well, you know . . .' I said, casting around for a euphemism for mad.

'Listen, doctor,' he said, putting a new cigarette into his holder, 'My sister only came in here for a rest, because she's exhausted. She needs a rest, that's all.'

'I know she's tired,' I said, as indeed she was: the thought scanner and the voices had been so active that she had not eaten or slept properly for three weeks. 'But I mean, how long has she been hearing things that aren't there?'

'But they *are* there, doctor.' The terrible truth then began to dawn on him. 'You don't think she's mad, do you doctor?'

'Well, as a matter of fact . . .' I said. 'Well, yes, I do.'

'Because she isn't.'

He turned to his duffel bag and drew out a small cassette recorder and ten full-length tapes. He had, he said, stayed up nights to record the voices of the neighbours taunting and insulting his sister, and to record the whirring sound of their thought scanner. To prove to me that his sister was not mad, he played one of his tapes, made at three o'clock one morning.

It came as something of a surprise to hear how noisy a council flat was at that time in the morning: doors banged, lavatories flushed, floorboards creaked. Then the patient's brother began a high-pitched hiss through his gritted teeth.

'Did you hear that?' he asked when he had finished.

'Yes,' I replied.

'That was the thought scanner.'

'No it wasn't,' I said. 'It was you, making a hissing noise.'

'Listen again,' he said, winding back the tape, and making me sit nearer to the speaker. When he played it again, he started to hiss.

'There, did you catch it this time?' he asked, switching it off.

I was by then bursting with suppressed mirth, tinged with irritation that there appeared to be no method of making him see sense. He offered me his ten tapes – fifteen hours in all of noctural domestic clatterings – to which he said I should listen in my spare time, though naturally he wanted them back as evidence when the case came to court. Acceptance of his tapes would feed his delusions, implying as it did that there *might* be something in them; but non-acceptance would destroy what little vestige of trust or faith he had in me. I took the line of least resistance and accepted them, saying that I should listen to them when I had a spare fifteen hours, but also asking why his mother had never heard the neighbours' jibes and taunts.

'Mother's stone deaf,' he said.

He and his sister suffered from a rare condition called *folie à deux*, first described by two French psychiatrists, Falret and Lasègue, over a hundred years ago. Their original description was startlingly appropriate to this strange couple. When two people, usually of low intelligence, one of whom is often physically ill, live together in unhealthily close association, shunning contact with outsiders, and one of them – usually the stronger personality – becomes deluded, the partner sometimes believes in the veracity of the delusions, though not quite with the unshakeable conviction of the one who originated them. In one point only did our couple differ from what Falret and Lasègue described: according to them, when the two people are separated, the originator of the delusion remains mad (there were no anti-psychotic drugs when they wrote) while the partner soon abandons his bizarre notions and realises their true nature. But in this case, both of them continued to believe in the neighbours' thought scanner, and even that they had moved it into the hospital. They applied to the housing authorities for a transfer to a flat in another part of the city, which amazingly was granted, and I do not know of their ultimate fate.

Sometimes it appeared to me that there were people in the hospital whose behaviour was as bizarre as that of any patient: namely the administrators. Part of the education of every doctor, as he makes his way up the hierarchy, concerns the administration of the hospital. He is co-opted onto committees where he learns what he never previously suspected, that hospitals do not run themselves, but require organisation. Unfortunately, there is a long tradition of hostility between doctors and administrators, to which I contributed in full. Our administrator was a short man whose ambition had once been to become an heroic tenor, bespeaking a vein of frustrated megalomania, or so I thought; but realising he would never progress beyond the chorus, he opted for the less glamorous, but more secure rewards of hospital administration. He was reported also to keep pet alligators which, if true, was a trait not altogether wholesome. It seemed to me that he was an empire-builder, more concerned with the luxurious furnishings of his office than with the rest of the hospital, an impression strengthened when he was able to buy an expensive office gadget at a time when there were insufficient sheets for the patients' beds, and no funds to buy them. When taxed with this apparent paradox, he stated merely that the money for his gadget came from a different 'vote' from that used for purchasing sheets, which for him was the end of the matter. In common with many administrators he seemed to feel that the hospital would run a lot smoother if only the doctors would cooperate and exclude the patients, who spoilt routine. He came to be my *bête noire*, as I was his. It was only towards the end of my time at the hospital that I discovered, by means of a staff outing, that he was a fellow human, amusing and cultured, who was by no means always as obstructive as I had liked to suppose.

I attended meetings of our joint medical-administrative committee, in which doctors and bureaucrats from several hospitals took part, my only contribution being intermittent facetious remarks. Such committee meetings seemed to generate considerably more heat than light, and I cannot recall a single issue that was resolved by them. The doctors, men on the whole of greater intelligence and education than the bureaucrats (who were then not quite so firmly entrenched as now), won the arguments on the intellectual plane; but it was the inertia of the bureaucrats that won the day when it came to practical results. One issue was brought up at every meeting I attended: a roof leaking over one of the wards. It had been leaking for eighteen months by the time I joined the committee, and for all I know it has not been repaired yet. Whenever it rained the bed underneath the leak was soaked, depriving the ward, which was always busy, of a much needed place. On one occasion (perhaps he had just been reading Edward de Bono's *Lateral Thinking*) a bureaucrat suggested that an incontinent patient he kept in the bed, so that it wouldn't matter when it rained. On another occasion, the man responsible for carrying out hospital repairs was called before the committee to explain why the work had still not been carried out. He explained that hospital repairs were done in order of seriousness and, frankly, a leaking roof over one bed did not rate very high, a hundred other more serious things cropping up every week. I pointed out that on this principle, the roof might *never* be repaired, and he admitted that this might indeed be so. One of the administrators then piped up that he wished doctors would express their appreciation of what *had* been done rather than constantly harping on what *hadn't*. This marked the introduction of the socialist realism school of hospital administration.

It was about this time that I started to investigate the archives of the —— Hospital, which were stored in the basement of a sister institution. I soon discovered that conflict between doctors and administrators was nothing new. Of course, a hundred and thirty years ago the hospital had been administered with incomparably greater efficiency than now, because then there was only one professional administrator, a hospital secretary paid the high salary of £400 a year, and board of governors consisting of prominent men of affairs with no time to waste. Even so, the physician-in-chief, a Dr Julius Freund, was constantly complaining, firing off repeated memoranda to the secretary and the board concerning the insufficiency of the hospital's out-patient facilities. At length he grew so frustrated by what he saw as their prevarications that he began, by way of protest, to examine out-patients on the table of the board room, on whose comfortable appointments no money had been spared. The secretary had a lock put on the board room door but the good doctor called a local locksmith to remove it. Once more he began to examine patients on the sacred table, but the hospital secretary intervened. A fight between the two men would have ensued had it not been for the timely arrival of the house surgeon, who separated the two men. In the mêlée Dr Freund called the chairman of the board, His Royal Highness the Duke of Cambridge, 'a damned blackguard', and it was this that proved too much for the board.

On this occasion the doctors did not pull together. As soon as it became clear that Dr Freund's position was irretrievable his deputy, who clearly coveted his position, began to tell tales. Dr Freund, he alleged, was in the habit of allowing a friend of his – 'not a medical gentleman' – to be present when he examined ladies. Dr Freund was dismissed his post for 'conduct unbecoming' a physician-in-chief.

There was conflict too between doctors and nurses, just as now. One night a patient whose leg had been amputated bled to death in the ward because the protestant deaconess nurses – who were paid £12.10s per annum and all the beer they could consume – were unrousable through drink. The doctors had no end of a good time moralising about the nurses. And I discovered in the archives another venerable tradition: depriving the patients of their rations. The hospital accounts showed that eight ounces of meat were bought her patient per day; but the ward records showed that patient ate meat only three days a week, and then only four ounces.

The very pleasure I derived from delving in the archives, from handling the written records and by their means transporting myself to another age, served me with a warning that I should not long be content with a conventional medical career, with a slow rise through the hierarchy to reach, ten years on, my final resting place – a consultancy. After two years I conceived a plan to go to India, not, as most adolescents do, to find out more about myself – I knew sufficient already – but to write a book, on a subject unspecified. But to do this I needed to earn more money, since my salary scarcely covered my restaurant bills. I therefore took a temporary position as locum to Dr Felder, whose practice was a few miles away, which I ran in addition to my job in the hospital. Sylph said he would cover my absences, which Dr Felder assured me would be short, by stalling if anyone called for me. Dr Felder said I should be able to finish his work in two hours a day: he must have been a very swift worker.

The practice had two doctors, but I never saw the other. Both he and Dr Felder ran extensive private practices in Harley Street and seemed to care little for the helot patients of the N.H.S., of whom between them they had six thousand. Their premises were small and cramped, no doubt to reduce the rent they paid. They had between them only one consulting room, and no receptionist, so that the doctor had to answer each telephone call himself. The records of the patients were kept in a floor-to-ceiling bookcase arrangement immediately behind the doctor's swivel chair. About half the time alloted to each patient was taken up with searching for his notes. One had to develop the skill of taking a medical history while crawling on the floor looking for his notes, if his name began with a D, an I, J or K, a P,Q or R, or a W,X,Y or Z. There were never less than forty patients, some of them present merely to escape inclement weather, and of course no appointment system, so that they complained both of the length of their wait and the brevity of their consultation.

The telephone was a constant source of exasperation in the middle of consultations.

'Hello doctor, should I take two green ones or three?'

'I'm very sorry, madam,' I replied, 'I don't know who you are but I suggest you take three.'

A woman called in a state of agitation. Someone had died the previous day of botulism after eating tinned salmon, an event which had been widely publicised on radio and television, but which I had somehow missed.

'Hello, doctor, I've just eaten half a slice of bread and butter and some salmon paste.'

I paused before answering.

'Thank you for calling and letting me know,' I said.

'No, but do you think I'll be all right, doctor?'

'Well I don't much care for it myself, but I don't see any reason . . .'

'Do you think I'll get botulism?'

'I shouldn't think so.'

'Well anyway, I'll be coming down to the surgery tomorrow for a check-up.'

'Not if you've got botulism, you won't be,' I murmured.

The patients were for the most part working class, with a very imprecise grasp of human physiology, and seemed to have only a vague notion of what previous doctors had told them, so that they knew only that they suffered from a 'cardiac heart' or a 'gastric stomach'. There was a sprinkling of middle class patients, however, from the fashionable squares nearby who, having read the previous week's *Sunday Times*, wanted the latest miracle cure for a disease they did not have, or to be reassured that they were not suffering from an epidemic which threatened the survival of the human race. But if any patient showed unequivocal signs of *real* illness, he was packed off at once to hospital, though this never happened more than once or twice a week.

It was during my period as locum that I made a momentous discovery: whalebone corsets are sometimes still worn by the matrons of east London. A fat lady in her sixties came one morning to ask for some pills for her cough. I asked her to undress, so that I could listen to her chest through my stethoscope.

'The other doctor never does that,' she protested.

As she climbed up on to the couch I began to realise why. She reminded me of a fat boy at school vainly trying to defy the laws of gravity by jumping over some apparatus in the gymnasium. By the time she had heaved herself up, exhausted, on to the couch, she had already used more than the three minutes allowed for each consultation. Then she began to undress. She had many layers to divest, some of cotton, others of satin, to all of which I should have had difficulty in putting a name. At last she was down to her final layer, which to my alarm I saw was a whalebone corset. If she took if off she (or I) would never get it on again.

'Never mind,' I said. 'That'll do.'

I slid the stethoscope between her molten, humid flesh and the back of her corset, which gripped my fingers like a wrestler's hand shake.

'Breathe in,' I said.

There was a crackling sound, like an army walking over dry twigs.

'Well,' I said, withdrawing the stethoscope and my hand, which I gave a good shake, 'I don't know about your chest, but your corset sounds fine.'

She grunted.

'I'll just give you some pills,' I said, writing a prescription.

'That's what the other doctor does,' she said.

When I had saved enough money to get me to India I resigned my post. A dinner was held in my honour in the occupational therapy department, complete with pavlova, and I said goodbye forever, as I thought, to the —— Hospital, which I knew even then I should always hold in affection.

My passage to India was not quite the turning point for which I had hoped. It was not that India was disappointing – having been there before I knew it could never be that – but rather that I suffered an absurd illness. This was not some terrible tropical plague contracted in the Deccan, which at least would have had the merit of romance, but some kind of viral illness that first manifested itself on the aeroplane *en route* to India.

I broke the journey and stopped off briefly in Syria. The aircraft landed at a most inconvenient time in the morning and, speaking not a word of Arabic, I found myself stranded at the dismal Damascus Airport. There I was befriended by an archimandrite of the Syrian Catholic Church who invited me, should I ever be in Aleppo, to stay in his cave. He drew his beautifully engraved card from under a motheaten and heavily stained black soutane. I noticed from the label on the inside of his beret that it had been made by the British Fez Company in 1950. We took a taxi together to the centre of Damascus, stopping to pick up a somewhat overripe belly dancer from a nightclub. The archimandrite strongly recommended an hotel and swept off into the Damascus night with his belly dancer (at my expense).

A room could not be found for me until break of day, this being the season of the Haj and the hotel full of Moroccan pilgrims *en route* for Mecca (about twenty to a room, as I later discovered); but if I cared to lie down awhile in the hotel restaurant, a room would be found for me in due course. In the restaurant a trestle serving table was made up as my bed, a lone waiter taking down the musty curtains for use as blankets. When dawn broke and my room was pronounced ready, I discovered in my bed a half-eaten bread roll and lots of prickly crumbs; on the floor were a pair of slippers with curled-up toes; and the table was strewn with blackening banana skins. I was disinclined to complain, however, lest I should be taken for the arrogant westerner; and since the sheets remained unchanged for the duration of my stay I slept on the bed rather than in it.

I passed my days in Damascus sitting idly in the Great Mosque, an activity – if that is the word – I found strangely satisfying. I discovered that the street stalls outside the mosque sold as good food as the best restaurants, at a fiftieth of the price, so I had little reason to stir. Feeling energetic I once strayed into some opulent suburbs in the bare brown hills above the city, and walking down a street of houses with marble facades I suddenly realised I was the only person there without a machine gun. It was full of guerrillas of one faction or another. Two silver Porsches drew up to one of the marble-fronted houses and from one emerged a bodyguard, from the other a man in a sheeny silver mohair suit who was greeted by an Arab in traditional costume coming from the house. They embraced effusively and at great length, from which I deduced they were sworn enemies, and so laughed. My amusement, however, was curtailed by the men with machine guns: they signalled to me in no uncertain terms that I should clear off.

In the freezing black of night I eventually loaded my baggage on to the aircraft to India, the theory of the authorities being that no man would put a bomb on board an aircraft in which he was himself to fly. This was in the days when fighters in sacred causes were not quite so eager for martyrdom as now.

In Delhi I stayed in a small but comfortable hotel in the diplomatic quarter, in whose garden, in the shade of a bougainvillea, sat an American girl, day in and day out, muttering either mantras or very complex calculations as to how much longer she could afford to stay in the hotel. The manager was a man of philosophical bent, who judged the truth of a philosophy purely by its age. Ancient Greek philosophy, in his opinion, was greatly inferior to Hindu, because it was a mere two and a half millennia old, whereas Hindu philosophy was at least two million years old.

I consulted a doctor, much used by the diplomatic corps, about my illness. He sent me to a pathologist for blood tests, a Dr (Mrs), who carried on her practice surrounded by domestic concerns, in the midst of children, mynah birds in cages, servants requesting instructions for luncheon, visiting friends, holy men and carpet salesmen. She was about to take my blood by means of a needle that was blunt from use and none too clean when I mentioned that I too was a doctor. Reluctantly she removed the dirty needle from the syringe and searched in her drawer, amongst the ink-pads, forms, old pens and rubber stamps, for a new, disposable needle.

'As you are a doctor,' she said, with the air of one conferring an inestimable benefit.

The tests showed nothing specific and I was assured that

despite my enlarged liver, swollen ankles and unnatural lethargy, I was not ill, to speak of.

I managed to make the acquaintance of some very rich Indians, one of whom invited me to a garden party at his 'farm' just outside Delhi. There he cultivated orchids, though he had a little wheat, 'only as an ornament', growing in small clumps in flower beds. As such, it was a great success, very elegant. The owner had a concession to make an important industrial material for the whole of India; next door to his farm that was of the Oberois, the hoteliers. He was a Jain, sufficiently orthodox to be a vegetarian, but not so devout that he swept the ground before him as he walked lest he should crush an insect with his feet. He sat under a white silken canopy on white silken cushions, plump and sybaritic, while the conversation of his guests tinkled around him, loosened by expensive French wines. Suddenly he clapped his chubby hands together and from the shrubs and bushes emerged twenty liveried servants bearing platters of exquisite vegetarian food. It was like the India of cheap romantic novels.

In spite of ill-health, but with the doctor's assurance that it was nothing, I travelled thousands of miles on the Indian Railways, hardly a rest cure, but balm to a spirit tired by routine. In Calcutta I stayed with my friend Dr Thacker, a paediatrician, whose labyrinthine home housed his extended family. One brother was a lawyer who practiced his final addresses before the mirror; another was a small-time film mogul who had once considered making a serious, artistic film rather than the cheap trash his studio turned out twice a month, but had rejected the possibility on the grounds of commercial unviability; the eldest brother was Big Boss, head of all the family's enterprises and coordinator of their efforts. There was no time of the day or night when the house was empty of guests, when a meal was not being prepared, when the sound of animated conversation could not be heard. My friend said that until he went to England he did not know the meaning of privacy; there was something both suffocating and profoundly reassuring about the all-encompassing household, whose cohesion nothing in the world could destroy.

We went together to the Marble Palace, a crumbling edifice of Italian marble, built in the early nineteenth century by a Bengal tax-farmer from his receipts. When that economical and lucrative, but also rapacious, method of tax-gathering ended, the family had fallen on hard times; but having in the years of their zenith become aristocratic – the head of the family was a rajah – they refused categorically to earn a living or sell their assets or live in a lesser style than that to which their birth now entitled them. And so they still kept a zoo, though there was nothing on which to feed the animals, and an emaciated deer scavenged the tufts of grass that grew in the cracks in the marble verandah. The rajah wandered the garden performing ritual ablutions in the tank and awaiting patiently the restoration of his fortune. Inside the palace, dark and dank, was an astonishing collection of heavy, luxurious Victorian furniture, all gilt and mirrors and plush, presided over by enormous statues of Queen Victoria and two of the subsequent King-Emperors. In a room the size of a football field, at the epicentre of the house as it were, stood a magnificent billiard table from which the covering white cloth was never removed. Stacked against the wall, facing inwards, were scores of paintings in heavy frames. The first we turned up was a portrait by Sir Joshua Reynolds.

I went up to Darjeeling, once a kind of Epsom or Ewell in the Himalayas. It had now, thankfully, been taken over by Tibetan emigrés, and in the surrounding hills, as the mists parted, one came across Buddhist monasteries, their small pennants flapping and snapping in the wind, their bells tinkling celestially. In the morning I arose early to watch the sun rise over Kanchenjunga, 28,000 feet high. A small crowd of reverent Indians gathered there too, and though they must have seen it break a hundred times before, when the dawn came up in all the tints of a watercolour by Edward Lear over that stupendous peak, they gasped and then applauded.

As I walked up one of the shabby, dilapidated streets of Darjeeling I was approached by a Gurkha.

'You are British, I can see,' he said. 'Let me shake your hand.'

It was cold and I was wearing gloves, which I removed to shake his hand. My small gesture sent him into ecstasies, panegyrics.

'Look,' he said, addressing a non-existent audience, 'look at the way he takes off his glove before shaking hands! That is British politeness, British culture, for you!'

Alas, he was drunk and his judgement was impaired.

I went down to the south of the country in the company of a Madrasi businessman who was strongly in favour of English as the national language of India.

'This Hindi', he said, 'is Latin and Greek to me.'

I embarked from the holy part of Rameshwaram for Sri Lanka, where the pier connecting the train with the ferry had not long before been blown away in a storm, with the loss of several hundred lives. On board I was befriended by Dr and Mrs Garunaratne, who had been visiting their son at the ashram of a fashionable saint in Southern India. Dr Garunaratne had once been chief medical officer for the whole of Ceylon and had then joined the World Health Organisation. He was spending a happy retirement firing off what he called 'stinkers' to the ministry of health about the constant deterioration of things since his retirement. His WHO pension in Swiss Francs allowed them to live well, come what might; but there had been a time, when he was studying in London, when they had been so poor that, to avoid having to pay for textbooks, his wife had copied them out longhand from the library.

I toured the island, visiting its holy Buddhist places and sitting under the famous tree grown from the branch of the bo under which the Buddha attained enlightenment. I managed somehow to insinuate myself into a group of Japanese pilgrims to the Temple of the Tooth, to attend a ceremonial uncovering of the dental relic. I spent a few days in Hikkaduwa, a coastal resort where German hippies tried to attain enlightenment by smoking bhang and arguing with the harrassed owners of the filthy guest houses about the lack of hot water. In the night the fireflies glowed tantalisingly and the hippies talked philosophy.

I returned to the mainland, making my way slowly up the east coast. I stopped at Puri, where once a year the Juggernaut was wheeled out to the ecstatic devotion of millions of pilgrims, and was for the rest of the year a refuge of second-rate hippies dealing in snakeskins, stuffed alligators and drugs on the long beach; I stopped at Bhubaneswar, with its exotic skyline of a hundred elaborately carved temples. I turned inland, to the holy city of Varanasi (Benares) on the holiest of rivers, where ancient wisdom manifested itself by men burying their heads in the sand, literally, and by the performance of other feats seemingly in contradiction to the laws of physiology. Who could fail to be moved by dawn on the Ganges? The left bank arrayed with its Maharajahs' palaces leading down to the burning ghats where garlanded bodies were prepared for cremation, the flames licking vivid orange and red against the sandalwood biers; the right bank a timeless tableau of Indian agriculture, buffalo dragging the plough slowly and rhythmically across flat fields inundated by the holy river, glistening silver in the early light; all to the continual chant of *om mani padmi hum*, sacred words made holier by their very repetition. The vultures that perched expectantly atop the palaces and wheeled in spirals in the white sky seemed not the loathsome carrion creatures of the imagination but an integral part of everything as it should be. The uncremated bodies of the outcastes, bobbing in the water wrapped in white shrouds, too lowly and contaminated to be consumed by the pure flames of fire, reminded one briefly of the harsh and rigid Hindu hierarchy of souls; but yet, however prosaic one's normal outlook, however down to earth or even subterranean, one comes away from the Ganges at Benares with a profound feeling of the illusoriness of appearance, of the essential oneness of the universe.

This mystical moment, however, does not survive the attempt to buy a train ticket at Benares Station, where all the philosophy in the world is not equal to one ten rupee note.

Inexhaustible though India was and is, no subject for a book struck me with the force of revelation. Besides, I remained ill; almost any exertion caused my ankles to swell, and excursions beyond my bedroom door became matters of grim determination. With my tail somewhat between my legs I was obliged to return to England, where my condition slowly improved, though without a doctor being able to tell me what had been wrong.

Once more the question of earning my living arose, and for a short time I was employed in a large and modern research hospital in a suburb of north London, where every facility was available, where the staff of every department were leaders in their field, and where life seemed to me intolerably dull. The suburb was one of neat rows of semi-detached houses, in which people lived semi-detached lives; a police car or an ambulance or even a stranger in the street produced a slight motion of the net curtains behind which housewives lived their lives of quiet desperation. As the thousands of commuters alighted from the trains every evening, one saw the word MORTGAGE written on every face, and when they died the words THREE PIECE SUITE would be engraved on their hearts.

The hospital itself had all the warmth of an airport terminal. Glass and steel and concrete are no doubt the very best of building materials from which, in an ideal world, all hospitals would be constructed; likewise would they have extensive asphalted areas around them for the convenient parking of cars. And yet, for all this perfection, all this planning, all this intelligent use of space, I felt myself – as a mere human being – out of place and almost superfluous. Just as the low ceilings stifled noise, so did the whole complex of buildings stifle personality, of the staff and patients alike. The doctor never met the secretary who typed his letters face to face, but dictated down the telephone to a centralised pool of tape recorders. This impersonality in the name of efficiency resulted in each letter having to be redictated and retyped four or five times before it even began to resemble what had been intended; but there was no fun to be had out of this imperfection, only irritation.

I worked for the best of consultants, two of the most eminent researchers in the country, whose findings stand the best chance of any I know to be truly epoch-making, if epochs are to be made in psychiatry (which I doubt). Their judgement was sound, their ideas clever and sometimes even brilliant; and yet, what little difference it made to the shattered lives of the patients! I found it difficult to be painstaking over minutiae which was what research, at least in this field, required; and where human behaviour was concerned I found the broad sweep of literature more illuminating than the narrow shaft of science. My lack of enthusiasm for research was compounded of two elements: sheer laziness, mental and physical; and a fear of what men will do to men once everything has been reduced to a technical problem, like teaching pigeons to play ping-pong.

At any rate I resigned and, like a creature of habit, returned to the —— Hospital. It was, from the point of view of a career, a step in the wrong direction; but as I walked down the short road to the hospital a fat West Indian woman whom I did not know approached me and said, 'Are you coming back to work here, doctor? Well God be praised,' and I was never happier to see the hospital gates and the porters' lodge. If I had worked in the suburb for half a century no-one would have recognised me in the street, let alone talked to me; possibly not even in the canteen.

During my absence Dr Gilchrist had succeeded in founding his special department for the elderly, and it was there that I worked. Unlike one geriatrician of whom I knew who never admitted a patient to his ward unless likely to die within three days, so that he could collect a payment – known colloquially as *ash cash* – for signing the form permitting a cremation, Dr Gilchrist had, as I have said, a marked affinity for the old. The principal, indeed the overwhelmingly prevalent, disease with which we dealt was senile dementia, a relentlessly progressive condition which deprived old people of their memory, their concentration and eventually their entire personality, until they were mere shells of human beings, robots with faulty mechanisms. It was more agonising a disease than any I had known, not for the patients themselves, who soon lost their awareness that anything was wrong, but for their spouses who, perhaps after fifty years of happy marriage, saw their partners degenerate slowly into incontinent, rambling figures who failed even to recognise their own children, who were utterly dependent on others for the performance of the simplest daily functions yet were quite incapable of gratitude or even understanding that something had been done for them. There were not enough hospital beds to take them all in, so that the burden fell often on their spouses who, in their twilight years, were obliged to scrub and clean and care as though for a baby, one moreover that would grow ever more helpless, ever more demanding, ever less appreciative. Quite often I was asked to kill the demented spouse before all memories of their previous happy life together were overwhelmed. It was a request with which I fully sympathised, but with which I was unable to comply. I found it difficult even to withhold antibiotics when the patients contracted pneumonia, a common way of complying with the wise injunction:

> Thou shalt not kill; but needst not strive
> Officiously to keep alive

Our demented patients had a huge day room to themselves, an entire former ward, round which they skated in a ghostly dance, uttering fragments of meaningless words, laughing or getting angry without visible cause, suddenly slapping a nurse round the face or upsetting a table. Mealtimes were horrible to behold: though shrunken in body and mind the patients had ravenous appetites, unchecked by table manners, so that by the end of each meal mashed potato and gravy appeared everywhere, in hair, on walls, on chairs and tables, on the floor, and even in beds. The night nurses put them to bed at seven o'clock in the evening, straight after they had eaten, the better to pursue their true avocation, watching television. The patients, needing little sleep, woke again at two or three in the morning, to resume their restless minuet around the day room, disturbing the slumbers of the now sleeping night nurses, who at once resorted to the doctor on duty, demanding that the patients be sedated until breakfast time (when they went off duty). At first the doctor might resist this unreasonable demand, telling the night nurses to put the patients to bed later in the evening; but in the end the nurses won, for it was in their power to summon the doctor from his bed five times a night until he surrendered and drugged the patients comatose.

It was in that winter that patients began to die of cold. By some mysterious process the total output of the hospital's heating system seemed to have been diverted to other parts of the building, so that they were as sultry as a tropical greenhouse; but the wards above them were of Arctic iciness. It was at this time also that the laundry ran short both of pyjamas and bedclothes, replacing the former with flimsy x-ray gowns and the latter with disposable paper sheets of minimal insulating capacity. There were a number of excess deaths that winter, but since they were of dements, whose lives seemed of little value to themselves or to others, no one made much of a fuss, though daily I contacted the person responsible about the bedclothes, as much for the pleasure of having him squirm and lie and utter false promises as to improve the lot of our patients.

One of our dead patients was the subject of a coroner's enquiry, though why she should have been selected for this posthumous honour was something I never discovered. I was the only witness. The coroner's court was a dismal little building with an entrance hall at whose reception desk expert witnesses like myself collected their cash payments in advance and in full view of the bereaved and waiting relatives. A pathologist's recorded commentary on a post mortem was relayed over the public address system as I collected my fee, presumably by way of entertainment: the emotionless voice of the pathologist droned on about the multiple stab wounds to the body ('that of a well-built Caucasian male aged approximately twenty-five'), from which he drew the unsurprising conclusion that death had not been from natural causes.

I entered the courtroom in time to hear the previous case. I was a little nervous, for though I was not aware of having been in any way negligent or incompetent, still it was possible I had overlooked something and the greatest fool, after all, can ask more than the wisest man knows. I need not have worried. The coroner was a doctor who evidently believed in the solidarity of the profession. The case before mine was that of a young woman who had gone to hospital having taken a large overdose. There she was told to go home, have a nice little rest, and in the morning she would feel better. Instead she was dead.

'I want to assure the realtives', said the coroner, 'that everything that could have been done *was* done.'

I knew then I had nothing to fear. I did not mention the freezing ward or the lack of bedclothes in the hospital.

Not all our patients were demented, however. And one tended to assume too easily that just as the wits diminish with age, so do the passions. From time to time we received a sharp reminder that this is not necessarily the case.

One afternoon an elderly couple was brought to the hospital by their distraught son. The father, aged seventy-eight was nearly as round as he was tall, and was so incapacitated by Parkinson's disease that he could walk only with the help of a walking-frame. He denied any comprehension of why there was alarm in the family. His wife, two years younger than he, was wearing an absurd lacquered wig, a temporary expedient to conceal a healing gash upon the crown of her head. She requested to speak to me alone.

One evening in the preceding week the pair of them had stayed up to watch the late night movie on television, something they had never done before. She was more interested in her crochet-work than in the film, which she gave only a passing glance. It was Alfred Hitchcock's *Psycho*, and she remarked during the murder in the shower that it did not appear to her a very nice film. She decided to go to bed before it was over, her husband staying on to watch the denouement.

She was woken an hour later by a blow on the head. She thought the roof was falling in. She felt the warm trickle of blood down her temple and heard a thump on the pillow by the side of her head. She made out the silhouette of her husband standing over the bed, walking frame in one hand, hatchet in the other.

'Whatever are you doing?' she asked.

'I'm going to kill you, I'm going to kill you,' he exclaimed, and made to bring the hatchet down once more upon her head.

He was slow-moving and clumsy, however, and she managed to grab his hatchet arm and topple him over on to his back where, fat and Parkinsonian, he was as helpless as an upturned beetle. She ran to call the police. When she returned he decided that if the police were coming he could not greet them in his pyjamas, so he asked her to help him put on a shirt and tie, which she did.

The police, though, treated the whole matter as a joke – whoever heard of a seventy-eight-year-old attempting murder? – and merely took the old man to live with his son, since his wife not surprisingly refused to live with him any more. But the old man's daughter-in-law did not want him either, and took an overdose by way of protest. There was nowhere for him to go but hospital.

What passion had moved this ancient axeman? It was jealousy. For the entire fifty years of his marriage this man, from the very first day, was convinced his wife was unfaithful to him, a conviction that only grew with time until *Psycho* showed him the way to still his fears. His wife had only to look out of the window to make an assignation; to pay the milkman at the door to be caught *in flagrante delicto*; to sigh to pine for her lover. The very evening of his murderous attack he had thrown the meal she prepared for him at the wall, shouting, 'Get back to your fancy man! Go on, get back to your fancy man!' No argument, no assurance, no evidence had any effect whatsoever on his conviction, and for fifty years they had lived in a hell of suspicion and accusation.

And the strange thing was, all his family were the same. His father and grandfather had been insanely jealous, as were his brothers and sisters. One of his brothers had run a pub, and every time his wife served a male customer he kicked her. The pub did not prosper, but even so she must have had sore ankles. The treatment of such jealousy, as one wise old psychiatrist remarked, is not medical: it is geographical. The only remedy is for the couple to be separated; and so, on the eve of their golden wedding anniversary, our couple went their separate ways, he to an old people's home where he sat benignly smiling in a chair, no-one dreaming of the violent, stormy passion which had only recently wracked his breast, and she to discover the delights of life without jealousy, a bittersweet discovery since her life was nearly over, most of it ruined by futile attempts to prove her innocence.

The day after Christmas we received another reminder that serenity is not always achieved in old age. A man who had retired recently from running a successful small business was brought to the hospital because he had, quite suddenly and without warning in the middle of Christmas dinner, grabbed his wife and tried to push her out of the fourth-floor window of their daughter's flat. He had never before offered his wife violence, and only failed in this strange attempt because his son-in-law restrained him. He had always been a selfish and unsociable man, but since his retirement he had become odder and odder. When out driving with his wife he would deliberately crash the car, just to give her a shock; or he would fill it with all the rubbish from their dustbins; or he would uproot all the flowers in their garden, of which he knew she was very fond. He said he did these things 'to keep her on her toes'.

We felt almost certain that there was some as yet undisclosed organic illness that accounted for his strange behaviour, and we searched for it with every means at our disposal: blood tests by the hundred, urinalysis, x-rays, computerised tomography, psychometry, electroencephalography, endoscopy; he saw neurologists, psychologists, gastroenterologists, endocrinologists, psychiatrists and chest physicians. Of course, any human being examined that closely displays abnormalities, both physical and mental, and we followed up these clues with dogged persistence, until all lines of enquiry were exhausted. We were forced at last to admit that the patient had tried to push his wife out of the window because he hated her and he was a very nasty old man; a discovery which cost the British taxpayer many thousands of pounds.

His wife, who had known this all along, asked me one day whether I could not perhaps kill him.

'We'd all be better off without him, doctor.'

'I'm sorry,' I replied, 'but this service is not available on the National Health.'

'Can't I go private, then?' she asked.

Shortly afterwards I was transferred to one of the large teaching hospitals, where I attended to the lunatics who from time to time wander into any great hospital, to the patients who went mad on the wards, to out-patients, to the constant stream of would-be suicides, and to alcoholics and drug addicts. The hospital had a great, if slightly self-regarding, *esprit de corps*, so that all who worked there were anxious not only for their own reputation, but for that of the hospital. The head of my department there was Professor Thomas, a man of the utmost eminence, though the reasons for this were lost in the mists of time: it seemed to me that his eminence stemmed now principally from his eminence, like a kind of habit. He was spoken of in hushed tones, simply as The Professor, with a kind of almost cringing respect. Yet when you met him he was quietly spoken, undemonstrative, still with a Welsh accent, physically rather like a teddy bear, who spoke good sense, was obviously very knowledgeable, but gave few outward signs of exceptional brilliance. No-one ever knew him raise his voice, lose his temper, or even utter an admonishment; he was never less than polite, friendly to all, and yet had accumulated in his hands a truly formidable amount of power. He was president of a learned college, president of a powerful national medical association, and secretary of a worldwide association of psychiatrists. I had always assumed that power was accumulated by grab, by destroying one's enemies, by displays of ruthlessness; but the Professor's route must have been different, indeed opposite. He advanced by diplomacy, by offending no-one, conciliating everyone and striking compromises. He dined out on his tact. Whether it was instinctive or achieved by the most rigid self-control, one could not but admire him for it. Only once did his famous balancing act fail him and, according to rumour, it cost him the knighthood that almost certainly would otherwise have been his. While he was secretary of the worldwide association of psychiatrists the issue of Soviet psychiatric incarceration of political dissidents arose and, by nature a trimmer and temperamentally unsuited to making grand but futile gestures, he worked – with temporary success – against the expulsion of the Soviet delegation from the association. Whether he was right or wrong to act in this way I am uncertain, but for once he drew much criticism and in place of a knighthood he was awarded a lesser honour – though he also received a Soviet decoration.

The consultant with whom I had most to do was Dr Partridge, a man of imperturbable wisdom who had also made contributions to neurochemical science. He was the very antithesis of the psychiatrist as popularly conceived: neatly dressed, well-ordered and of self-evident sanity. He was capable of inspiring instant confidence in patients, who I am certain would unhesitatingly confide in him their innermost (and usually disreputable) secrets, knowing that they were stones that went to the bottom of a very deep pond. He had achieved an equanimity in the face of human folly that I knew I should never be able to emulate.

There were other consultants attached part-time to the department, some of them psychotherapists. As a group of men and women I had always found psychotherapists rather smug, wearing their perfect comprehension of others rather on their sleeve, as it were, and never giving it a rest. They were well and even elegantly dressed, giving much attention to small details of their appearance, especially shoes; they seemed all to live in the fashionable inner suburbs, where advertising executives and other intellectuals gathered. Their social origins and etiolated, Henry Jamesian outlook on life made them almost uniquely unfitted to understand the sordid reality of most of our patients' lives; they liked their patients intelligent, coherent, articulate, educated, of good basic personality and with only quasi-philosophical problems (Who am I really? What is the meaning of life?) to solve. When they agreed to take one of your patients they gave the impression of doing you a stupendous favour: but if ever you questioned any of their interpretations of a problem, they immediately turned and asked what the matter was with *you* that you found the interpretation so threatening? (Freud, of course, was a past master of this tactic, a kind of intellectual terrorism, as was Marx.) They claimed to be unexercised by the question of the scientific validity of their method and theories.

My patients were somewhat more varied than they had been at the —— Hospital, coming as they did from a broader social spectrum. My first patient there was a German spinster who now lived in Lewisham, yet another wasteland of bureaucratic architecture, who came because she was miserable and lonely, her only social activity outside work being attendance at sad little evening classes in literature run for the benefit of the lonely at the local polytechnic. It was clear that she was one of those unfortunate people for whom intellectual pursuits are a substitute for life, but who have themselves little intellectual distinction. She had lived through the Nazi era, which she witnessed with the clear vision of the growing child, and had known near-starvation in the aftermath of the War, but these were things of which her neighbours had no experience and in which they had no interest. She longed to reminisce and to have a little intellectual conversation, and every two weeks or so she had an hour of my time. She mentioned that she had been born in Trier, and when I remarked that Trier was also the birth place of Karl Marx she almost wept with joy. She had lived in England for thirty years, she said, but I was the first person she had met there who had known that fact. When she came I encouraged her to dwell on her memories rather than on her miseries, and somewhat naïvely even encouraged her to write her memoirs. This was something she had always planned to do, she said, because it would be wrong for her experiences to die with her. I agreed, and even promised to help her with the English, but her first attempts destroyed the sustaining illusion that locked in her head was a fine volume of memoirs which she would one day write. It came as a terrible blow when she saw that she was incapable of giving literary form to her memories: she would have been happier never to have made the discovery, going to her death with the comforting thought *if only I had had time, if only I had had time* . . . She forgave me my clumsiness, however; when the time came for our last meeting she brought me a present and asked, not without embarrassment, whether she might kiss me.

My patients were varied in manner, circumstance, temperament, character and complaint. There was a well-to-do suburban housewife who had such a dread of running blood that when her young son had a nosebleed, to which he was unfortunately subject, she felt so ill that she had to retire to bed for two days leaving her frightened son to fend for himself. Psychotherapists had only interpreted her condition; the point, however, was to change it. (As a child she had witnessed a horrible accident in the street and seen blood running like rain down the gutter.) I instituted a course of behaviour therapy and before long she was so much relieved of her dread that I was able to take her to the hospital blood bank and pour time-expired blood over her hands without her flinching. I exulted in triumph, for unequivocal success was not often mine.

There was a man referred to me by a surgeon who had performed no less than ten operations on the man's groin (where he had once had a hernia), and had at last come to the conclusion that the patient's complaints of intolerable pain had more to do with his mind than his body. The man did not look like someone in agony: he was obsequious and smiled blissfully as he described his allegedly terrible sufferings. It was somewhat surprising that the surgeon had taken so long to appreciate that this was no straightforward surgical case.

The man's wife had a mild pulmonary ailment which prevented her from doing any shopping or housework but which, strangely enough, did not prevent her from going to play bingo twice a week. As a result of his wife's ailment, the patient had had to cook and clean as well as earn their daily bread. His father, too, had been an invalid, bedridden by a wound received during the Great War – in the groin. He was able to walk but not to work, and was comfortable only when reclining on a couch. Curiously, his wife – the patient's mother – developed blinding, constant, incapacitating headaches some years after the end of the Great War and was therefore unable to look after her husband, care of whom devolved upon the patient. His childhood and youth were spent tending his father while his mother retired to bed to nurse her headaches. He had been obliged to postpone his marriage until his father died. And he had married an invalid of doubtful incapacity.

'My parents were wonderful people, doctor,' he said. 'And I love my wife. She's a wonderful woman. We'd be so happy, only this pain in my groin . . .'

It was difficult not to see satire in his fatuous smile, but he resolutely refused to draw any connection between his past life and his present condition. I did not think it wise to press the point. Better he should 'suffer' his spurious pain than be forced to acknowledge the futility of his sacrificed life. He had decided to spend the rest of it in bed as an invalid, the only method known to him of avoiding drudgery and achieving contentment.

One morning I was called to see a man who had wandered into the hospital and claimed he could remember nothing at all of his previous life, not his occupation, his address, nor even his name, until he woke in the early hours in a cinema auditorium in Fulham. This was, he said, his very first memory of life. He wandered across London and decided to avail himself of our services as he passed the hospital. A famous neurologist, Sir Charles Symonds, disbelieved in the genuineness of *transient global amnesia*, as it is known, and used to take the 'patient' into a room where he addressed these words to him:

> I know from experience that your pretended loss of memory is the result of some severe stress at home or at work, and I promise that if you tell me what it is I shall say to your relatives that I cured you by hypnosis.

He had never known these words fail to produce the required effect, but I doubted whether, without his striped trousers and black jacket, I had the presence to carry them off. My patient stoutly maintained he had emerged fully adult without a glimmer of a past in the Fulham cinema, like a butterfly from its chrysalis as it were, but my scepticism did nothing to restore his memory, even when I pointed out that his accent indicated he came from the North East of England and not Fulham. I resorted to more drastic measures. I put him on a couch and injected him with a drug to make him sleepy, repeatedly asking him his name and address as he drifted into unconsciousness. I felt like an agent at the Gestapo. Just as he was closing his eyes he murmured an address which I caught and wrote down. While he slept I asked the police to trace the address, and before long I was given a telephone number to ring, in the North East of England.

'Hello,' answered a woman, whose clipped tone indicated that she was a person of few, but telling, words.

I explained who I was and why I had called, and asked whether anyone answering the description of my patient had gone missing.

'Yes, me 'usband.'

'For how long?'

'Three days.'

'Did you contact the police?'

'No.'

'Why not?'

'This is the fourth time 'e's done it.'

It appeared that rather than face his wife with bad news he lost his memory and personal identity. The bad news this time was that he had been fired from his job as a bus driver for being drunk on duty. The last time he had been fired he had gone wandering to Glasgow where, as she put it, 'the doctors put 'is 'ead in a big machine,' to make sure there was nothing wrong with it. I told her that he would be returned shortly to the bosom of his family.

'There's no 'urry,' she said.

I went to inform the patient of his name, and that he was married with two children. He received the news blandly, as though it concerned a long-forgotten acquaintance. I also told him he would shortly be returned whence he came, news which he also received with indifference – *la belle indifférence*, in Charcot's phrase.

I decided to travel with him, to witness the happy reunion. We took the train together to the North East of England. He looked at the countryside with the bemusement of an alien to the planet. Was it acting? I am not sure. As we approached the grimy, once-industrialised wasteland of his native city, I asked him whether he began to recognise anything. He shook his head. If it was an act it was a good one, and he was keeping it up.

When we reached the station we allowed the platform to clear, until there were only two of us and a small, thin woman in mauve trousers of artificial fibre left upon it. She walked towards us, her movements sharp and nervously aggressive, like those of a ferret. No wonder he loses his memory, I thought; the only thing surprising being that he ever recovers it. Her thin lips were white and bloodless; she looked set to give him a piece of her mind. At the last moment, however, seeing that he had an escort, she decided on a less vengeful greeting. With a gesture that would have chilled an icicle she flung her arms around her neck and exclaimed:

'Thank God you're 'ome.'

He disengaged himself from her embrace and took a step back.

'Who are you?' he said. 'I don't think I've ever seen you before.'

We took a taxi from the station to their home, a journey completed in frigid silence. It was hardly the time for pleasantries about the weather. At their home, a small terraced house, two children – pallid as though raised like unseasonable vegetables in a greenhouse – ran out to greet their father, but he denied all knowledge of them and they shrank back perplexed.

The patient examined the contents of the front room with mild but detached interest while his wife made a cup of tea – for me, not for him. When she returned with it on a tray she said:

'I can't 'ave 'im 'ome like this. 'Ell 'ave to go to the bin, it's the only answer.'

Life there, she said, was so awful that it would powerfully jolt his memory. I thought she was probably right. An ambulance called for him (the hospital had one of those deceptively rural names, conjuring up images of orchards and cherry blossom rather than of locked wards and shrieking patients), and I returned to London.

The bane of almost every hospital are the patients who take overdoses, usually with no intention of harming themselves, but to bring a husband or lover to heel. Nearly a tenth of all emergency medical admissions to hospital are of self-poisoners, and they receive scant sympathy from staff who consider they are quite busy enough without this time-consuming and futile addition to their work-load. It was an attitude which, try as I might to fight it, I came increasingly to share, for I saw little reason why people should turn their private woe into public burden. Neither kindness nor understanding seemed to stem the tide; on the contrary, I received the impression, the result perhaps more of prolonged irritation and frustration rather than of strict observation, that the more attention the overdosers received the less were they able to conceive of solutions for themselves, and the more dependent on others they became. I began to wonder, as I saw a crop of self-poisoners every day, whether a hefty fine would not be more appropriate than empathy and false promises of help to come. This was certainly the view of the casualty department staff, who washed out the stomachs of the overdosers not so much for medical reasons, but in the vindictive hope that so unpleasant a procedure would discourage them from repeating their action (it was a vain hope). Once a young girl, well-known to the hospital for her repeated overdoses, swallowed the contents of a bottle of mild analgesic, which she assumed was harmless because it was so widely available without prescription. But she miscalculated: blood tests showed that she had irreparably damaged her liver. It was not without a certain exultation that she was informed of her unavoidable and imminent death (she was still conscious).

'But I didn't mean it,' she said. 'I don't want to die!'

What sweet revenge it was on all the patients who had so tormented staff by taking overdoses!

Patients often held the threat of suicide over us like the sword of Damocles. I was once called to see a girl of twenty who was in psychotherapy with a social worker. The latter was at the end of her tether because the patient, who slashed her wrists regularly, was at the window threatening to jump out unless the social worker agreed to devote even more of her time to her. I pointed out to the patient that as the window was not very high up she might only break her ankle, which would be ridiculous as well as painful. Why not go to a window a couple of storeys higher up? Or better still, find another building altogether – a small favour to ask.

'Pig!' she said, but she did not jump.

I told the social worker, who was shocked, that she should detach herself somewhat from the patient, for whom she felt an unhealthy degree of responsibility. This was not medical or clinical advice, but ethical.

Representatives of another rarer, stranger and altogether in-comprehensible group of patients – or 'patients' – found their way to me from time to time. These were the people who went to one hospital after another faking symptoms to gain admission. In time they became expert not only in those symptoms most difficult to disprove, but those which aroused most anxiety amongst doctors and provoked the most investigations. When unmasked, these 'patients' left the hospital unabashed and sought out another. Not long ago an article in the *British Medical Journal* traced the career of one of these hospital addicts; he had undergone thousands of x-ray examinations, including barium meals and enemas, thousands of blood tests, and several quite serious operations. In all, he had cost the National Health Service since its inception between one and ten million pounds. A new development in this field was that women had learnt to fake their children's illnesses, to gain the attention of paediatricians. Mothers put blood and glucose in urine samples; they induced fevers artificially; they witnessed epileptic seizures that never happened.

Sometimes these fakers would fool me; sometimes I would expose them. I saw a lady who made a habit, or almost a profession, of slashing open her own abdomen: it was the forty-third time she had done it. Wiser men than I had failed to prevent her, and now her abdominal wall was so scarred and friable that it was impossible to sew it back together. I saw too a good-looking but unintelligent young labourer who was convinced his nose was too big, and he sought an operation to change its size and shape. He had already undergone two operations in Harley Street, which used up all his savings. Though there had been nothing wrong with his nose in the first place, and the Harley Street surgeons had given him two more perfectly good, but different, noses, he was still not satisfied. He sought yet another operation, this time on the National Health, but it was refused because it was his mind, not his nose, that was deranged. He rejected all solutions other than a new nose, however, and he went away once more determined to save his wages to buy a new nose in Harley Street. As Bernard Shaw once remarked, if you pay a man to cut off your leg he'll do it for you. But the young man's story had the air of a Greek tragedy about it, moving inexorably to his suicide once it dawned upon his slow brain that no-one could give him the nose of his dreams.

It was my powerlessness, as well as my complete lack of comprehension, that began to tell on my nerves. I did not have the self-confidence of the psychotherapists, who believed that by mere cogitation in a chair all would be, or had been, revealed unto them. There never was a case they failed to understand, and yet I found their theories almost as bizarre and convoluted as the behaviour they were attempting to explain. It seemed to me that we were playing on the shores of the ocean of human misery, whose depths were still uncharted and indeed unfathomable.

It so happened that while conducting a medical out-patient clinic one day I diagnosed a rare condition in a patient which had been overlooked by several doctors more distinguished than I, including a professor or two. There is a peculiar scale of values in academic medicine whereby he who diagnoses the rarest condition is valued more highly than he who treats a common one well, and this *coup* of mine – a fluke no doubt – opened up vistas of what, in the conventional sense, is called a brilliant career. An eminent professor offered me a research bursary but I knew, such were my scientific talents, that if I researched for a century I should never discover anything of real significance. Not many researchers do, and I was not the discovering kind. While not completely devoid of ideas or imagination, I lacked the patience to follow them up in painstaking and frequently boring detail. The prospect of spending hours poring over dry and humourless scientific journals in the library did not enthral me, and I knew that once I was sucked into that world of research, where an almost hysterical enthusiasm reigns and one's work is so much the centre of the universe that one seldom pauses to consider its wider significance (or insignificance), I should never escape. The world still seemed to me larger than any institution, and having seen an advertisement for a position in the Gilbert Islands, in the South Pacific, I decided to make a complete break and apply for it.

The professor who offered the bursary remarked that if I preferred to lounge on a beach under a palm tree in the South Seas rather than take the opportunity he was offering me of discovering the cause of schizophrenia, then so much the worse for me. I naturally wondered whether, flying in the face of a career, I had made the right decision, or whether I was ruining my life for good and all; but a still, small arrogant voice within me whispered that even if it were research that interested me (which it was not) I should be more likely to discover something important in a place where little or nothing had ever been done than in a great hospital where every patient was researched to distraction. Now, several years later, I still do not know whether I made the right decision: perhaps it is mistaken to seek an unequivocal answer in such matters. At any event, to the South Seas I went.

SIX

The Gilbert Islands

THE FIRST Pacific island on which I set foot – very briefly – was Guam where, as the ubiquitous slogan had it, *America's Day Begins*. It was from here that the B52s set out on their bombing raids on Vietnam; but it was now a staging post for Japanese tourists, glazed by their long flight, on their way to and from Los Angeles. They bought duty-free goods at the airport shop as though it were a sacred obligation. People in Guam wore baseball hats and said 'Have a nice day'.

My route also made necessary a short stay in Nauru, a tiny island ten miles in circumference, in the midst of the azure ocean. The only hotel was then managed by an Australian woman with sky-blue eyelids who was in a permanent state of exasperation at the *kanakas*, as she called them, because they never did anything properly except, as she put it, 'eat and fuck'. (She insisted on maintaining standards nevertheless: no-one might enter the bar after seven o'clock who was not warning socks). The worst of it was, the kanakas were cheeky. Since Nauru's independence in 1968 – it had been till then an Australian-governed territory – the Nauruans had become, on a *per capita* basis, among the richest people in the world. They had gained control of the phosphate mining industry on the island, and even those who did not own land with phosphate deposits – worth $120,000 per acre to the owner, as much again to the state in taxes – were paid a pension from the age of 18, given free water, power and telephone calls, and housing at a rent of $9 a month. Imported goods were free of duty and a bottle of Scotch, brought 12,000 miles from the Highlands, cost less than $3. It was scarcely surprising then, that Nauruans, when they consented to work at all, were not easily badgered into working hard.

Nauru was once known, in the days of traders, beachcombers, blackbirders and missionaries, as Pleasant Island, and for a short unspoilt stretch just beyond the hotel it was possible still to see why. There was a long, fair beach in an elegant sweep, fringed by gracefully inclining palm trees whose green fronds were met by the snowy spume of the blue and white breakers that crashed in soothing rhythm against the curious coral pinnacles, the size of a man, that dotted the reef. Beyond the narrow fringe of palms was a gentle slope, covered with the emerald green shrubs and trees of the salt and sandy soil, whose luxuriance gave a misleading impression of fertility. If you were lucky as you walked along the beach, a fairy tern, dazzlingly white and with bright eyes of shiny jet, would hover above your head as though from curiosity. You saw frigate birds and boobies; out to sea, describing their slow, gentle, perfect arcs out of the surface of the water, a school of dolphins. It was enchanting, but it concealed a harshness and a precariousness which modern life, for all its ugliness, had overcome. If the rains failed there were terrible droughts, in the days before water was brought by tanker; and the fish could disappear for weeks on end. When nature was bountiful, life was leisurely; but when it withheld its bounty, much life was extinguished.

But most of Nauru had, in any case, changed beyond recognition. Apart from a few short stretches, the narrow coastal strip was now littered with untidy tin-roofed shacks and houses, surrounded by the rusting hulks of numerous wrecked cars. These were the homes of the Nauruans, millionaires amongst whom lived no differently from the others, except for bigger radios and more powerful cars. Small grey Polynesian pigs rooted around the household rubbish, while at the height of the day Nauruans lay on mats in the shade of frangipani trees, sleeping off the heat. Nauruans are among the fattest people on earth, consuming an average of 7000 calories a day. More than half of them are diabetic.

There was no anchorage off Nauru, for beyond the reef the sea plunged to a depth of two miles, so a high cantilever deposited the mined and crushed phosphate rock into the holds of waiting ships tethered to giant buoys. Along the shore, beyond the cantilever was the crowded labour camp, where lived the contract labourers from Hong Kong, the Philippines, the Solomons and the Gilberts, each with their own small quarter. These were the people who actually worked the mines, at wage rates determined by racial origin. Next to the labour camp were two rows of Chinese general stores, crammed full of cheap junk and the large cassette players with which the islanders proudly returned home. The torpid Chinese merchants sat all day among their merchandise in black slippers, baggy grey trousers, and off-white undervests. They looked doped by opium; several of them were millionaires.

Inland, in the centre of the island, were the phosphate works. Phosphate was discovered in Nauru in 1900 and mining began at once, while the island was still a German possession. At first the mining was done by hand, but now great metal machines, like robotic praying mantises, crawled over the landscape, scouring out the precious rock. First the vegetation was mercilessly rooted out; then the grey rock was grabbed and transported to an implacable, remorseless crusher; and finally the end product rolled its way on a conveyor belt out to the cantilever high above the reef. At the end of the process the landscape was left a hostile, eerie moonscape, coral pinnacles forty and fifty feet high sticking upwards like the monoliths of some primitive religion. When first exposed to the atmosphere the coral was a bleached white, but with time it oxidised and darkened, so that where the mining had begun it was almost black. A few straggly creepers clung to the oldest pinnacles, as though the process of evolution had had to start all over again, life having once been totally destroyed. In a few years the whole of the island will have been mined out and the Nauruans obliged to seek another home.

I returned several times to Nauru and came to know it quite

well. It never lost for me its bizarre atmosphere of unreality and impermanence.

It was four hundred miles across the wide ocean from Nauru to Tarawa, where I was headed. Seated comfortably seven miles above the water, with the certainty of arriving at a predetermined destination, it was difficult to appreciate the full magnitude of the achievement of the first settlers of the scattered islands of the Pacific, their daring and intrepidity, as they journeyed in canoes from South East Asia into the greatest emptiness on earth, with no knowledge of what they would find.

Tarawa is a coral atoll in the shape of a V, each arm of which is about fifteen miles long. Between them is the lagoon, most often a brilliant turquoise, but capable of turning almost any colour – pink and gold at sunset, grey in the rain, milky green when the sky is overcast. The land is nowhere more than ten feet above sea level, a thin ribbon not more than a few hundred yards from ocean to lagoon side. When the tide goes out the reef is exposed and the area of the land surface doubles. One could stand among the coconut palms and see both the cobalt of the ocean and the aquamarine of the lagoon.

The humid heat of the island struck me with the force of a jetstream as I stepped into it. Astride the equator, neither the temperature nor the length of day ever varied much in the Gilbert Islands. At night, when the breeze dropped and the air became still, it seemed if anything to grow hotter. If ever you felt cold in the Gilbert Islands you knew you had a fever.

I was met by Dr Hardinge, the surgeon at the hospital. He was a tall, gangling figure with a slight stoop who wore what I imagined to be pre-war Royal Navy shorts, which came to just above the knees. His long socks left little of his thin legs exposed to the tropical sun and though he was only in his late thirties he gave you the immediate impression he was born forty years at least after his time. He had a mobile, expressive face, and there was a slight aura of failure about him, like a Chekhovian doctor. It was impossible not to warm to him at once. He was a brilliant mimic, so that when, for example, he issued a thundering denunciation of 'papism' in the voice of the Rev Ian Paisley, it was hard to believe that the unscrupulous clergyman was not actually present. But for the most part his conversation consisted of gentle complaint about his lot in life. His wife had not liked life on the atoll, finding the other expatriate wives dull, dowdy and narrow. She had gone home, leaving behind the large handloom that had been her only consolation. Dr Hardinge had no desire to return to England, quite the contrary, but his wife's refusal to live anywhere else drew him back. He was all too aware that his career had not been a great success, and sometimes he fell back on that typically British consolation, of enumerating his relationship to the gentry. I have never quite understood why being the second cousin twice removed of a bishop or an admiral or a baronet compensated for a lack of personal achievement, but I suppose one should not deny people their consolations where they find them. We had long talks together, from which I came away with a not unpleasant feeling of worldweariness. He was a lost soul, not untalented, who had never found, and never would find, his true métier. He was lacking in the deforming singlemindedness necessary to pursue a distant or difficult goal, and it was this fastidiousness that made him attractive.

We drove together the few miles to the village of Bikenibeu, where the hospital was situated. The southern stretch of the atoll was now the administrative centre and capital of the newly independent Republic of Kiribati, pronounced *Kiribus*, a local approximation to the word Gilberts. Independence from Britain had come, by pure coincidence no doubt, within a few months of the exhaustion of the colony's only land resource, the phosphate of Banaba. It was my first glimpse of 'urban' Tarawa, as it was sometimes called. It wasn't really urban, even though 20,000 people – a third of the population of the Gilbert Islands – crowded on to its three square miles. Except for those in government employment, a small minority who were housed in six grades of housing according to rank, people lived in homes of traditional Gilbertese construction: raised platforms a foot or two above the ground, with thatched roofs and opened to the sea breeze. At night, or when it rained, screens were lowered. The coconut palm and the pandanus provided all the materials that were necessary for the construction of a comfortable house: the timber framework, the string with which it was lashed together, the mats, thatching and screens. Beside the houses were the outrigger canoes, prized possessions of almost religious significance, in which the men caught the staple fish. Even Gilbertese with a money income lived largely by subsistence, and few indeed were they who could not, if the need arose, have returned to their traditional way of life, a way seemingly in perfect equilibrium with its environment. The versatility of the coconut palm and the fecundity of the sea afforded them a kind of social security that no monetary provision could ever equal.

At the centre of every village was the *maneaba*, a large communal meeting house under whose roof elaborate customs were followed. Every man had a place in which to sit, according to his clan, his ancestry and his seniority. The flouting of custom by a Gilbertese in a maneaba was a grave offence, punishable in the old days (and very occasionally even now) by death. On Tarawa the customs were less rigidly observed than elsewhere and the maneabas were often constructed of cement and tin rather than of coconut and pandanus. The traditional maneabas however were magnificent structures, built exactly to an ancient and invariable plan without a trace of metal. They were up to fifty feet high, cool and airy, whose steeply sloping thatched roofs came to within four feet of the ground, so that one had to stoop to enter. As well as the venue of all celebrations, maneabas served as shelters for visitors, and the place where the old men sat and told their yarns the livelong day.

The hospital was close to the ocean, a series of one-storey buildings connected by an open causeway roofed by thatch. This roof seemed to be undergoing perpetual repairs by gangs of prisoners who wore rough and baggy blue shorts, a yellow stripe to signify regular prisoners, a red stripe to signify murderers. The wards were at right-angles to the ocean, with a door at each end, so that from the entrance one caught a glimpse of the deep, restful blue of the water. A cool and grateful breeze blew through them, and the sound of the waves must have soothed the patients. At any rate, they showed an astonishing capacity to sleep, sometimes more than eighteen hours a day. A curious thing about the Gilbertese was that they slept with their eyes half-open which gave them the Hippocratic facies of impending death, and the doctor a very nasty turn, until he got used to it. Another problem was the man in charge of the hospital sewage pump who had a habit of discharging the sewage precisely as the tide went out.

Beyond the main hospital was the Mental Wing, surrounded by a high wire fence which, however, was no match for lunatics who had climbed the highest coconut trees almost since the time they learnt to walk. Beyond the Mental Wing was a small leprosarium, and then a row of spacious bungalows along a coral path shaded by broad-leafed breadfruit trees. My home was along this path. When the tide was in, the Pacific Ocean was within five yards of my door: I was told that one of the previous occupants of my house was so frightened of tidal waves in the night that he always went to bed in an inflated life-jacket. He had to be repatriated for lack of sleep. I, on the other hand, found the repetitious roar of the waves so soporific that my problem was in staying awake.

On my right lived Dr Hardinge. On my left lived the manager of the national airline, an energetic antipodean full of unorthodox commercial ideas. He lived there with his wife. She was a quiet woman of retiring habits, monosyllabic until about four o'clock in the afternoon, when she quickly became drunk on whisky (she had the largest bottle I have ever seen, five feet high and two across). After that she was loud and abusive, using language that embarrassed even her husband, who was very far from a prude. If anyone called he carried her, protesting, into the bedroom. Once a thief broke into their house and stole her engagement ring. Her husband's only comment was 'I wish he'd taken my wife and left the ring'. Not long afterwards they were divorced. She returned home, he went to California to set up his own airline. Some time later, he was replaced in the house by a naive young Australian volunteer who had lived all his life on a fruit farm in rural New

South Wales, to whom I related unlikely stories just for the pleasure of hearing him exclaim 'No? Fair dinkum!'

I started work at once. The hospital was not more than ten minutes' walk from home. I met the staff and made friends with Dr Tomati, a very capable doctor and the best amateur tennis player I have known (he was once to represent Fiji until it was discovered he was ineligible), and Dr Storm. The latter had enjoyed life to the full, though not always in ways of which the early missionaries would have approved. Three parts Gilbertese, he was the grandson of an Irish trader who had stayed in the islands. Perhaps it was from him that Dr Storm inherited the profoundly un-Gilbertese habit of saying precisely what he thought, however uncomplimentary, rather than fudge matters with forms of words and outward conciliation. This made him unpopular with some traditionally-minded Gilbertese, and when he stood for parliament, the *Maneaba ni Maungatabu*, he lost heavily. During his election campaign he tried, unsuccessfully, to suppress his own personality, to gain more votes. One morning he came into coffee almost at bursting point.

'I try to be nice to the patients,' he exploded. 'But I just can't manage it.'

He and his friend, Dr Biribo O'Halloran, an anaesthetist who retired to run a night club on the edge of the lagoon, had an inexhaustible fund of stories. Although the islands were peaceful and gave you the impression that nothing ever happened there, one day being precisely like another, they had both lived lives full of incident. While at school they had witnessed the Japanese occupation and the recovery of the islands by the Americans at the Battle of Tarawa. Dr Storm told me of the time he and a friend had been lost at sea in their canoe for ten days. There was nothing like it, he said, for turning a man (temporarily) religious: he had prayed as he had never prayed before. His friend went mad and started to hallucinate a voice calling his name, to which he responded by diving out to sea in the direction of the supposed voice. Fortunately he realised his error in time and returned to the boat. Dr Storm had given up hope when they found the sixty-mile long net of a Japanese fishing vessel, to which they clung until it was hauled in, causing some surprise to the fishermen. The experience, I am glad to say, exerted no lasting reformatory influence on him. One night afterwards, somewhat the worse for wear, he missed the only road on the island while on his way home and drove out to sea, realising that something was wrong only when the waves began to lap round the accelerator pedal.

The Gilbertese were marvellous survivors at sea, as indeed they had to be. If they drifted only eight miles or so from the shore of one of the low islands, even with its tall fringe of coconut palms, it disappeared over the horizon. An error of a few degrees in that immense ocean might mean drifting for hundreds or even thousands of miles without sight of land. It was hardly surprising, considering the numbers of men who went out daily fishing in their canoes, that every so often some went missing. The surprise was rather how many survived two, three or four weeks adrift on the ocean; and many people believed the Gilbertese fishermen were possessed of arcane knowledge which helped them endure. The most astonishing story of all was that of an old man (he died in 1983) who had been on Banaba during the Japanese occupation. The Japanese were in retreat and decided, on the kick-the-cat principle, to massacre all the Gilbertese on the island. The man was warned of the impending massacre by a Japanese officer who had grown fond of him, and advised him to set out in his canoe. He was adrift for *seven months* until he reached one of the islands of New Britain off New Guinea, weak but not permanently the worse for his ordeal.

Apart from Dr Hardinge there were three other expatriate staff in the hospital when I started work there. The pharmacist had invaluable knowledge of the cheapest source of every drug, vital for a poor, importing country like Kiribati. He had acquired his knowledge from his private pharmacy in Zambia, where he had made a considerable fortune selling Africans the laxatives and patent medicines in which they placed a touching, and lucrative, faith. His assets in Zambia had been frozen, of use neither to him nor to the Zambian government, for interest and rents accumulated in his bank accounts there untouched and untouchable. A tolerant and humorous man, he felt no bitterness, for he had few illusions about the provenance of his fortune, besides which he had managed to export enough capital to make him modestly prosperous.

Miss Arlington was a tall, middle-aged woman with that genteel Scots accent so well adapted to complaint. She had been an expatriate most of her adult life, and took the not untypical expatriate view that her present country was hell on earth, but her last one had been heaven. She was particularly fond of Malawi where, she said, she had been a friend of Dr Banda – 'such a perfect gentleman'. Her main complaint about Kiribati, other than the difficulty in finding potatoes, was the presence of so many biting insects: mosquitoes, cantharides beetles, and cane bugs which came out of the furniture and bit you while you were playing bridge. For this she held the past colonial régime principally responsible.

'Why,' she was heard to ask on a dying fall, 'didn't the British *do* something about the insects?'

She had come to Kiribati as an adviser on nursing, though she admitted she had been so long an administrator that she no longer knew 'one end of a patient from another'. One day, with an epidemic of dengue fever, a viral disease unpleasant but not usually fatal, approaching the islands from across the Pacific, I gave a talk to the hospital staff to prepare them for its onslaught. At the end of my talk, Miss Arlington observed:

'Well, it sounds as though dengue is worse than malaria.'

Somewhat taken aback, I replied that malaria killed more than a million people every year; very few died of dengue.

'Yes, I know, but poor Midge Potter's headaches with dengue were so much worse than mine with malaria.'

Thus the tragedy of Midge Potter's headaches tipped the balance in favour of dengue as the more serious disease.

We did not get on well together. She thought me arrogant and brash; I thought her falsely genteel. And yet she could be an entertaining and generous hostess. In retrospect, our disagreements seem petty and unnecessary, though they were compelling enough at the time.

James Denton-Smith was an administrator in the Ministry of Health. He was one of the very last colonial officers ever to be recruited, coming out to the Gilbert Islands straight after having completed a degree in geology at Oxford. He had been a district officer on the island of Butaritari, whose inhabitants were famous for their drunkenness and their predilection for dogs' meat. There he had found a wife, Maria, a large girl unusually fond of practical jokes, like jumping out from behind a door and shouting 'Boo!' They were both of them fat, with vast appetites; he was capable of drinking a great deal without any perceptible effect on his speech or behaviour. He wore long khaki shorts such as had held together an empire, and had in his time done everything from trying to promote a smoked fish industry to acting (successfully) as defence counsel to a murderer. He was that rare thing, an efficient and imaginative administrator, capable of using his intelligence to grasp essential technical detail; but it was his very ability, together with a certain intolerance of fools, that made him enemies, for where torpor and mediocrity flourish, energy and talent are not well received. Once, when asked by a visiting dignitary what was Kiribati's most valuable export, he replied 'Requests for aid'.

I soon had responsibility for the Mental Wing, the medical and the tuberculosis wards. A new Mental Wing was under construction, but the old was still in use at the time of my arrival. No-one had taken any interest in it and though it was only twenty years old it had the aspect of a primaeval Central American political dungeon. It was built of concrete on three sides of a square, with a narrow, dark corridor running alongside the cells, some with doors of iron bars, others with solid metal doors with Judas-windows. The patients slept on concrete blocks, unsoftened by bed clothes, next to the walls, with a tiny barred window above them. There was a small hole in the bottom of the wall leading to a drain outside, through which the cells were sluiced out with a hose. All lights had long since ceased to work and the patients spent twelve hours of every day in total darkness. There was a constant faeculent smell in the building, so that to enter it even briefly produced a profound and lingering nausea. And a few of the patients were attached to the wall by a chain around their ankles eighteen inches long, so that they could scarcely move. They ate, slept and relieved themselves where they were chained; two of them had been so chained without a moment's release for more than two years.

The staff consisted of untrained orderlies and an old nurse, Sam, who was kindly and remarkably longsuffering. So too were the orderlies, who worked in these frightful conditions without being brutalised by them. Their only weakness was for the patients' weekly allocation of tobacco. They all smoked an evil, rank, molasses-soaked preparation from New Guinea, sold in ingot-like blocks. One of the orderlies was a giant of a man, I should guess six foot eight, who had only to loom in the background to quieten the most refractory of patients, though he was neither violent nor, as I believe, particularly strong. More than once I was glad when he interposed himself between a patient and me, though of course I made it a point of honour never to show fear.

I decided at once to release the patients from their chains, and briefly feeling like the Pinel of the Pacific (there is a famous painting of that revolutionary psychiatrist releasing his patients from bondage in the Bicêtre), I ordered their shackles removed. At first Sam refused to comply, saying it was too dangerous to be contemplated: the patients would be violent. I said that nevertheless it must be risked, and I should take the blame for any untoward consequences. Then Sam said the patients could not be released because the keys to their chains were lost. I suspected this was the *real* reason for their continued close incarceration, which I brought to an end with a hacksaw.

Of the two patients, Maribo and Reroa, who had been chained for two years to their respective walls, Maribo said 'Thank you' and merely walked away as though he had been only momentarily detained, while Reroa took the opportunity to run out, climb up the coconut tree in the Mental Wing's yard, and shower the tin roof of his erstwhile prison with coconuts. Everyone had to take shelter until the coconuts were exhausted. I thought this no mean achievement on Reroa's part after two years of bondage, but the rest of the staff saw it as a vindication of the policy of enchainment. And I must admit that giving them their freedom, relatively speaking, had remarkably little effect, either for good or evil, on their condition. They both continued to hallucinate threats against them and occasionally to lash out at those nearby whom they mistook for their tormentors. Otherwise they were friendly and even had a sense of humour. But alas for Reroa, who had once been the best scholar in the best school in the whole colony: he suffered from the liver disease that carried off a considerable number of the Gilbertese prematurely, even by the standards of their reduced life expectancy.

Oddly enough, these patients from the other side of the world would not have been out of place in the —— Hospital or in any other institution for the mad. They walked with that zombie-like shuffle that proclaimed them at once as long-term patients. Some of them had been given huge, perhaps even record, doses of tranquillisers (and sleeping pills three or four times daily). For example, a powerful tranquilliser that is normally administered by injection once every two weeks or month, was given to some patients twice a day, again with very few effects either good or evil. And like the patients at home, they resented any attempt to stir them from their apathy. Their only strong desire, drugged or undrugged, was to do nothing, to sleep, and while unavoidably awake – a moment awake being a moment wasted – to let their minds empty of all content, as though rapt in some Zen meditation.

With the misplaced zeal of the tyro I decided to rehabilitate the patients through useful activity: the raising of vegetables. Since the soil of Tarawa was saline and infertile I decided upon hydroponics as the method to use. I sought forty-four gallon drums for division into two, and made enquiries after fertiliser.

But my efforts were entirely misguided, for not only were the patients immoveably apathetic, but the Gilbertese were simply not a cultivating people. Their only crop, other than coconuts for copra, was *babai*, a coarse taro that grew in swampy pits dug for the purpose. Even then babai was not an everyday or staple food; worse still, it was tended only by women, and practically all our patients were men. To ask them to cultivate vegetables, which they neither wanted nor liked was therefore as inappropriate a suggestion as it was possible to make.

Nevertheless, I called a meeting to discuss my project. Reluctantly and slowly, the patients gathered in our yard under a small, delapidated maneaba which had been built, presumably, to make them feel more at home. Some had almost to be carried from their cells, for though it was mid-morning they had gone back to sleep after breakfast. Meals – fetched from the kitchens in buckets – were their only voluntary accessions to full consciousness.

Outside the wire fence gathered the lepers from the nearby leprosarium, to laugh at the lunatics. They, in their self-obsessed or purely vacant way, seemed not to notice. I addressed them.

Surely, I said, it was better to do something constructive, something worthwhile, than to waste their lives just staring up at the ceiling? They would never be fit for discharge if they did that. And was not their diet monotonous? Rice and fish, fish and rice? Well then, how about growing vegetables to supplement and vary it? Later, maybe, they could keep pigs and chickens.

My ideas had a soporific effect on some of the patients, who snored loudly, but Reroa approached me and kicked me on the shins.

'You are trying to make slaves of us all,' he said.

A few months later we moved from the dungeon-like old Mental Wing into the new one, which had been designed by an eminent Canadian professor of psychiatry, who had been righteously appalled at prevailing conditions when he visited. His optimistic design required a few amendments because he omitted to include anything so coercive as a lock, let alone a fence or secure rooms for disturbed patients. This was an oversight because nearly all our patients were strong young men, admitted against their will on account of violently disturbed behaviour. The professor had evidently envisaged a time when the Gilbertese mad would seek their own treatment rather than having to be dragged to the Mental Wing by four or five hefty policemen; but in three and a half years, I never saw a patient admitted there voluntarily. In the days before there was a Mental Wing at all – so I was told – a man who went mad in a village would be tied up, and if after a time he failed to recover his senses, he would be pinioned to a coconut log and floated out to sea. Those who were mad without being violent or destructive were tolerated and cared for. But this drastic method of dealing with violent lunatics was entirely understandable in the circumstances, for in the confined environment of the atoll, with its delicate social equilibrium, little patience could be shown the unbiddable. More than once the question flitted across my mind whether a country nine-tenths of whose population were still subsistence fishers and gatherers could really afford to keep at public expense such unproductive people for up to forty years.

And if our European humanitarianism might not be appropriate to these exotic surroundings, what of our law which had been transplanted wholesale there? The paraphernalia of the rules of evidence, chief justices, courts of appeal, etc., had been set up, though there was little doubt most of it was incomprehensible to the Gilbertese people. (The Chief Justice was a former Battle of Britain pilot who once, while celebrating, fell off a ferry from Betio to Bairiki. On being rescued half-drowned, he demanded that the ferry return to search for the shoe he had lost in the water.) In a Gilbertese village, where it was impossible to hide anything, everyone knew who had transgressed against custom –a living reality, unlike the dead letter of the law – and the transgressor was punished in accordance with custom by the old men of the village. James Denton-Smith knew of cases where adulterers had been crushed to death by logs and their bodies disposed of without any intervention by the forces of the law, which in any case would have been quite powerless since they required witnesses to act, and none would have been forthcoming.

One evening, while on duty in the hospital, a woman appeared, deeply gashed by many stabwounds. She was accompanied by her husband and both of them were drunk. At first she claimed not to know the identity of her assailant: she had walked out of her hut in the dark and been set upon. But then her husband fell on to the bed next to hers and started to snore stertorously. She at once told us that *he* was the attacker, but she had been afraid to say so in front of him. He still had the knife with which he had attacked her about him, and he had recently been released from gaol having served a five-year sentence for murder. The police were called and he was led away.

About a week later I was again on duty when a man was brought to hospital with a gash across his neck. Had it been a fraction deeper he would undoubtedly have been killed. I was surprised to learn that it was the same man who had attacked him as had attacked his wife the week before. He had been released on bail and that night had gone to a bar where he had become drunk. He took out his knife, went up to the man who was a stranger to him, said 'I'm going to kill you', and cut his throat.

The next morning the police asked me to talk to the man, who was in their lockup, to determine whether he was sane. He had sobered up by then, but showed no remorse; he was not concerned with the fate of his victim, and took the attitude that these things happen. I reported that the man was not insane but – surely a conclusion it required no training to reach – was very dangerous especially when drunk, having attempted to murder two people in the space of a week, and having also a conviction for murder. In that case, said the police, they would have to release him again on bail; for if he were not detainable in the Mental Wing, they could charge him only with wounding, a charge for which the granting of bail was mandatory. I protested. Surely, I said, the charge should be attempted murder; but the police, whose understanding of the law was fragile, insisted on releasing him.

That night, while the released man was sleeping in his hut, a group of ten villagers entered and stabbed him to death. His ragged corpse was brought next morning to our mortuary, where it attracted a festive crowd (as did any corpse). But the whole episode must further have lessened respect for the European's alien system of law, which had so signally failed to protect the community. The police had applied it only mechanically, without understanding; but it was in any case better for everyone that the man should die than that he should be fed and housed free of charge for the rest of his life. This was so obvious to the Gilbertese that it needed no statement.

And this was a viewpoint with which at least one colonial governor, according to Dr Storm, had agreed. When a man was sentenced to imprisonment for murder he ordered that the prisoner should receive dental treatment under anaesthesia, from which the man would unfortunately never wake up; and this was an order which no mere colonial medical officer would dared have disobeyed.

The patients in the Mental Wing were, as I have said, for the most part very disturbed indeed. When I arrived one of them had not spoken for three years, not a single word. In an attempt to demonstrate the power of drugs to the staff, and thus to gain their respect, I injected him with a stimulant, methylamphetamine, with which the hospital was curiously well-supplied. Almost as the needle penetrated his vein he began to talk, and the staff drew back amazed at this apparent miracle. Alas, it was beyond my powers to make him talk sense, and for two days a dammed-up flood of paranoid nonsense poured from his mouth, night and day, until the staff were exhausted listening to it. Thereafter, he lapsed back into his mute condition which on the whole the staff preferred, though he had sudden outbursts of destructiveness. They preferred also the kind of injections that rendered a struggling, violent patient almost instantly unconscious, the natural condition of most of our patients.

One of my first patients was a prisoner with the physique of a grizzly bear. He had broken away from a prison work party, run into a school, and there set upon the newly arrived English headmaster, whom he might have killed had the children not called for help. The man had a long history of assault, and had once murdered (or twice, if the rumour was true); but it was evident that he was quite mad and had been so for many years, which accounted for his numerous unprovoked attacks on passers-by. Asked about the latest incident, he said the Queen of England told him to do it, that he might extract information about an American aircraft that had crashed in the Gilberts during the war; and he went on confusedly to talk about being granted an airline as a reward. He broke off his sentences to receive further instructions from the Queen, who told him sometimes to remain silent. Very large doses of tranquilliser soon suppressed his royal hallucinations, but they left him a shambling, amiable shell of a man, with a grin of empty fatuity, plagued by the side-effects of the tranquilliser, a severe tremor and a restlessness of his feet as though ants were crawling over them as he sat. He attacked no-one while he took his drugs regularly; but I have since heard that after I left the islands he ceased taking them and resumed his obedience to what he assumed were Her Majesty's commands. Again I wondered whether perhaps the Gilbertese way – in the circumstances – was not the best.

Soon afterwards I received a patient who acted on even higher authority, namely God's. He was a young seminarian, and he was brought to the hospital by the Catholic bishop. I asked him why he had brought the patient.

'Well,' said the bishop, 'he spends all day praying.'

The patient was indeed in the grip of a religious mania but this, too, yielded to the onslaught of tranquillisers.

One of the two principal reasons for admission to the Mental Wing was temporary madness caused by alcoholic excess. (Australian beer has done far more harm in the Pacific than all the French nuclear tests.) The Gilbertese tended to drink not at all or to lose control. They had an expression *Full drunk*. A man was not full drunk if he could still walk. The toll of motorbike accidents along the single road in Tarawa was truly terrible: I saw men too drunk to walk being lifted by their friends onto their machines so that they could ride home. Not infrequently they failed to make it, but somewhere on the way crashed headfirst into a coconut tree. One night a drunken pair rode home. The passenger was a man who some years before had lost a leg in a drunken motorbike accident, and now used crutches to walk. One of his crutches caught in the spokes of the rear wheel and he was catapulted headfirst into a tree, whence, falling back into the road, he was crushed by a passing vehicle. The driver was also killed. The passenger's brains were spread across the road and in the morning I saw stray dogs eating them. I thought I had seen everything, but I blenched at this.

More gruesome still was the story of a man brought from the island of Tabiteuea whose inhabitants were famous throughout the Gilberts for their aggressiveness. Having drunk continuously of the fermented toddy of the palm tree, he began to hallucinate voices threatening to kill him. He ran away, but the voices followed. Deciding to kill himself rather than deliver himself up to his persecutors, he climbed a coconut tree and jumped. Alas, he did not die, but only broke his back; and the voices pursued him still. He took the sharp knife he used for cutting toddy and slit open his belly. But still he did not die, so with his own hands he pulled out his intestines and bit through them. He was still alive when he reached the hospital, and indeed his life was saved by the surgeon. But his legs were paralysed by the fall, and I had hardly the heart to tell him to drink less, for whatever the original reason for his overindulgence, he had twice the reason now.

I went to the two prisons on the island, one in Betio and the other in Bairiki, to interview all the prisoners who had killed unlawfully. I talked to twenty-one murderers in all. At Betio prison I found the gates unlocked and all the warders gone to lunch. (One of the prisoners subsequently 'escaped' and murdered another man.) The prisoners were lying around in the shade. When one of the warders returned I told him I should like to speak to all his murderers.

'Good idea,' he said. 'We have fourteen.'

Of the twenty-one, one was mad (he murdered his sister

because he hallucinated her insulting him); one murdered his own son who was trying drunkenly to rape his sister, not for the first time; while all the others were drunk at the time of their crimes, which seemed to be otherwise unmotivated. *Pro rata*, there would have to be 20,000 such murderers in Britain. And prisoners whom the Gilbertese considered *dangerous* were not kept in Betio or Bairiki at all, but two thousand miles away, on Christmas Island.

I am not sure I can explain this patent inability to cope with the blandishments of alcohol (common to many aboriginal societies). It is said that until the irruption of Europeans into the islands in the early nineteenth century, the Gilbertese knew no alcohol, though to ferment toddy is the easiest thing in the world. Once introduced, however, they took to it with gusto, so much so that the later colonial authorities, alarmed at its effects, tried to suppress it. Until ten years before independence, the Gilbertese needed a special licence to allow them to drink, a licence which was revoked in the event of misbehaviour; but in the changed climate of anticolonial sentiment it seemed anomalous and arbitrary that Europeans could drink as much as they liked – and often they liked a lot – while permission for the Gilbertese was so grudging and partial. Since it was out of the question to apply the same regulations to Europeans (there would have been a mutiny), the restrictions had to go.

Perhaps it had something indirectly to do with the extreme smallness of the islands, which necessitated a tightly-controlled society in which people did not freely express their emotions, antagonisms and disagreements, and all had to obey sometimes irksome customs. The islands, though beautiful, were a limited and limiting environment, and it was my impression that those who knew something of the outside world drank to forget. Education did not help; on the contrary, it made the frustrations all the worse. Alcohol was a release; moreover, it was widely accepted that a man who was drunk had temporarily lost responsibility for his actions, and therefore could say and do things which normally would be unacceptable, without being called to account. But perhaps – as they say in Russian novels – this is all nonsense.

In *The Lancet* one day I read an article about youths in Britain who sniffed glue and organic solvents. The author concluded that it was the hopelessness of the slums, the despair, the unemployment and the ugliness of degenerating industrial society that made them do it. I wrote to *The Lancet* to tell them that in the Gilbert Islands, as far removed from degenerating industrial society as it was possible to imagine, many youths, even on the untouched outer islands, had taken to sniffing petrol fumes. They did it not because they were wretched, but merely, in their own words, 'to feel different' – *nota bene*, not to feel better. Subsequently I published a small survey in which I showed that Gilbertese with schizophrenia had sniffed petrol far more often in their youth than Gilbertese of similar age and background without schizophrenia. I suggested that the petrol fumes might have had lasting neuropsychiatric effects (though it was possible that the schizophrenia first manifested itself as an avidity for petrol fumes). The survey was later reported in *The Times*, but very inaccurately; if so serious, or at least solemn, a newspaper could misrepresent something from the cold and dry pages of *The Lancet*, what of foreign wars and political revolutions?

The only expatriate with whom I had to deal in my psychiatric capacity was a bureaucrat with a harridan wife. They lived lives of mutual torment. Once he had chased her along the beach behind their house, brandishing a carving knife. Eventually he grew depressed and would not speak. His wife brought him to me: it was no fun tormenting a mute.

'He's depressed, doctor,' she said. She was scornful of his weakness.

I gave him electroconvulsive therapy and before long he was manic. He wrote reports and letters fifty pages long; he made grandiose plans; he talked incessantly; he never slept.

His wife brought him to hospital once more. She looked a bit paler, less self-confident, this time.

'Can't you make him depressed again, doctor?' she asked.

When the Europeans came to the islands they brought with them not only the Bible, alcohol and metal implements, but tuberculosis. I had seen a few cases before, but none so florid. About a third of all the patients in the hospital had tuberculosis of one form or another. But the Gilbertese regarded the hospital as a place of last resort, after all else had failed. Almost everyone in the islands believed himself possessed of arcane medical knowledge, and that the plants to be found there were sufficient to cure all ills: and since nine out of ten illnesses cure themselves, the success rate of any inhabitant was certain to be high. When herbal medicine had failed, it was assumed that malign magic must be at work, and it was only after counter-magic had also failed that the patients, often *in extremis*, were brought to us. Since such patients often *did* die, in fact, the idea that the hospital was a place only of last resort was reinforced. Sometimes one had the impression that people were brought to hospital only in order to die, so that others might retain their faith in local traditions of magic and medicine, the demonstration of powerlessness of *our* kind of medicine being an important prop to that faith. For a doctor it was very frustrating but perhaps, overall, it was better that the Gilbertese should retain the beliefs of their own culture, even when they resulted in avoidable deaths, than succumb to the rationalism of an alien culture.

In any case, success in the hospital never challenged that faith to the same degree as failure reinforced it. A pretty young girl was brought to the hospital from Christmas Island because her legs had grown weaker over several months until now they were paralysed completely. She was an important member of a dance troupe of whom her father was leader. He was convinced that her weakness was the effect of magic worked on her by the leader of a rival dance troupe. Hence he refused to allow her to seek medical attention, relying instead on magicians. Eventually, and very reluctantly, he allowed her to come to hospital. Examination showed that two of her vertebrae had collapsed, leaving an ugly lump in her spine as well as paralysing her legs. She had Pott's disease, tuberculosis of the spine, of which paralysis is a late and often irreversible complication. Once started on antituberculosis therapy, however, she recovered the use of her legs slowly but surely. There was no reason why she should not have recovered completely, apart from the deformity in her back, but one afternoon her father appeared at the hospital slightly the worse for drink – and said that our medicine was no use, it was magic she needed. He wanted to take her away and a fight nearly ensued. He was evicted and his daughter continued her recovery. But this success was not attributed to our treatment, rather to the magic which continued to be performed on her behalf outside the hospital. We were confronting not so much an individual belief as a whole cognitive system.

There were other cases that illustrated the same point. Early one evening a young woman was brought by her relatives because, shortly before, she had covered herself from head to toe in her own excrement. Not surprisingly, this was more than they could tolerate. A week before she was brought she had given birth at home in the village. A day or two later she began to have a fever, and both she and her relatives believed it was caused by the spirit of her dead brother-in-law taking his revenge on her. A magician was called, and he gave her a protective magic garland and some magic oil. Her fever, however, not only failed to abate but grew higher, and then she started to hear the voice of her brother-in-law threatening to rape and then to kill her. The magician was again called, but his prescriptions availed nothing. At last, to keep the spirit away, she covered herself in excrement. It was certainly repulsive.

In the early part of her pregnancy her husband had died. His brother had then claimed what he regarded as his rights over her, but she rejected him. This rejection was the motive for his revenge. Then he too died, not long before she gave birth. It all seemed to fit together.

In fact, she had puerperal sepsis and a few injections of penicillin cleared it up. Her fever abated, she no longer heard the voice of her brother-in-law. But this was not the curative effect of penicillin; it was the magic acting at last. She had been brought to hospital for us to perform the menial task of hosing her down.

Belief in spirits was universal. When our radiographer died suddenly at home of a heart attack, his deputy would take no x-rays in the department for several days, throwing open the normally shuttered windows to let out his restive spirit.

A great many of our patients suffered from acute and life-threatening diseases of the kind which it is gratifying to treat because it is precisely for these diseases that modern medicine is so unequivocally and uniquely effective. (But, as I have said, a hundred successes did not equal one failure in public estimation.) Tuberculosis of the lungs, spine, kidneys, hip, abdomen, lymph nodes of the neck, and membranes of the heart and brain, yielded to our treatment, as did pneumonia, meningitis, typhoid, dysentery, amoebic liver abscesses, septicaemia and hookworm, the latter causing the most profound anaemia I had ever seen, with blood levels of haemoglobin that I should not previously have thought compatible with life. Of course, treatment of individual cases did little to alter the prevalence of disease, however important it was to the individuals concerned; but I had little faith in public health as it was developing in the islands under the auspices of the World Health Organisation, either. This is something to which I shall return.

Sometimes one doubted whether the patients whose lives we had saved appreciated it. A patient was brought from Butaritari with meningitis, from which he had been unconscious for three days. In hospital he remained unconscious for a further four days, until we had given up hope, though we continued the treatment. Suddenly, unexpectedly, he regained full consciousness and sat up. I asked him how he was feeling, hoping for paroxysms of gratitude.

'Constipated,' he replied.

If I could at that moment have given him back his meningitis, I should unhesitatingly have done so.

The Gilbertese were not immune from worry over minor ailments, as one unthinkingly assumed people intimately familiar with real dangers must be. One afternoon a prominent member of the cabinet consulted me because every day, after lunch, he felt an almost irresistible urge to sleep, especially if he read official papers. *Then* he went straight to sleep. All I could suggest was that he forwent his lunch or his official papers.

And now I have a confession to make, which causes me much embarrassment. Although in the event I stayed more than three years in the Gilberts, I never learnt more of the language than simple questions after health. For this serious omission I can offer several excuses: I was never sure how long I should stay, it was a language spoken by only 60,000 people in the world, it had no written literature, the nurses and doctors with whom I had to deal all spoke English, my social life was almost entirely among the expatriate community; but none of these excuses satisfied me. It was laziness combined with an attitude of cultural superiority I should certainly have condemned in others. Now I am aware I have compounded this mistake by misleadingly dwelling too long on the sombre side of life in the islands, which inevitably obtruded itself upon me because of my work. For life as a whole was certainly not sombre there.

Even on Tarawa, the most crowded by far of the islands, the island where conflict between aboriginal culture and the tawdriest aspects of our synthetic but abundant way of life was most acute, the tempo of existence was pleasantly relaxed, people not having yet learnt that getting and spending are the chiefest pleasure and highest good of mankind. Nobody was ever in a hurry, but being city bred I never managed to reduce my pace by walking to the slow but dignified amble of the Gilbertese. They found my haste very funny, and as I passed them I could hear their giggles. Even when I had nothing to do I walked like a commuter late for work; but even when they had somewhere to reach by a specified time they walked at the speed of an old man out for an evening stroll. I could not slow down, they could not speed up. Here was an unbridgeable gulf, the physical manifestation of a completely different apprehension and valuation of time.

The Gilbertese were not perhaps the most beautiful people in the world, but their movements had a simple, unhurried grace. They were personally very cleanly, and when their smooth brown skin glistened with bathing, and their heads were garlanded with frangipani or hibiscus, they were very attractive to see. They were reserved, and even those who had lived in the islands for many years felt they would never fully understand or know them; yet they smiled readily and were fond of jokes. They were exquisitely polite, with elaborate forms of greeting, and were willing to go to considerable lengths to avoid giving offence to the point where it was impossible to tell what they really thought. They were the most uncompetitive of people; though naturally good at games like tennis they attached no importance to winning. In school races, the leader of the field would hang back to allow the others to catch up. They had a code of hospitality such that guests were looked after as long as they cared to stay (it was a reciprocal arrangement, of course); and they had a profoundly egalitarian attitude to material goods. A relative, no matter how distant, had only to ask for a valued possession – a radio, a kerosene lamp – and it was granted him. Of course, the new owner might quickly be dispossessed by a distant relative of *his*; the whole system redistributed what little wealth there was in the islands so that no-one became rich while his neighbours remained poor. It discouraged individual enterprise and effort, but it discouraged unhealthy possessiveness. What was mine today might not be mine tomorrow, so that possessions were held in usufruct rather than freehold, as it were.

The Gilbertese retained a charming informality (except about those traditional customs they held important) which often appeared to outsiders as incompetence. The fact was that their scale of values was incommensurable with that of the expatriates who had come mainly to assist them in technical or administrative matters. Often they had little understanding of why they were asked and paid to do something so completely alien to their previous way of life, and therefore they performed their allotted tasks as though propitiating a powerful foreign deity, the outward form of the various ceremonies being more important than their content or meaning. The nurses would mark temperature charts with obviously absurd readings, for it was the mere act of filling them, rather than the information they were supposed to convey, that was important. A routine was difficult to establish, but once established was equally difficult to change. There once must have been an English matron in the hospital with an obsession for giving patients enemas before operations, who thoroughly drilled their necessity into her staff, and this had been successfully transmitted down the generations. Emergency operations were held up while unnecessary enemas were performed, even at the cost of life. It was a brave nurse who thought for herself.

There was a weekly flight to Christmas Island from Honolulu, and a man was employed there whose only job was to switch on the navigation beacon once a week in preparation for the arrival of the aircraft. The beacon was twenty miles from his home and he thought it would be more convenient if it were next to his house where, without informing anyone, he moved it. When the aircraft arrived the following week it received a signal to land far out to sea, but fortunately the pilot saw the island and chose to believe his eyes rather than the signal.

Who could blame the beacon keeper? To have explained it by reference to the emission of invisible waves which guided the aircraft would have sounded as fantastic to him as the explanation of illness by magic did to me. Even the purpose behind incomparably simpler instructions was sometimes misunderstood. There is a story, perhaps apocryphal, of a government clerk who had been instructed never to deliver over government property without a duly signed requisition order. One day someone rushed into his office to ask for a fire extinguisher, for the building next door was on fire. He asked to see the man's requisition order.

This lack of understanding was both frustrating and charming. Who could be angry with thieves who broke into a house and, seeing a typewriter, sat down to play with it and left a piece of paper with their names proudly typed upon it? Who could fail to be charmed by a local radio station on which 'Here is the local news' was once followed by a silence and then the announcement

'There is no local news'? Or where the only international telephone operator in the country has 'gone for breast feeding'? Or
wish to change a country where the President still wore no shoes
and climbed a coconut tree to cut toddy?

The scale of life was small and humane. The celebration of the
first anniversary of independence was held in the National
Stadium, a coarse football field in Bairiki with a small breezeblock
stand along one side. When the national flag – the sun rising and a
frigate bird flying above blue waves – unfurled, it was upside
down. The police bandmaster stood with one leg in an ant's nest
and went through agonies of nose-twitching while trying to stand
to attention as his boots, socks and legs crawled with ants. When
the students of the Marine Training School marched past the
President, their leader ordered 'Eyes left' for some unaccount-
able reason, for the President was on their right, throwing the
boys into terrible confusion. All this was not taken as an insult to
the national dignity, as surely it would have been anywhere else in
the world; rather it was the occasion of innocent laughter.

It would have been impossible for anyone in the Gilbert Islands
to become high and mighty. Everyone was too close to subsistence, too equal in the face of nature, for that. One night some
friends of mine heard a peculiar rustling in the land beyond their
small garden. They went out to investigate and discovered a
cabinet minister crawling in the undergrowth, collecting the
empty beer cans that Gilbertese drinkers had carelessly tossed
away. These he cut into two, filling each half with water and
freezing them with a stick in the middle. The resulting flavourless
ice-lollies he sold to children at ten cents each, to supplement his
ministerial salary which, though large by Gilbertese standards,
was small by others. This source of income, however, came to an
end when his electricity supply was cut off for non-payment of
bills; so many of his relations had descended upon him, attracted
by the convenience of electricity, which not one in a hundred
Gilbertese enjoyed, and which made life so much easier, that his
electricity bills alone were larger than his salary. A man in such a
situation was unlikely to be smitten with megalomania.

The naivety of the Gilbertese about the outside world could be rather touching. Those who had never travelled beyond the islands knew of the world only what they had seen in the films shows under the stars in their village maneaba: an odd melange of Filipino gangsters, Kung Fu fighters, Count Dracula, Korean women wrestlers, Roman legions, cowboys and Indians, Mongol hordes and Zulu Impis, whose fictional nature was only dimly perceived, so that I was once asked where Superman lived.

There were other sides to the Gilbertese character which were less attractive, at least to outsiders. They neither forgot nor forgave an injury done them. They might take their revenge many years later, when the original injury might, one supposed, have been forgotten. They were almost entirely lacking in public spirit and were seemingly concerned only for the welfare of their own extended families. H.E. Maude, the former governor and student of Pacific history and anthropology, told the story of how he one day saw a woman drowning out to sea. He asked some men with canoes who were standing on the shore watching her plight why they did not rescue her. 'Why should we?' they replied. 'She is not our relative.' And certainly the Gilbertese displayed a callousness towards the sufferings of those not of their lineage which foreigners were bound to find repellent. One afternoon a truck taking children on an outing overturned and spilled them out on rocks. Sixteen were hurt, three seriously. They were brought to hospital, followed by an almost triumphant crowd of onlookers. Soon there were so many of them that we, the doctors, could not move from patient to patient. The crowd wanted so desperately to see the injured, to have a full view, that they swarmed into the wards even through the windows. No appeals or threats moved them, and they found the distracted howls of the parents of the injured amusing rather than pitiful. James Denton-Smith tried to clear them away by brandishing a broom handle, but they were like flies at a sore: no sooner brushed away than they returned. We called the police to clear the hospital, but they were no better than the rest. There was no disguising the distastefulness of this scene for the viewpoint of outsiders.

But the remarkable beauty of Gilbertese life was to be found on the other islands. Tarawa had been touched and tainted a little by the cheapest and most worthless aspects of our civilisation which were, however, the easiest for people of a materially simpler culture to appreciate. It was sad to see the pictures that the children at the élite state secondary school on Tarawa chose to adorn the cupboards round their beds, which revealed presumably their dreams and aspirations: advertisements for Marlboro cigarettes, Bacardi rum, Oscar de la Renta, and the like. The outer islands remained truer to Gilbertese traditions.

Each Christmas I stayed on the island of Abemama with Dr Frank Belling, who lived there with his family. Robert Louis Stevenson stayed on Abemama for six months before moving on to Samoa, but there was no residue of his time there. Frank was an experimental pathologist (one day he will be a professor) who decided before settling finally to a life of microscopic examinations of tumours that have killed people to spend a few years as district medical officer on Abemama. He was a man of very precise mind, who never held opinions on any subject beyond what was strictly warranted by the evidence, and who never did anything but he did it well; both he and his wife liked Abemama, but in the end the general level of bureaucratic incompetence drove him with relief back to his pathological laboratory.

Abemama was unpopulated by comparison with Tarawa. It was a relief to walk along the coral road through the coconut groves in complete solitude and silence, other than the swish of the sea. The waters around the shore were so translucent they seemed actually to transmit a brilliant light. Irridescent yellow and electric blue fish darted tantalisingly among the coral and on the beach small crabs with inquisitive black eyes on stalks and one crimson claw – the other drab – fled down their holes at the approaching footfall. Across a shining turquoise passage was Abakoro, an islet with a fishing village. Everywhere one found shells; a hundred different molluscs of tasteful pastel hues and swirling geometry, including the pearly nautilus. Further up the island, in a small bay, was the crashed hull of a Japanese flying boat, a relic from the war. It was well preserved in shallow water, a tribute to the workmanship of the time.

Nearby among the coconut trees was a crashed American bomber, whose fuselage had been mined for forty years for such sheet metal as the islanders required. The arrival of the Americans in Abemama was an event so momentous that the old men talked of it still in the maneabas. Frank had heard the story so many times that it bored him stiff; but the old men never tired of relating the miraculous material abundance that the arrival of the Americans seemed to presage. So many cigarettes, so much chewing gum! The Gilbertese took to the latter at once, and now all the women chewed it, making a peculiar clacking noise with it between their teeth, so that when first I saw a film under a maneaba I looked around me for cicada-like insects. When the war was over, the Gilbertese petitioned that the islands remain American rather than be handed back to the impecunious and parsimonious British, but their petition was denied. It was a fortunate escape, for the British policy of meanness turned out in the long run to be far wiser than the American policy of open-handed subventions. The wretchedness and degradation of the American territories in the Pacific, swamped as they have been by well-meaning generosity, are such that I have never met an American who has not hung his head in shame after visiting them. The Marshallese, similar to the Gilbertese, have been crushed and extinguished by the weight of baseball hats, soft drinks, popcorn, ice machine, airconditioners, bubble gum and cake mixes.

One Christmas a whale was beached a mile away from where we stayed, and the villagers had an unaccustomed surfeit of meat. Within a few days the whale was no more than an implausibly large skeleton smelling rather of rotting fish, with a few tattered sinews hanging from the bones. It was a small whale, as whales go, but its vertebrae, which each weighed many pounds, made conveniently sized stools.

At full moon, with the tide out, we went night fishing among the rock pools. The air was so clear that it would have been possible to read by moonlight, whose beams caused the rustling palm fronds to glow silver when they struck them. We caught a multitude of small fish and had a prolonged struggle with an ugly, powerful moray eel, with vice-like jaws lined with needle-sharp teeth, and a slimy body that seemed immune to the blows of our machete. We leapt about in the pool to avoid its ferocious bite (and also the strokes of our own machete). When finally we scooped it into our bucket, it snaked undulatingly in what we assumed to be its death slither. But in the morning it was slithering still in the moisture of its own slime, until we gave it the *coup de grâce*. It was surprisingly good eating, grilled in tinned butter.

At another time of the month the reef danced at night with the bright lanterns of the octopus gatherers, who winkled the creatures out with great skill from their crevices in the coral. The lanterns seemed to have a life of their own, for from a distance it was impossible to see who was holding them. They all appeared at once, a hundred at a time, for octopus could be caught only during a short phase of the lunar cycle. A man caught fifty to eighty a night, though each was small and provided only a morsel of food.

Each Christmas we attended the dancing in one of the maneabas. There was no question of the importance of dancing in the eyes of the Gilbertese. People who were feckless in their performance of any government-ordained task were meticulous in their preparations for dancing, practising for several evenings a week months in advance. A night of traditional dancing was no mere eruption of animal spirits, but a solemn undertaking of truly artistic intensity. After every such evening, Frank Belling saw one or two girls who had taken part who were so overcome by the emotion that they required sedation.

A good-humoured but excited and expectant crowd gathered in the maneaba, filling it with bodily warmth. A few hurricane lamps hanging from a beam in the roof shed the only light for miles around, though the black, cloudless sky was studded with a miraculous profusion of stars. The atmosphere under the high sloping roof grew tense and emotional. Somehow one never forgot one was on a narrow strip of coral in the vastness of the ocean. The dancing began, and as the hours passed it grew more passionate. The girls were clad in grass skirts, blackened with an aromatic pitch whose scent filled the air; around their black hair shining with coconut oil they wore tiaras of plaited and pointed pandanus and frangipani; around their waists they wore strings of cowries, tied with human hair; around their arms they wore bands of flowers or – too often these days – plastic substitutes and coloured tinsel; too often also they wore white bras. The men wore finely woven pandanus mats around their waists which they slapped to intricate rhythms; some sat round a flat sounding box nine inches high and five feet square which they beat in hypnotic unison.

The men swayed, clapped their hands, swung their arms from side to side, and stamped their feet, all as one. The women, who danced separately, stood out at the front in a line of three or five, sometimes with identically clad tots of three in another line before them, their arms outstretched, their hands quivering to the music. They turned their heads suddenly, jerkily, from one direction to another, the expression on their faces being that of some kind of transcendence. They went forward and back in little steps, sometimes very slowly, sometimes faster, but always with grace. There was nothing spectacular in any of the movements, rather they were subtle and fine-tuned, so it is difficult to convey their cumulative impact, which was – even when one was ignorant of their evident symbolism – very moving. As the hours went by one entered a trance-like state, and left the maneaba as though intoxicated. It seemed then as though the island were the centre of the universe, and nowhere else mattered.

As soon as I returned to Tarawa I was once more engulfed by the social life of the expatriate community. I do not suppose that as a community we were very interesting – we were, for the most part, respectable administrators, lawyers, teachers, doctors, accountants, economists and engineers, all nevertheless trying to escape a stultifying life at home. A few came to restore foundering marriages, a universally disastrous proceeding. We ate in each others' homes, went for picnics, played tennis, gossiped. Life had a peculiar timeless quality, like a still from a film. On the Queen's Birthday the High Commission threw a party, hired the police band, planted the Union Jack in the lagoon, and everyone got drunk at British Government expense. There were cricket matches between the British and Australian expatriates in which, despite protestations of lightheartedness, each side played desperately for the honour of its country. The Australian team, including the portly Australian High Commissioner, once appeared with T-shirts bearing the legend BURY THE BASTARDS. Unfortunately they lost, and the manager of the Bank of New South Wales, the only bank in the country, who liked to win whatever he played, stalked off with a face of thunder, contemplating letters about the overdrafts of the English team. A few cans of ice-cold Australian beer – liquid gold, they called it – restored his perspective.

One of our community's chief luminaries was Alwyn Jones, a man of Micawberish optimism, whom neither misfortune nor disaster could long repress. In spite of his name he claimed to be Irish (his father had been chaplain to an Anglo-Irish aristocrat, and Alwyn had studied in Ireland). He was without doubt the most loquacious man I have ever met, quite unstoppable in his logorrhoea. He could finish a bottle of whisky at a sitting, and though a little drunk after the first glass, he never seemed to grow any drunker. His stream of consciousness was legendary. He was a long-term expatriate who had spent years in Africa, and by comparison with *his* stories, those of the Baron Munchausen were plausibility itself. His house was full of zebra skins, elephants' feet, antelope horns etc., all of whose original owners he had, of course, shot. It was a brave man who asked him about them. Once at a dinner party he claimed to have shot fifty zebra in an afternoon.

'What did you use?' asked the pharmacist. 'A machine gun?'

His wife went through exquisite tortures as he told his preposterous stories, but she was very fond of him. He was capable of talking an entire company to sleep after dinner, but far from taking offence, he never even noticed. When they woke he was still talking. In the days when there was still a Governor of the Gilbert Islands he once persuaded the radio station to allow him to give a talk. He rambled as usual without ever coming to the point, if there was one, but unfortunately for him the Governor was listening and he sent a short message to the radio station: 'Get that man off'. In mid-sentence – no, in mid-word – the voice of Alwyn Jones faded away to be replaced without any explanation by music, as though there had been a coup.

Nothing daunted, he found an outlet in Tarawa's weekly paper, *The Atoll Pioneer*. The articles he wrote were multifarious in subject matter, but the only one I recall concerned the migratory habits of crabs. Unfortunately, owing to a typographical error, it appeared under the title:

THE EQUINOCTIAL MARCH OF THE ARABS

(The same newspaper once published a picture of some rather stolid and fierce-looking girls from the island of Maiana at an island party with the caption: *Maiana Beauties Doing The Cook*.)

But when Alwyn Jones left the islands we all suddenly came to the realisation that he was irreplaceable, there wasn't another man like him in the world, and that he had never said, drunk or sober, a nasty or disparaging word about anyone, among the countless millions he had unleashed upon the world. This was far more than could be said for the rest of us, amongst whom malicious gossip was endemic, like a disease. He was one of the best-hearted men I ever knew, which was why his wife still loved him.

Of course, islands like the Gilberts attracted drifters, beach-combers, cranks and confidence tricksters like a magnet attracts iron filings. There was an inevitability about it. Not long after my arrival an American came with Texas real estate for sale. His desert land had been thoroughly prospected and found utterly useless for any human purpose, and he therefore called it Green Acres. In the Ellice Islands he managed to persuade the government to part with half its annual budget in exchange for some of these Green Acres. He was less successful in the Gilberts, but even there he relieved more than one man of his few dollars.

For several seeks I was host to an American called Jonas who had a degree in mathematics and had been a missionary volunteer in New Guinea. Instead of returning home at the end of his tour, he became a trader in ethnic artifacts, and he also went round the Pacific relieving old men of their caches of old coins which they kept hidden under their beds. These he melted down for their silver content, of far greater value now than the face value of the coins. For more than a month my house was like the lumber room of an ethnographical museum, with grass skirts, mats, coral necklaces, conches, sharkstooth swords, dried puffer fish, walking canes, nineteenth-century biscuit tins and beer bottles, tin whistles, clamshell adzes, coconut husk vases, cowrie belts and hardwood pestles, all awaiting classification and labelling, crowding me out entirely. Jonas spoke with the gentleness of Anthony Perkins playing a psychopath, and had recently been deported from New Guinea for reasons upon which he did not enlarge.

The islands were also visited by the celebrated, indeed world famous, crank, Erich von Däniken. He had heard there were some giants' footsteps imprinted on rocks on the island of Arorae and he wanted to see them. No doubt he could think up some bizarre theory to explain them afterwards. He went to the airline office to buy a ticket, and was by now pretty well used to people fainting away at the very mention of his famous name. At Air Tungaru, however, they merely asked him to spell it, and even then got it wrong.

The giants' footsteps were not impressive, but that of course did not prevent him from writing a book.

Most of the beachcombing types came from Australia or New Zealand. There was something buccaneering and disarmingly frank about them. I was having a beer with an Australian one evening as the sun was going down lilac and gold and crimson over the lagoon.

'You know, it's not true all Australians are uncultured,' he said. 'Some of my friends are fucking cultured.'

Most of the antipodean beachcombers were heavy drinkers. It was a way of life with them. An Australian trader consulted me one day because of a serious drink problem he had.

'I only had ten cans yesterday, doc,' he said. 'And today I haven't had any. I just don't feel like it. Today's the first day in ten years I haven't had a drink.'

I looked at him. He was yellow; he had hepatitis.

'Well,' I said, 'you've got hepatitis. That's why you don't want to drink. What's more, you mustn't drink for at least three months.'

'Oh!' he said.

'And I see from looking at your hospital records that sometimes you vomit blood in the morning.'

'Yeah, that's right.'

'It's not a terribly good sign, you know.'

'Oh, isn't it?' he said. 'I thought everyone did it.'

He returned three months later. To my surprise he had not touched a drop.

'Hey doc!' he said. 'I feel terrific. I haven't felt this good in years. Why's that then?'

'Why do you think?' I asked.

'I don't know. You're the doc, you should know.'

'Well, for the first time in ten years you haven't got a hangover.'

'Oh.'

A look of deep cogitation passed over his face like the shadow of a cloud over a field on a summer's day.

'Does that mean I can go back on the beer?'

As one might have expected, the sexual code of these people was not strict. One New Zealander, whose purpose in being in the islands was never quite clear, used his housegirl, who was herself far from pretty, to procure nightly partners for him. If what she found failed to please he would say:

'Take that *thing* away and get me another one.'

The reward was always the same: the bus fare home. Bad girls in the Gilbert Islands went under the expressive name of *nikiran-roro*.

There was an old trader to whom the Gilbertese government had extended citizenship, a decision it came much to regret, for he was seized by litigation mania against that very government. He was short and enormously fat, so that you thought he must have some glandular disease; he had flaming red moustaches the shape of buffalo's horns, which looked as though they used up his substance. His past was widely believed to have been very chequered, a belief he did nothing to contradict. I do not know whether he spoke Gilbertese, but I never understood more than one word out of two of his English, and that one word was always the same expletive. But he was nevertheless a shrewd business-man who rarely failed to make a profit on a transaction. Money, though, was no longer his great goal; rather, making a fool of the government, whatever time or effort it cost him. The government responded by directing restrictive regulations at his businesses. One evening he was at a party where a government minister in his cups offered him a government trading company for $50,000. He took out his chequebook and gave the minister a cheque for that amount. Next morning he sold the company to a third party for $100,000. In the meantime the minister, having sobered up, realised what he had done and refused to deliver up the company. A court case ensued in which the minister – to win – had to admit in the witness box that he was so drunk that he had not known what he was doing, and furthermore so drunk that nobody could have supposed that he had. The trader lost his case, but he had not brought it to win. Discomfiting the minister was satisfaction enough. The government retaliated by refusing to licence his ships. It was the trader's boast that he had fathered twenty-four children in the islands, a feat that looked beyond his present physical capacity.

There were several half-caste dynasties in the islands, founded by traders like him. They passed their surname from generation to generation in European fashion, unlike the Gilbertese who merely took their father's first name as their surname. They were still traders, but also took jobs as harbourmasters, captains of inter-island vessels, and the like. Their ambiguous social position made them sometimes eccentric. An old man, the head of a prominent half-caste family, was brought to see me by anxious relatives because he had not eaten for many days. He was still well-covered with flesh, for he had once been a very fat man, but he was listless and indifferent to his surroundings. He wanted only to die, he said, and that was why he refused to eat. This was no sudden whim, as it transpired: on retiring from his job as carpenter and boatbuilder three years before, he decided that his life was over, so he went to bed to wait for death, first making himself a coffin which he kept next to his bed so that his relatives would not have far to lift him when he died. He had been waiting now for three years, consoled only by the proximity of his coffin and the beer he drank. I found nothing physically wrong with him that could not be explained by a three year residence between the bedclothes, and I returned him to his beloved bed and coffin where, a few months later, he died.

There were Chinese half-castes too, usually traders. The richest family in the whole country was generally agreed to be the Lee Ho's, whose stores were universally known as Bing's, Bing being the nearest somebody could come to pronouncing Bill, the first name of the founding Lee Ho. But though they were rich – or *because* they were rich – the next generation was going to the bad. The eldest son was an alcoholic at the age of twenty, continually crashing cars and motorbikes, getting into fights, spending money freely, disappearing abroad for months at a time, and contributing nothing to the business. Some of the other children were beginning their slide down the same slippery slope. Within a few years everything that had been built up would be smashed to the ground. It had the inevitability of a Greek tragedy.

One group of foreigners in the Gilbert Islands who should not escape mention are the missionaries. Having read Somerset Maugham's brilliant though polemical (as I then thought) short story 'Rain', I started out with a general predisposition against missionaries. Later I discovered just how little exaggeration there had been to Maugham's portrait of the American protestant missionary, Davidson, and his wife. Davidson was drawn from a model whom Maugham must have met on board ship. In the story, Davidson's mission islands are mentioned as far-flung coral atolls about ten days' sailing from Pago Pago, a description that fits the Gilberts very well. Davidson tells how he brought about the expulsion from the islands of a trader called Fred Ohlson:

> Fred Ohlson was a Danish trader who had been in the islands a good many years. He was a pretty rich man as traders go and he wasn't much pleased when we came. You see, he'd had things very much his own way. He paid the natives what he liked for their copra, and he paid in goods and whisky. He had a native wife, but he was flagrantly unfaithful to her. He was a drunkard. I gave him a chance to mend his ways, but he wouldn't take it. He laughed at me.
>   Davidson's voice fell . . . and he was silent for a minute or two. The silence was heavy with menace.
>   'In two years he was a ruined man. He'd lost everything he'd saved in a quarter of a century. I broke him, and at last he was forced to come to me like a beggar and beseech me to give him a passage back to Sydney.'
>   'I wish you could have seen him when he came to see Mr Davidson,' said the missionary's wife. 'He had been a fine, powerful man, with a lot of fat on him, and he had a great big voice, but now he was half the size, and he was shaking all over. He'd suddenly become an old man.'

While delving in the archives in the National Library, James Denton-Smith came across the name of a trader who had left the islands suddenly and inexplicably in the 1890's. His name was Fred Ohlson.

The Davidsons disapproved of the native lava-lavas. Mrs Davidson says: 'It's a very indecent costume . . . Mr Davidson thinks it should be prohibited by law . . . At the beginning of our stay Mr Davidson said in one of his reports: the inhabitants of these islands will never be thoroughly Christianised until every boy of more than ten is made to wear a pair of trousers.'

While browsing in the archives, I came across the following statement in the report of a North American missionary for 1892: 'The natives will never be Christianised until they are made to wear trousers.'

As for the native dancing, that too had the Davidsons' disapproval: '. . . It's not only immoral in itself but it distinctly leads to immorality. However, I'm thankful to God we stamped it out, and I don't think I'm wrong in saying that no-one has danced in our district for eight years.' Judged by the missionary reports of the time, this was a mere transliteration of something Maugham actually heard. The missionaries were *obsessed* by the need to put down the dancing, and they used the metaphors of guerrilla warfare in their reports. When dancing reappeared in a 'pacified' area, one of them wrote: 'The dancing party has been active again.' Mrs Davidson could have written that.

But it was one thing to dislike missionaries because of a short story, another altogether to dislike them face to face.

The Catholics were represented mainly by nuns: a few Irish and many Australian. There were also still a couple of very ancient French sisters, one of whom died aged nearly 100, not having returned to France for seventy years. There was also an old French father, now in his eighties, whose mind was perfectly clear, and who lived in the seminary next to the bishop's house. When one saw him in his cell-like room, contentedly reading books of devotion in preparation for his meeting with God, owning nothing at the end of his long life but the shirt and trousers in which he stood, happy in his total poverty, one could not remain unmoved.

The nuns were active, as teachers and in other ways. It seemed strange and almost comical to hear these white-clad figures speaking with abrasive Australian accents. They were strongly opposed to all contraception except the natural method pioneered by Dr Billings.

'Remember lydies,' one of the nuns used to repeat, as a kind of *bon mot*, 'Drie dies are syfe dies.'

It was alleged that some of the nuns were quite unscrupulous in their opposition to other forms of contraception, telling credulous Catholic woman that the intrauterine device gave rise to deformed babies, the contraceptive pill to cancer. Of the dangers of repeated childbirth they said nothing; but yet they were good women, utterly devoted to the welfare, as they saw it, of the Gilbertese.

A young father on an outer island, a charismatic, had started a movement in favour of faith healing. This, of course, was the last thing we doctors wanted, but there is no doubt his methods caught on quickly. Frank Belling knew of several cases where he had prayed young children to preventable death. In the hospital on Tarawa prayer groups used to gather round the bed of seriously ill patients, with the instinct of vultures; each member of the group spread out his arms and held hands in a chain round the bed, closing his eyes, uttering emotionally charged prayers, and singing high-pitched hymns. I once warned them to be careful, otherwise the patient would levitate and bang his head on the ceiling.

The Catholics exerted considerable pressure on their communities to contribute financially to church projects. They and the protestants were in strong rivalry, each sect having been taught that the other was the Devil's snare and delusion. Neither side of the great divide held with the new policy of mealy-mouthed ecumenism. And one of the ways in which this rivalry manifested itself was a competition to build the biggest church (of cement and breezeblock). I once received a request from the Catholics for a donation because, it said, the Catholic people were suffering terribly as a result of their efforts to build a vast new church in Bikenibeu. It had never so much as crossed the mind of the framer of this request that an alternative way of reducing their suffering was to halt the construction of what in any case was certain to be an architectural monstrosity.

The Catholics were tolerant of human foibles, however; drunkenness, dirt and dancing had never exercised them deeply, as they had the protestants. The infant mortality rate among Catholics was much higher than among the protestants, and this was not the result of larger families, since the protestants practised little more family planning than the Catholics. But the government was frightened of the statistics and, perhaps wisely, neither published nor acted upon them. As for religious life, it attracted a number of young Gilbertese women. It was a refuge from the drudgery, the subordination to men, the not infrequent beatings and the physical exhaustion through yearly childbirth that marriage often entailed. It attracted few men, on the other hand.

There were Mormons and Seventh Day Adventists in Kiribati. The Mormons had recently decreed that people with skins as brown as the Gilbertese could, after all, reach heaven, though not apparently without wearing long black trousers, white shirt and tie, and plastic identification badge. A southern baptist church, the Church of God of South Carolina, had also reached the island. (The rule was that no church could proselytise without first building a school.) The pastor of this church when I arrived was Brother Marvel, a well-covered man who was excessively fond of chocolate, to judge by the quantities he bought on the rare occasions it reached Bing's store. Strangely enough, his wife – whom he never addressed other than as Sister Marvel – fitted almost exactly the description of Mrs Davidson:

> She was a little woman, with brown, dull hair very elaborately arranged, and she had prominent blue eyes . . . Her face was long, like a sheep's, but she gave no impression of foolishness, rather of extreme alertness; she had the quick movements of a bird. The most remarkable thing about her was her voice, high, metallic, and without inflexion; it fell on the ear with a hard monotony . . . like the pitiless clamour of the pneumatic drill.

Sister Marvel was unnaturally pale, as though she shunned the sun as the source of leprosy; she usually looked as though she had just bitten on something extremely sour, like a lemon.

Brother Marvel had come to the Gilberts from Barbados, where the exuberant religiosity of the people had been precisely suited to his expansive style of preaching. The reserved Gilbertese, however, he found much harder to enthuse. They never spoke in tongues or shouted *Glory Hallelujah*! I decided one Sunday to attend his service.

The church was a plain brick hall. On the floor sat the Gilbertese congregation, dressed in snow-white shirts or blouses and equally white lava-lavas. The contrast with their smooth brown skins was very striking. The altar was a table on a raised platform and it was there that Brother Marvel stood. To his right was a lectern, behind which was a Gilbertese assistant; to his left, on the extreme edge of the platform, sat his wife.

There were a few hymns, during the singing of which someone handed a slip of paper to Brother Marvel to tell him who I was. When the hymns were over, Brother Marvel drew the attention of the congregation to me.

'We have a medical doctor in our midst,' he said. 'We are very glad to see him. We welcome him with all our heart.'

And then, to my horror, he asked me whether I wouldn't like to stand up and give a little testimony to someone he called *The Lorr-erd*.

The whole congregation was looking at me. I stood up.

'Thank you very much,' I said. 'It's very nice to be here.'

Then I sat down. It wasn't blasphemy, but it wasn't exactly testimony either. The man behind the lectern began to translate what I had said into Gilbertese, and Brother Marvel shot him a look as if to say 'Don't be such a bloody fool'.

This slight setback, however, did not put Brother Marvel off his stroke for the main event of the service, his sermon. He took as his subject 'the efficacious fervent prayer of righteous men'. He managed to compress quite a lot into a comparatively short time, from sin and Satan to everlasting bliss. He was daily expecting 'the End of the Whir-erld', though this did not discourage him from sending his young daughter back to the States to get educated. In three-quarters of an hour he ran through the gamut of human emotions. He sobbed, he laughed, he implored, expostulated, exclaimed, remonstrated; he went down on his knees, he climbed up on the altar, he flung his arms wide, he raised them up, he cast himself down into the congregation, he mopped his brow, he was overcome; and every two minutes he stopped for it all to be translated.

The man behind the lectern translated without intonation, matter-of-factly, as though the End of the Whir-erld were the cancellation of a train departure or a slack day's trading on the stock exchange. The congregation watched and listened to Brother Marvel without any change of expression. I formed the opinion that they came only so that their children might be eligible for the Church of God school.

After the service Brother Marvel asked me how I had liked it. I said it was very nice. He said it was difficult to get these people to take their salvation seriously, the most urgent question facing any man.

From time to time Brother Marvel preached over the radio. He was quite unable to preach, however, without his gestures, and so one heard his voice fade away and then return as he went out of and came back into range of the microphone. Sometimes one heard him crash into the walls of the empty studio as he flung himself about.

Strangely enough, my evident lack of religious enthusiasm did not discourage any of the missionaries from consulting me. I discovered that most of them interpreted their least twinges as death-throes, and evinced no particular anxiety for an early reunion with their Maker. They were hypochondriacs.

Brother and Sister Marvel were replaced after a year by Brother and Sister Farb. Brother Farb was a lean, greying man whose perpetual affability was temperamental rather than ideological. He always wore a red baseball hat with a slogan embroidered in Coca-Cola script: *Jesus Christ, He's the Real Thing.* Sister Farb was a retiring woman who never wanted to be a missionary, and would have been happy to continue as the preacher's wife in a small town in Georgia, baking cakes for Bible study meetings. She was in the Pacific on Christian sufferance. Her husband, however, came from a circus family and had seen something of the world. I had the impression he had found Jesus relatively late in life and like St Augustine had sinned a little before doing so.

Because he knew by direct acquaintance what he exhorted everyone to abjure, and because he was so palpably a kindly man, I thought his religion entirely sincere.

The traditional protestantism of the London Missionary Society flourished on the outer islands. The work of the missionaries had long since been taken over by indigenous pastors, who were the most important, as well as the richest, sleekest and fattest, men on their islands. There was no doubt that the villages under their sway were pleasantly clean and neat, sober and hardworking. There was great emphasis on the externals. of religion. For example, on the sternest of islands there were bylaws forbidding people to be anywhere on the island during Sunday church services other than in church or at home. A bell was tolled an hour before midnight on Saturday to warn the night-time fishermen to return home (or be fined). Social pressure to conform was intense; but whether religion meant anything more than outward show I do not know.

Dr Storm told an irresistible story from the time of one of the last colonial governors, of a protestant pastor and his daughter who had been sent to New Zealand for education. The pastor heard through another Gilbertese living in New Zealand that his daughter had taken up with a man there, and he wrote to her in great distress, admonishing her to retain her virtue at all costs. Not receiving a satisfactory reply, he ordered her to come home; but she then wrote to tell him that she loved this man, that he was going to marry her, and that he was, moreover, a millionaire. She knew her father well – probably better than he knew himself – for this not only placated but delighted him. She wrote him letters about her fiancé's houses, his farms and horses, and his yacht. He relayed these letters proudly to his flock. His self-importance grew. He was impatient for her return so that he could display the rewards of his righteousness. Eventually she returned, but without him. He was to follow, she said, in a few days' time in his yacht, and to prove it she brought with her engraved invitations to all the senior members of the government and civil service, including the Governor himself, to a cocktail party on board the yacht when it arrived. The forthcoming party was the only topic of conversation among the expatriates. Those who had not been invited reviled those who had; while those who had smirked complacently. On the appointed day all offices closed early, for the party was to start at four in the afternoon. Everyone dressed up to the nines; the Governor donned his ceremonial uniform, coloured sash, sword of honour, and white helmet with fluttering egret feathers. They all strained their eyes scanning the horizon of the lagoon for the elegant outline of the yacht. At five o'clock it still had not appeared. Then the pastor's daughter arrived, distractedly waving a telegram. Her beloved fiancé had suffered a heart attack *en route* and alas the yacht had turned back for New Zealand. Regret any inconvenience, stop.

Thereafter the fiction could not long be maintained. The Governor had been made to look a fool. The pastor's daughter went insane, the only route of escape left to her; while the gullible pastor resigned in shame, financially ruined (his daughter's elaborate lies had required expensive props), never to seek prominence again. Is it not written, *Pride goeth before destruction, and an haughty spirit before a fall*?

The latest missionaries to reach the islands were those of the Bahai faith. They were unusual in that they did not proselytise. Presumably they won converts purely by force of example. Not far from my house, on the lagoon side of the island, lived a Bahai couple from New Zealand who had missionary visas but never undertook missionary work as conventionally conceived. In what they believed, other than general benevolence and religious tolerance, I never discovered; but we became friends nonetheless. They lived in a house built only of local materials, unlike the missionaries of the Church of God, who lived in an American suburban enclave. Stephen Pendereski was the son of a landowning Pole who lost everything in the war and its aftermath, and went as a refugee to New Zealand. He was something of a *littérateur*, with a degree in English which it had taken him several years to complete. He was still sufficiently a child of his generation to think Thomas Pynchon the greatest author since Homer;

he admired opacity in writing. He wanted to write himself, I think, but a certain fastidiousness and mock-aristocratic languor prevented him. Perhaps he was just afraid to discover whether or not he possessed any talent. His wife Cynthia, on the other hand, was an accomplished painter, with a very distinctive style. She was one of the few artists in New Zealand able to make a living solely by her art. She took inspiration from the landscape and small towns of her native land. She must have had it in mind to become the Gauguin of the Gilberts, for what artist could come to the South Seas without such a thought? Having little artistic imagination myself, I found it difficult to conceive how the brilliant colours of the Gilbert Islands could transfer to canvas without intolerable vulgarity, more Tretschikoff than Gauguin. Her husband was building a studio for her, a shelter on stilts overlooking the lagoon, and I look forward impatiently to her solution of this artistic problem.

Our life in the Gilberts was quiet and uneventful, I suppose, but just as one learns to savour material goods by being deprived of them, so we came to cherish events. They were few and far between, but such was the foreshortening of time we experienced there – or was it just that we were growing older? – they seemed sufficient to occupy our minds, and we were never bored. There was, for example, the South Pacific Forum, attended by heads of Pacific governments, including Malcolm Fraser of Australia and Sir Robert 'Piggy' Muldoon, of New Zealand, the latter impressing everyone with his enthusiasm for accepting hospitality. These two could find nowhere clean or comfortable enough for them on the island and slept on board ship out to sea. One Prime Minister forgot his suitcase and sent his jet back to fetch it, in the meantime having to make do with whatever he could find at Bing's. The King of Tonga's brother was so fat he had to be transported in a London taxi (once the Governors' official car). All other vehicles were unable to accommodate his bulk. The heads of government held their deliberations in the parliament building and I was deputed to hold myself in readiness outside in case one of them should have a heart attack or fall comatose from boredom. At the party afterwards I heard one of Muldoon's advisers, a woman who was trying very hard to eliminate all traces of a New Zealand accent, ask a small, dark-skinned man what he did for a living.

'Well actually', he replied, 'I'm a Prime Minister.'

Then there was a general strike: food became scarce, there was no electricity, and the water supply was inconstant. In an act of ethnocentrism stunning in its crassness, a British Labour government had once sent as *aid* (sic) a trade union organiser to start a union among public employees, who until then had hardly thought of such a thing. Of course a grievance was soon found, the Government proved inept at handling it (failing even to answer letters), and before long a general strike was called. Though the grievance appeared small, feelings grew bitter as the strike progressed: men still at work were intimidated and threatened with death, firesetting started, and the police, still barefoot, were issued with ancient rifles and helmets. One man was shot in the foot while setting alight a maneaba. Once again it appeared that the Gilbertese emotions were held in a kind of Pandora's box which it was better not to open. The union had forgotten, or had not been told, one very salient fact: that conditions for a strike by unskilled workers are not propitious where ninety-five per cent of the population is unemployed. The strikers were simply sent back home and replaced by men anxious for a chance to earn some money.

The whole episode set us thinking about the purpose of aid. Few of us knew the Gilbertese well enough to say what was good for them. I think they did not know themselves any longer. Our presence was disturbing, creating patterns of consumption for an élite for which there was no economic base. Having brought them religion we were now irreligious; having covered up their nakedness we now told them they should dance bare-breasted; having condemned them for the infanticide and abortion by which they once limited their population, we now told them to limit their families. We from Europe and America were used to changing our minds, our manners and our morals every few years; but the

Gilbertese were not. I wondered whether some future writer might not write about us as Somerset Maugham had written of the missionaries.

One aid organisation in particular became my *bête noire*, perhaps because I saw it close to. This was the World Health Organisation. When I arrived in Kiribati its representative there was an Indian from Kenya, now a British citizen. He had played a part in eradicating smallpox from Bangladesh, and he was a highly competent, experienced doctor. He was charming, handsome, humorous, immensely hospitable; but he was sceptical of large and inspirational schemes to transform everything at once such as the WHO was then, as now, promoting. He even had enough breadth of vision to question whether everything needed to be transformed. After all, the Gilbertese were not unbearably miserable or wretched, even if their infant mortality rate was twelve times Sweden's. He was not a public health evangelical.

Unhappily, he was soon replaced by another, compared with whom Davidson was but a vacillating agnostic. He too was charming, socially; unfortunately I thought him less than fully competent. Only a highly bureaucratic organisation could have tolerated him for more than a moment. Worse still, he believed himself possessed of Revealed Truth, which had been vouchsafed him at an American school of public health. He had learnt whole textbooks of jargon, whose obscure terms he recombined in sentences that were almost, but not quite, English. This was how he elucidated the WHO's slogan *Health For All By The Year 2000*: ' "Health for all by Year 2000" simply means that before the Year 2000 (ie 17 years from now) all the people in Kiribati should have a level of health that should be interpreted in real terms to our existing economic, social and religious conditions.' He poured forth such a stream of circulars that in a few months he had created a paper shortage in the country and had used 3000 duplicating stencils (one circular for every 20 inhabitants). Though he had once qualified as a doctor, he had forgotten many of the technical aspects of medicine. He talked – and wrote – endlessly of 'intersectoral cooperation', and of 'vertical and horizontal integration', but never of why no kerosene had been despatched to refrigerators on the outer islands, thus vitiating the whole of the immunisation programme. Mere practicalities were beneath his notice: his job was to 'motivate' others. To this end, he sent his circulars to the unfortunate nurses on the outer islands:

> Daily recording of information especially those related to the 37 Family Planning and priority diseases with regard to their situations as problems, the health related services provided to try to solve these problems and the operations of the Ministry of Health and Family Planning infra structure in the field through recording in HIC household folders and health centre or dispencery administration log books (designed by HIC) by the MAs and PHNs and HIC household cards by the Health Aides.
>
> The VWGs request the supports of the health aides, ASIs, PHNs, the MAs or other intersectoral extension worker with regard to matters that they cannot do or obtain for their health related activities organised in relation to the population problem and the 37 priority disease at the households, certain houses, village meeting places, the health centre, the dispenceries or the central hospital as regarded appropriate or feasible.

Unfortunately, he took any criticism by expatriates as being motivated by ill-will or by embittered colonial sentiment. He was, moreover, in a noble tradition of WHO incompetence in the islands. In 1977 there was a cholera epidemic, for the suppression of which the WHO sent 2,000,000 tablets of sugar-coated potassium chloride, of no conceivable use in such a situation, and three tons of pure phenol, with which a Burmese expert had advised disinfecting the lagoon. The tablets fed the ants in the pharmacy; while, fortunately for Tarawa's supply of fish, the phenol arrived after the epidemic had subsided. No-one was quite sure how to dispose of it once it had arrived, however; it was thought that an expert in phenol disposal might have to be called in.

Of course, I should not like to suggest that everyone who works for the WHO is incompetent. Those experts seconded to it from universities and research institutes really *are* expert. I remember with admiration the visit of Professor Shivaji Ramalingam of the University of Malaya, who came to study the mosquitoes of Kiribati at the behest of the WHO. He had devoted a quarter of a century to the study of the taxonomy of mosquitoes (at least 3,200 species are known, and more are discovered each year). The extraordinary thing about Professor Ramalingam was that he truly *loved* mosquitoes, the only man I have ever met who regarded them other than as a pestilential curse, sent to test Man's faith in a benevolent deity. He spoke of them tenderly, with the light of adoration in his eyes; he spoke of their habits with tolerance, amusement and even veneration. Strangest of all, while he was talking he managed to fire you with his enthusiasm, so that for a short while you forgot it was a mosquito that had driven you half-mad the night before by buzzing in your ear. He made the taxonomy of mosquitoes seem the most important subject in the world. He went searching for eggs and larvae, pupae and imagos, with as much gusto as a child on a nature study outing. Great was his delight when he discovered a fifth species in the Gilbert Islands (only four had previously been known), *Aedes marshallensis* I think it was. He gathered their eggs and nurtured them in muslin-covered pots until they metamorphosed into adult mosquitoes, whereupon the cleaner of his hotel room, thinking Oh dear, all these mosquitoes have got into his pots, sprayed them with her insecticide aerosol. Professor Ramalingam was devastated. When he came to the hospital next morning he was almost in tears.

> – All my pretty ones?
> Did you say all?

The only thing the Gilbert Islands lacked, from the point of view of the medical entomologist, was insect-borne diseases (other than occasional outbreaks of dengue whose visitations, however, were not nearly as frequent as those of the medical entomologists).

By far the worst effect of the WHO, however, was the

atmosphere of suspicion and intellectual dishonesty which it so successfully fostered. The WHO, having semidiplomatic status, was unlikely to be a vehicle for the gathering and dissemination of unpleasant truths, but it nevertheless came as a surprise to discover that almost *any* disagreement or even questioning was dismissed as arising from the most discreditable of motives. The representative once told a visiting paediatrician that there was no tuberculosis or malnutrition among the children of Kiribati, at a time when all the children in the children's ward, which he had never visited, had tuberculosis or malnutrition, or both. Of course, the paediatrician did not believe him, for even in Switzerland, let alone in Kiribati, it would be possible, if one looked hard enough, to find cases of tuberculosis and malnutrition.

As though with the credulity of the newly literate, who are so proud of their accomplishment that they believe everything they read must be true, the WHO representative had only to put something down on paper for it to become, *ipso facto*, the truth. This was an attitude he managed to communicate to a large proportion of the Gilbertese medical profession, so that they came to believe that shuffling papers was their true vocation, that nothing written down had to be checked against reality (for paper *was* their reality), that office work was vastly more important than any other, and even that the care and cure of patients was degrading, harmful and retrogressive work that could and should be left to menials, insofar as it was done at all. It was a great pity, for while they were good doctors, they were very bad bureaucrats; there were enough of them, moreover, to give adequate medical coverage to the entire population, unlike most poor countries.

The WHO gained its ascendency by two means, the augustness of its name and the disbursement of funds, which were enormous in the context. The Gilbertese were insufficiently self-confident to challenge the opinions of the WHO representative. If they failed to understand his meaning they assumed the fault was with them rather than with him. When I recommended a change in the drugs we used for the treatment of tuberculosis because an alternative was cheaper, more effective, easier to administer, preferred by the patients and with fewer undesirable side-effects, the only argument produced against such a change was that the WHO had not recommended it. Mentally, the Ministry of Health had been recolonised.

And the WHO representative dangled the carrot of overseas travel – understandably a choice reward – constantly before the Ministry, providing it acquiesced in his domination. Many nurses were sent to the Philippines, at not inconsiderable expense, to learn to insert intrauterine devices, though on their return they inserted not a single such device, both because the patients did not want them and because they were unavailable. Moreover, there was someone well-qualified to teach insertion already in the island.

Stranded on an island a few hundred yards across, it was all too easy to see things out of proportion. The island was the centre of one's universe and one's frustrations came to seem of transcendent importance, of significance to the whole world. The WHO became a nightmarish obsession, and I even had T-shirts printed with the absurd definition of Health For All By the Year 2000. (Since the constitution of the WHO defines health as not merely the absence of disease but the presence of complete physical, psychological and social wellbeing, the slogan is itself absurd, with as much meaning as *Come to Marlboro Country* or *My Goodness, My Guinness*.) I began to overlook the pleasant and relaxed life I still led on Tarawa, or that in practice I was left completely alone to produce miracle cures or decimate the population at will. On leaving the Gilbert Islands I wrote an article for *The Sydney Morning Herald* which reflected the whole country in the distorting mirror of my obsession. I portrayed the government and the civil service very unflatteringly, to say the least, gratuitously causing offence. It was not so much that anything I said was untrue; rather that any number of truths about a subject do not add up to the Truth about it, if the perspective is distorted. Hence my article, though sincere, was misleading, and I apologise to the Gilbertese government for it. For what I have said about the WHO, however, I make no apology; I regret only that my powers of expression are not equal to the depths of my outrage at its degeneracy and dishonesty – at least, in the Gilbert Islands.

As residence on the island came to destroy perspective, so it led from time to time to a longing, physical in intensity, for a change of scene, to see a mountain, a river, or even just a hill. The time between home leaves seemed eternal, though when they came they were magnificent: the islands being almost antipodean to Britain, I went leisurely round the world. Sometimes the months hung heavy in the Gilberts, though the days went quickly; and it was during the *longueurs* that getting off the island appeared a matter of imperative necessity for the preservation of one's sanity. One also wished for reassurance that the outside world existed still.

I was fortunate to be twice called to Nauru which, if not exactly a metropolis, was at least a change. The first case was that of a twenty-five year old man who had property worth $750,000. He was both diabetic and epileptic, and had been admitted to hospital so many times in one kind of coma or another that he had been reduced, mentally, to the level of a three year old. His relatives gave him slips of paper inscribed with the words 'I want $20,000 in cash', and pointed him in the direction of the Phosphate Commission, where his money was held. They waited round the corner with a box of Fanta and swapped it for the money. He thought it a good bargain. So far they had extracted $80,000 in this manner, but the matter had come to the attention of the authorities, and it was brought before the Court of Protection. The question at issue was whether the man was capable of directing his own affairs. The relatives, of course, maintained that he was: they had more cases of Fanta they wished to exchange.

Only the most cursory examination was necessary to establish that he was unfitted even to be sent shopping, let alone manage an estate of $750,000. He was grotesquely fat, his eyes almost obscured by the flesh of his cheeks, the rolls of fat at his flanks so large that when he walked he spread his arms like a tightrope walker; the bulk of his thighs was such that when taking a step each leg had to describe a semicircle to avoid the other. His expression was vacant; he knew neither the time nor the date and had no notion of the purpose of the proceedings.

Seeing at once that their case had collapsed, the relatives asked how long he could be expected to live: a shrewd question, for the Court of Protection would sequester only that proportion of his wealth necessary for his upkeep during his lifetime, leaving the rest for him to squander as he might.

'Not for long,' I replied, only half-jokingly, 'if you have much to do with it.'

Which of course they did, for they were the ones who administered his insulin. What easier than to give him an 'accidental' overdose of insulin and withhold food? They had a point, however, for he could not be expected to survive even as long as the average Nauruan, who rarely lived beyond the age of fifty. The Nauruans were the clearest counter-example known to me of the public health axiom that rich people live long.

The second time I was called to Nauru was to see a boy of thirteen who had killed the young daughter of a Gilbertese worker by throwing a stone at her from a passing bus. His defence counsel thought I might be able to come up with something by way of extenuating circumstances, but though I thought from the outset this was most unlikely I consented to go, for I was anxious at the time to get off Tarawa.

I waited in an office for the young prisoner to be led in. The airconditioner fitted poorly into the breezeblock wall and uttered a kind of death rattle. I passed the time by reading *The Melbourne Law Review*. At length the prisoner was led in, and I received a shock. I was expecting a grossly fat, profoundly unattractive youth. The young murderer was, if ever the word can be applied to a human being, beautiful. He was like a fine wild animal straining at the leash of captivity. He was slim but well-proportioned; his features were of astonishing perfection; his eyes had a liquid clarity; he moved with lithe grace; his nostrils flared slightly with defiance; his skin was flawless. He was, I discovered, the personification of heartless evil.

I wondered as I questioned him whether his was an exceptional beauty, or whether perhaps all Nauruans had been like him until the Europeans introduced them to the glories of tinned foods and soft drinks.

The prisoner had ridden round the island on a bus, throwing stones at people from the windows. It was a fashionable game just then among Nauruan youths of his age, who saw no point at all in school. Why bother, when there was no subsequent struggle for livelihood? I asked him whether he was sorry for what he had done. No, why should he be, it was a good shot. Had he realised the game was dangerous? Yes, that was its point. Would he play the same game again? Yes, if he were bored. Even if it meant killing a passerby? Yes – especially if that is what it meant.

Boredom was the problem facing the Nauruans, killing them almost literally. It was boredom that induced youths to mount huge stereophonic speakers on to the backs of cars and drive incessantly round the island to music so loud that the ground vibrated, until they entered a trance and crashed. It was boredom that incited them to eat their piles of rice a foot high crowned with a large tin of corned beef, four or five times a day, and drink Pepsi or Fanta by the twenty-four tin carton. A nutritionist found a Nauruan who consumed 14,000 calories a day. They knew this mode of existence was soon fatal, that practically all of them would succumb to the complications of diabetes before they were fifty; but the knowledge did not stop them, it only spurred them on. More than once I came across spontaneous but strangely dispirited picnics in what remained of the Nauruan bush.

The Nauruans were hardly well-known, either individually or collectively, for the wise use of their resources. The police chief imported at great expense a Lamborghini sports car (the island, remember, was ten miles in circumference) only to discover that he was too fat to get in it. The owner of a brand new car and his passenger were so incensed when it ran out of fuel that they set fire to it and next day bought another. Dr Storm told me that a

Nauruan friend of his was so anxious to impress him with his wealth that he used $20 notes as lavatory paper.

As for the Nauruan government, it had invested in, amongst other things, the largest office block in Melbourne (known locally as *Birdshit Tower*), and an international airline, with one Boeing (five in all) for every 800 Nauruans. No-one was certain how much Air Nauru was losing, except that it was a lot; the forceful president, Hammer de Roburt, said that it was prejudicial to the interests of Nauru for anyone other than himself to know the extent of the losses, or the disposition of Nauru's other investments. Sometimes the aircraft flew thousands of miles with only one or two passengers on board. He said that the airline was Nauru's gift to the less fortunate (or at least, less richly endowed) parts of the Pacific, which would otherwise have been without an air service.

And while I was in Nauru I was asked to see another prisoner, who had served eight years in gaol as a murderer, with a view to recommending his release. The man was enormous, both fat and strong, now in his late twenties. He was not intelligent and, having played truant throughout his schooldays, was illiterate. He had played the games that had swept Nauruan youth in the wake of films shown there, so that after *Tarzan*, for example, he had hurled his even then considerable bulk at the small grey pigs, pretending they were lions, and wrestled the squealing, terrified creatures half to death. By his own admission, he had been exceptionally cruel. He had taken delight in soaking cats in petrol and setting them alight.

As he grew older, he and his friends took to driving drunkenly round the island in stolen cars. One evening the police gave chase. He and his friends abandoned the car and ran off into the bush, taking a case of beer with them. The police were too fat to follow. They drank the beer and went to sleep. Next morning they came across a girl walking through the bush and, still drunk, started to rape her. The police, however, had not forgotten them and had instituted a search. To stop the girl from screaming as the police drew nearer the prisoner put his hand over her mouth, but forgetting his weight and strength, asphyxiated her. He gave himself up, for there was nowhere to run.

The dead girl's parents, however, were born-again evangelicals, and soon set about forgiving him. He bowed under their religious ministrations, and now they regarded him as their own son, whom they visited daily. To make restitution to the feline world he had so grievously wronged, he kept cats for whom he cared tenderly. The warders tried to tempt him every so often with beer, but he refused it always. He never said or did a cruel thing, and accepted his punishment as entirely just. In quarrels he turned the other cheek. Despise evangelical Christianity as I might, I was forced to admit that for Nauruans it appeared to offer the only earthly redemption. A small but growing band of them had forsworn their degenerate and pointless existence for the false certitudes of cheap religion. But at times there are matters more important than the truth.

Towards the end of my time in Kiribati, my outlook grew more and more unbalanced by the cult of evasion I thought I detected in the Ministry of Health. I was therefore relieved to be asked, three months before I was to leave the islands for good, to serve for a time as medical officer on Christmas Island, two thousand miles from Tarawa (and thus the Ministry), on the other side of the International Date Line.

Christmas is one of the largest coral atolls in the world, a hundred miles round. The population was only about 1000, most of whom lived in the main settlement, called London (there was also a Paris and a Poland on Christmas). It was uninhabited until the British moved some Gilbertese there, and at independence the island was included in the new republic. It had achieved brief notoriety in the early sixties as a base for British and American nuclear tests. The British soldiers were told to turn their backs on the flashes, but the myriad seabirds of the island, given no such order, were blinded. In various parts of the island one came across long ranks of rusting military vehicles, abandoned when the soldiers departed; or concrete foundations littered with a hundred enamel wash basins, the remains of washrooms where National Servicemen had sluiced themselves down at unearthly hours in the morning under the irascible gaze of a sergeant.

Shortly before I arrived on Christmas, all the twelve million or so seabirds that normally lived there took mysteriously to wing and deserted it. James Denton-Smith reassuringly pointed out that all the seabirds had left Krakatoa a few days before it erupted. This was the only geological remark I ever heard him make, although he was a geologist.

My time in Christmas, however, was undisturbed by eruptions. The island was largely treeless and desolate. Some salt pans were being developed for exportation of commercial quantities, but work on the project had halted and the pans were windswept and eerie. I worked only in the mornings, for a thousand people do not occupy a doctor full time, even if many of the children are malnourished. (Some Gilbertese mothers had the unfortunate notion that to give fish to children under the age of three made then greedy and selfish as adults. Health education made no impression on this belief, except that when mothers brought their malnourished children to the doctor they knew exactly what to answer the question, What do you feed your child?). The afternoons I spent reading, holding myself in readiness for an emergency that never arose.

Nearby lived a young American from Los Angeles who ran a small store. He had come to escape the frenetic pace of California and after a year on Christmas had decided to stay for ever. He arranged a fishing expedition in his small, flat-bottomed aluminium boat. My last fishing expedition, overnight with Dr Tomati, had ended if not in disaster then in disgrace, with seasickness and an urgent longing for death. I had enjoyed it at first, watching the flying fish, piscine Cruise missiles, propel themselves at high speed for hundreds of yards over the surface of the water; and catching bonito, mullet and barracuda. In the dead of night we heard something strike our boat; and in the morning we discovered the broken-off beak of a garfish that had penetrated the wooden hull. By morning, however, I was more dead than alive, interested only in regaining land, which unhappily persisted in pitching and rolling for some hours afterwards.

With few illusions, then, as to my qualities as a sailor, we pushed the little aluminium boat over the reef and jumped in. The boat was so shallow that it seemed every wave must overwhelm it. We trawled with a hand line and feather lure in the deep blue water just beyond the reef, and within two hours the boat was so full of fish – trevally – that one more catch might sink us. And every time we stopped to haul in a fish I noticed that twenty or so sharks circled our boat a few feet below the surface, patiently awaiting a meal. I grew nervous. Every time our line taughtened forcefully with a bite I was certain it must be a shark *this* time, and was all for cutting the line before it devoured us, boat and all. My companion laughed at my nervousness, but I was relieved all the same to reach the shore with our more than adequate catch. The pleasures of sea angling were, I decided, not altogether unalloyed.

As part of my tour of duty I visited the islands of Fanning and Washington, a few hundred miles to the north. These too had been settled by the Gilbertese under a British scheme to reduce population pressure on the Gilberts, and there were about four hundred people on each. Until recently, they had been run as copra plantations by the large Australian trading company of Burns, Philp, but the expenses had long outrun the revenue, and the company sold out to the Kiribati government. This change was viewed with apprehension by the islanders, for the resources of the company, with a turnover at least fifty times greater than the national product of Kiribati, were infinitely greater than those of the government. Indeed, now that the Burns, Philp ship no longer called, the only way to reach the islands was by the light aircraft flown by an oceanographer from the University of Hawaii, who called once a month to check a meteorological recording station on Fanning. Even this slender lifeline to the outside world was about to snap, for the university's lease had nearly expired, and was not to be renewed. Thereafter the islanders would be at the mercy of such tramp steamers as called.

The oceanographer was a tall, distinguished-looking American, quietly spoken but with an air of authority. He was born and raised in Hawaii, and was, therefore, a Pacific islander, of a kind. (Hawaii is now a realm of holidaymakers, squeezed into ill-fitting shorts and browsing on sky-blue icecreams). He and his father once nearly changed the course of world history. Early on the morning of December 7th 1941 they were flying their private aircraft out of Honolulu when they saw the approach of the Japanese fighters and bombers. They radioed a warning but were not believed.

This was not a story he was anxious to relate, as a vulgarian might, at every opportunity; indeed, he was a man who spoke so little, and thought so much, that almost any casual conversation seemed intolerably noisy, like interference on a radio. I had been told he was a brilliant mathematician, and was somewhat in awe of him.

Washington was a small island with a strange brown freshwater lagoon in its raised centre, quite unlike the other islands I had seen. Its reef caused the waves to break with extraordinary force, and to unload a few tons of cargo from a vessel offshore was a hazardous business, taking a longboat several days. It was beautiful enough, but it is of Fanning that I think when I wish to recall the beauty of the South Seas.

Even now I cannot recall Fanning without experiencing powerful emotion. The island was in the form of a perfect ring, its jewel-like lagoon six miles across. The land was mostly covered in coconut groves but there was still an area where the original forest of Pacific atolls grew (the palm was introduced to the Pacific by Man). This forest was enchanting beyond description. The trees were tall and broad, white-barked and with the brilliant green foliage of fresh spring buds, though they were evergreen. There was a cool reticulation of shadows in the forest, and the ground rustled and clattered with a veritable carpet of scurrying land crabs. And deep in the forest – or so it seemed – the beating of the waves upon the shore was still audible, and the occasional cry of a seagull.

Fanning had once been a line station of the Cable and Wireless

Company, on the route between Australia and Canada. There were eleven company houses, red-tiled and airy, left in a clearing as a monument to its enterprise. They had broad, stone-floored verandahs with rattan screens to cut out the glare. They were arranged in two parallel rows of five, with the General Manager's house, slightly grander than the rest, standing at the head. Between the houses grew hibiscus and bougainvillea, now un-pruned and wild. Seniority in the station had once been expressed by how close you lived to the General Manager; but now the houses were empty and echoing. If Somerset Maugham was right, what passion, what envy, what intrigue must they once have seen!

I stayed in one of the houses, its only furniture a bed and a cane chair. I watched the sun go down from my verandah, turning to flaming crimson as it reached the canopy of the palm trees. It was a strange sensation for a modern man to be so completely isolated from the rest of the world, beyond all help and assistance, beyond all communication. I could not help thinking it was the best place in the world to survive the next war. I can hardly believe I was ever there.

The only occupied house was the one in which the oceano-grapher stayed. I went to him for dinner. He had donned a lava-lava and sat on the verandah, sipping beer. He called his Gilbertese wife to meet me, and she approached shyly, by stages, clinging to the wall and giggling. She was young, less than half his age, but they had two children of nine and six. He had been coming to the island every month for many years, and their liaison was stable. He spoke no Gilbertese and she would admit to little English, but there was obvious affection between them, though he was far from being a demonstrative man. I felt I was intruding, for with the termination of the university's lease, these were their last days together. The air was heavy with regret, made all the more melancholy by the unbearable beauty of the surroundings.

The brilliant daylight dispelled the atmosphere like a morning mist. I watched the white-capped waves hurl themselves against the reef. The heavy scarlet flowers of the hibiscus danced gently on the breeze, and the sweet scent of frangipani wafted tantalisingly on the air.

I returned to Tarawa. Was it really so very different? I do not think so now; yet I lacked the sense of proportion to see it then. After three and a half years, my mind had transformed it from near paradise into imagined hell.

Oh the mind, mind has mountains.

I wanted to leave the islands to recreate my life anew, and I did so.

EPILOGUE

A life is not a story, though it has a beginning, a middle and – I presume – an end. I have no simple conclusions to draw from the first half of my earthly existence. On the whole I have derived pleasure from the complexities of life, and would not care for them to be reduced to a few simple principles of easy application. But I have at least learnt that if I have failed to live up to the ideals of medicine as a profession, the fault lies with me and not with the profession, as once I thought.

I have not had a single all-consuming ambition. I no longer deride such ambition, for without it there could be no progress (and few great crimes either). From the outset I knew my powers were not equal to worthwhile scientific work, and I was too proud to trim ambition to capacity. Besides, the world appeared too interesting for me to plough conscientiously only one small corner of one small field. The penalty I have paid for my restlessness is that I no longer belong anywhere in particular: a train is as much home to me as a house.

When I applied for a position a little while ago, the chairman of the selection board, remarking on my disordered career, asked me what was my ultimate goal.

'To have an interesting life,' I replied.

This struck him as reprehensible and irresponsible. What if everyone insisted on an interesting life?

Perhaps he was right. I don't know.